Bill Burrus
Feb 2014

My
JOURNEY

My
JOURNEY
A Postal and Unique American Experience

Bill Burrus

Brown Books Publishing Group
Dallas, Texas

My Journey: A Postal and Unique American Experience

Brown Books Publishing Group
16250 Knoll Trail Drive, Suite 205
Dallas, Texas 75248
www.BrownBooks.com
(972) 381-0009

A New Era in Publishing™

ISBN 9781612540948
Library of Congress Control Number 2012954445

Printing in the United States
10 9 8 7 6 5 4 3 2 1

For more information or to contact the author, please go to:
www.BurrusJournal.org

Dedication

I dedicate this book to the person who is the axis of my life: my wife, Ethelda, who provided the foundation of support as I traveled my journey. My hope is that this book will serve as a record for future generations of the Burrus family. Hopefully, each will make contributions and live a life as full as mine.

To my daughters: Valerie Jean, Doni Mari, Kimberly Elayne, and Kristy Lanette; and son: Richard Antwon

To my grandchildren: Sharmecia Brown, Vadon Brown, Richard Brown, James Barker, Jammal Barker, Donny Ali, and Krisea Ansarah

To my great-grandchildren: Chastity, Alisha, Taliya, Keonte, Donivan, Evonnie, Tashari, and Tamesha

And very special cousins, nieces and nephews

Table of Contents

Part Four: Assuming the Reins

Foreword

The American dream unfolds before your eyes as you read this compelling saga of a bright young black man who left the hills of West Virginia because he dreamed of a better life.

In Wheeling, West Virginia, Bill Burrus knew that racism and discrimination would plague his life forever because of the color of his skin, so he ventured to Cleveland, Ohio, at the age of twenty-one. From there, Bill takes you on a phenomenal journey from his first day as a postal employee through his gradual rise to becoming the first African American ever elected by the membership as the president of an international labor union. It is a journey that took him all over the world and gave him power and influence reserved for the highest offices in the land.

Becoming president of the American Postal Workers Union did not occur overnight; this journey with Bill takes you through his trials and tribulations, along with the post office and national union politics that got him to the presidency. Bill Burrus is honest, forthright, and even self-criticizing as he chronicles details inside the American Postal Workers Union, where you can see both accomplishments and failures. *My Journey* is candid.

—Louis "Lou" Stokes, Congressman, Retired

Preface

Special thanks and appreciation are due my friend Robin Bailey, who served as my right hand at the Washington level in all union administrative matters and was always there when a task needed attention. Her assistance in the completion of this book has been invaluable.

In compiling my thoughts for this book, I looked back over my life and concluded that I have had great relationships with my father, William H. Burrus Sr.; my sisters, Billie Jane and Effie Marva; my mothers, Gertrude (Pat) and Blanche; and my wife, Ethelda. Each of these persons provided the nourishment of family and supported my journey to success. A special thanks to my cousins for being family: Wilbur Burrus, Marilyn Webb, Wanda Helms, Sandy Winborne, and Pat Russell McCloud. Moe Biller and Doug Holbrook were foundational to my union career, and though we disagreed on a number of issues, we maintained our collective focus on improving the lives and conditions of postal employees.

My life journey has included thorns and roses, and here I attempt to reveal the many aspects of my personality and make sense of the many facets of my efforts. At the time that Moe, Doug, and I achieved leadership positions in the postal arena, the compensation for postal employees wasn't enough for them to live the American dream. We were able to elevate their employment status and wages to levels deserving of their efforts. As a result of our successes, children have attended college, families have been nurtured in peaceful neighborhoods, medical conditions have been attended to, and individuals have been afforded respect and dignity in the workplace.

As John Donne said, "No man is an island," and the events of the time defined my place of existence, influencing my reactions to the world. During my career, the world was transformed by war and protest through social upheaval. Technology and trade altered occupations and shifted wealth, in response to which adjustments had to be made to the battles working people waged to hold on to their place on the social ladder and to climb the steps upward for greater reward. The American Postal Workers Union is the vehicle for representing the interest of postal workers, and I was privileged to serve in leadership positions.

The postal labor leaders before me—Stu Filbey, Jim Rademaker, Vince Sombrotto, and Moe Biller—transcended generations and laid the foundation for labor's progress. I inherited their strengths. My contributions were built on their foundation. Hundreds of my coworkers and associates influenced the efforts that led to my successes. Many served as role models while others were mentors and lifted me up in my climb to the top. I would be remiss if I did not take this opportunity to express my personal appreciation and extend a public acknowledgement of their contributions. *My Journey* is in fact *our* journey, during which I was privileged to serve. And to my many, many coworkers—the APWU office employees, staff, and fellow officers at the local, state, and national level; International Presidents led by President Rich Trumka; and specifically the members of the APWU National Executive Board—I thank you.

Introduction

The United States Postal Service has a rich past paralleling the growth of the nation, and it has fulfilled the mission "to bind the nation together" as recorded in the Constitution. Following the discovery of the New World and the settlement of the vast and fertile lands, the Pilgrims had the need to communicate, and during the early seventeenth century, mail service was initiated within the American colonies. In 1639, mail delivery by independent entrepreneurs served postal routes in Boston, New York, and Philadelphia to replace the British Crown System that had been imported from England. Benjamin Franklin was appointed the first postmaster general in 1775. With the signing of the Declaration of Independence and ratification of the Constitution, government-controlled mail services were formally established by the Post Office Act on February 26, 1792.

In 1829, Postmaster General William T. Barry was added to the president's cabinet and the position of postmaster general has continued as a part of the federal government to date. US postage stamps were introduced in 1857, and the post office began contracting with the private sector to transport air mail in 1926. Postal reform on August 12, 1970, established the United States Postal Service (USPS) as an independent entity of the federal government, replacing the Post Office Department. But even though the Postal Service continues as a federal agency, it is operated exclusively from postal sales and service and does not receive any tax revenue for its operation. The Postal

Service provides mail service to each address six days per week, exclusive of federal holidays, serving the continental United States and its territories, including Guam, Samoa, Puerto Rico, and the Virgin Islands. Mail deliveries were reduced from two to one per day in 1950.

The USPS presently processes and delivers 40 percent of the world's volume of mail at the cheapest rate in the developed countries. The Postal Service is the second largest US employer with 560,000 employees (a reduction from 800,000 in 1999), is expected to deliver about 150 billion pieces of mail in 2012, operates the largest fleet of vehicles (220,000), has an annual budget of $69 billion, and provides services through the largest network in the world, including 31,000 locations. Electronic alternatives have challenged the USPS's primary source of revenue in single-piece, first-class mail volume. Total mail volume has historically tracked national economic activity, so the prolonged and deep recession has adversely affected mail volume. Notwithstanding the competitive communication alternatives, it is expected that mail will continue to play a vital role in the communication needs of the civilized world.

My postal career overlapped with and was influenced by the Post Office Department and the U.S. Postal Service; thus *My Journey* is a chronological record of the period leading up to and following that change and its impact on postal workers and the American public. I trace the efforts of the dedicated employees and leaders of the postal unions as they worked on behalf of postal employees to elevate them to the middle class.

My story is one of a black kid who, with the help of others, overcame major obstacles and rose to positions of influence, affecting the lives of millions of postal workers and the mail services. The world has turned many times since I began my fifty-three-year career, and *My Journey* is my recollection of people and events within the postal community over this snapshot of time. Life is good.

PART ONE:

Finding My Way

CHAPTER 1

Learning to Distribute Mail

The date was February 22, 1958. It was unremarkable, overcast, and Cleveland cold, but it was the day that I began my postal career—one that would be responsible for millions of lives and take me around the globe, interacting with people who would shape the world and my life to come. I had recently been discharged from the army after serving three years and having celebrated my twenty-first birthday on December 13. I was prepared to begin my journey to places unknown. *I wanted to taste the wind and feel the fog.*

Four years earlier, I had graduated high school with honors as the class salutatorian, but I could not attend any of the four colleges in Wheeling, West Virginia, because they would not admit "coloreds." It was the same year that the Supreme Court ruled in Brown v. Board of Education that schools were required to integrate "with all deliberate speed." I had no idea how West Virginia would interpret the timeline, so the only option for higher education was a colored school—State College in Institute (Charleston), West Virginia—but it was far from home. My best friend, Donald Turner, had informed me that he was enlisting in the army. Even though I was employed as the town bank's custodian, there was no future for me in Wheeling, so I joined the army with him. The three years of service would serve as a stepping stone as I prepared to embrace the opportunities that lay waiting in places where I had not been, among people I had not met, doing things I had not done.

Upon my discharge from the military and a brief period in Steubenville, Ohio, I went to the apartment of my older sister, Billie Jane, on Parkwood Drive in East Cleveland. I had previously visited her when I was taking the postal test several months before but had returned to Steubenville to await the score. I was aware that I stood a good chance of being hired when I was notified that I had passed with a score of 91.5 with the five points added because of my veteran's status. Though there had been a massive fire at the army records center in St. Louis and my files were destroyed, eventually the Post Office Department was able to provide confirmation of my service and provide the military credit. The required physical exam followed, and I was instructed to report for duty on February 22.

I traveled by bus from 105th and St. Clair Avenue to Public Square, where I departed to walk the distance of five blocks to the Cleveland Main Post Office, a large stone building built during the Great Depression above the train station and mall dominating the Warehouse District. Throughout the bus ride, I was in deep thought about what lay before me. I had received employment offers from the United States Post Office and Standard Oil of Ohio, where my brother-in-law worked, and both employers requested that I report to work on the same day. I was tempted to accept the offer by Standard Oil because it paid more, so I called my father in Detroit to ask his advice; he responded that the decision was mine but "those government jobs are pretty reliable."

At the time, the president of the United States was Dwight Eisenhower, the postmaster general was Arthur Summerfield, first-class postage was three cents, and gasoline was twenty-four cents

4

per gallon. The world was a far different place and on that first day of employment my objective was merely to get through the day.

As I entered the imposing building, I was apprehensive; I had no idea where I was going or what to expect. Upon arriving in the designated room, I listened to a brief introduction to the rules of employment before my group of twenty-two rookies was escorted to the work floor—and *wow!* The room was cavernous, measuring two city blocks long and a block wide. It was filled with row after row of yellow cartons perched on shelves. We were informed that these were "cases" in which mail was deposited according to the address on the envelope. Ashtrays were affixed to the cases to accommodate the many smokers. It was the City Division mail distribution area, and I would soon be placing letters in the corresponding pigeon holes of the assigned case. My first thought was, *So this is where my mail goes, but how do they distinguish one letter from the other?*

Distributing Mail

In the letter sorting section where we were assigned, the post office had designed a system of casing mail that could be mastered by anyone with average intelligence and dexterity. You read the address on the letter and deposited it in the corresponding bin positioned in numerical sequence starting in the bottom lower left hole of the distribution case. This was five years before the adoption of the national zip code (which occurred in 1963), so the distribution of mailed items was determined by the number assigned to the community where delivery was made. In 1958, the post office in Cleveland divided the city into alphabetical units and each alphabetical designation was further divided into numerical sections, so each postal zone had a letter and number attached, beginning with A-2, B-3, C-4, and so on.

The suburbs bordering the city were identified by the name of the community and were integrated into the numbering sequence. Thus Shaker Heights, Ohio, was assigned the number twenty in the postal scheme; mail destined for a resident in that community would be addressed to Shaker Heights, Ohio 20. In reality, most mail for that area would simply be addressed by the sender to Shaker Heights, Ohio, and it was the distribution clerk's responsibility to sort it to zone 20. This distribution system was difficult to master, especially for new clerks who didn't know the city, and my productivity was less than average. At that time, the strategy of postal officials was to overwhelm the volume of mail with sufficient numbers of employees so the lack of efficiency of a few employees would be compensated for by others who were more experienced. During those years, postal employment was a revolving door, for many did not adapt to the unusual hours, the low pay, and the scheme study requirements. Among the new employees were political appointees who would not have career status but would continue employment for years.

As a typical government agency, the post office was highly regulated. Similar to the military, it even had rules and regulations for sorting mail; some bureaucrat with nothing better to do had defined the preferred means of mail distributing, instructing clerks in the proper way to extract mail from two-foot-long plastic trays positioned on the ledge of the letter case using the "official posture." There were precise instructions on how much mail to retrieve from the tray with each extraction, how to elevate it to the chest, and how to bend one's arm at a ninety-degree angle when moving forward to the designated bin. Everyone seemed to ignore these guidelines, but I was new and feared supervisory disapproval, so I tried.

We were given the option to perform the task of mail distribution while sitting or standing. I tried sitting, but the seat provided was designed as a means of medieval torture to those stupid enough to try to relax while casing mail. In less than one hour, I experienced excruciating pain in my back and legs as I contorted my body to conform to this strange device that I later learned was referred to as a "crutch." It was constructed of metal tubing with a platform and a foot rest. It could be moved up and down, but no position was comfortable. The upholstered seat could not be adjusted to a flat position. It appeared that the department's objective was to make you uncomfortable while casing mail, and it had succeeded. I elected to lean on the seating device, and the pain subsided over time to the point of being just uncomfortable. (Much later in my career, I devoted much time and energy to finding an ergonomically designed replacement, but despite my best efforts, the crutch is still torturing postal workers today.)

The supervisors informed us that special attention should be given to the letters marked "Air Mail" and "Special Delivery," both of which required additional postage, with special delivery receiving the highest priority. There were specially marked bins in the letter case where airmail and special deliveries were to be deposited for regular retrieval by a designated employee for dispatch to the Airmail Processing Facility located at the Cleveland Airport. At that time, the Cleveland Main Post Office processed mail for thirty-seven delivery stations; airmail was processed at the AMF located on the grounds of the Cleveland airport and special delivery and parcels at the parcel post annex, a separate building several miles from the main post office.

Mail was brought to the dock by truck from street collection boxes, the airfield, and trains arriving from distant locations. Upon arrival at the main post office, the mail sacks were unloaded onto carts, which were essentially platforms with wheels and handles, referred to as "nutting trucks." They were pushed onto the freight elevator and transported to the distribution floor where they were stacked into a pyramid—and when I describe it as a "mountain" of mail, I do not exaggerate. Mail sacks were piled more than six feet high. The mail handlers were in charge of extracting the mail from the sacks, and it was dirty work. Many of the mail sacks contained debris and dust—and on occasion dead animals—that had been extracted from the street collection boxes. The mail handlers would remove the mail from the sacks in an operation known as "dumping." True to form, postal management had developed precise rules to govern the process and prevent individual letters from being lost in the thousands of sacks filled with mail. There were inspections and final inspections to ensure that every item had been removed, but despite these safeguards, there were stories of letters being found many years later in otherwise empty mail sacks in some obscure location.

My job was to read the written addresses on envelopes and deposit them in the corresponding bins. Most of the letters were handwritten, as this time was years before the widespread use of computers and return envelopes, and for letters with messy handwriting, it was the postal employee's job to interpret the intent of the sender. For the letters with addresses of delivery that I did not know, I was instructed to deposit them in a special bin to be processed by a more experienced clerk. I filled this bin very quickly because I was new and had absolutely no knowledge of the postal distribution scheme.

Minutes stretched into hours while I struggled to familiarize myself with the tasks; after six painful hours—with no lunch—I heard the announcement that Group 32 was instructed to end tour. Clocks with a second hand were positioned on every wall to facilitate mail dispatches, and watching the passing of time, second by second, hour by tortuous hour was unavoidable. I departed the building and as I ended that first day of employment, I hoped that the letters that I had misdirected more often than not found their destinations. I had been trained by my father that I should do all my work to the best of my ability.

Having completed my first day as a postal employee, I walked to the bus stop for the return trip to my sister's apartment, which required an additional ten-block walk after the bus ride. I had time to contemplate what I had gotten myself into. Was this the beginning of a career, or should I review the "Help Wanted" section of the paper for something else? Since I left the army in June, regular permanent employment had been elusive. I had worked since the age of eleven, beginning with a paper route, then picking blackberries and selling them to neighbors for two dollars a quart, and progressing upward to cleaning the family's hair dressing salon, attending to the attached newsstand, custodial duties at Fulton National Bank and Horn's department store, and then the wide experiences of three years in the army. I was mentally prepared for permanent employment, and I knew that I needed a regular job. President Eisenhower's conservative economic policies had not generated expansion in the steel and auto industries. The path taken by the generation before me was not available, so it was the post office or what?

On the following day, I made the long walk to the bus stop, repeating the ride to Public Square for another day as a substitute clerk, earning $1.67 per hour with no work hour guarantees or any other rights that I was informed of. The orders were that I was to follow the instructions of the supervisor assigned to Group 32 without delay. I was directed to my assignment and resumed the activity of putting letters in the case pursuant to the instructions given on the previous day. I continued this activity for weeks, and over time I developed a rhythm and formed alliances with other new hires in my group, some of which developed into lifelong friendships. Lloyd Hayes and Al Steel were my closest companions, and we developed personal relationships that would last throughout my Cleveland career. Al Steel was near my age, so we connected as peers. Lloyd was of my father's generation; he became more like a mentor.

Schemes

From day one of employment, I was informed of the requirement to be tested on "schemes," the knowledge of postal zones that determine how the mail is distributed. Each geographical area was dedicated to a specific delivery zone—primary sortation—and then to a specific letter carrier—secondary sortation—for delivery. These multiple delivery points were combined into schemes, and each clerical employee was required to memorize the assigned schemes. I was assigned the Cleveland City scheme and H-8 Delivery Station as a secondary scheme, so I had to know the entire primary sortation city scheme (consisting of seven or eight zones), plus the secondary scheme of H-8.

I was born and raised primarily in Wheeling, West Virginia, with stints in foster homes in the Ohio Valley, Columbus, and Toledo. After serving three years in the army, I returned to Steubenville to connect with a jilted girlfriend, Barbara Turner, who had formed a relationship with the proverbial Jody, so I had no knowledge of Cleveland, its streets, or geographical layout. Because I was not a native of Cleveland, I knew absolutely nothing about the city, so committing the entire city to memory was quite challenging.

As a child, I spent several summers in Cleveland with my mother, Gertrude, and Jimmy Foreman, who owned a hat cleaning shop on Quincy Avenue. He collected numbers (the lottery in the colored community) and always had a container full of coins that my mother would raid and distribute to Jane and me. My grandmother on my mother's side, Arizona Rushin, lived with us over an apartment on Fifty-Ninth and Quincy Avenue, but because of Mother's concern for my safety, I was limited to a two-block radius to explore the neighborhoods; I learned very little about the city.

Each postal address was a name to be committed to memory. A single street like Euclid Avenue was delivered to by letter carriers in five different delivery zones, so I had to memorize the specific address that changed delivery from one to another. Therefore, I was forced to commit to memory over five thousand bits of information, which was no different from the other three thousand distribution clerks—but most of them had the advantage of knowing streets by name and could visualize their locations.

Each clerk was tested twice annually on knowledge of sections of the Cleveland delivery scheme until completion of the city's cycle—a period of approximately six years—and then the clerks were tested once each year. For mail destined outside the Cleveland mailing community, there was a similar schematic system, but I was never assigned schemes for the state of Ohio or other states, so I had no interest in understanding the scheme construction applied.

To assist clerks in the memorization of schemes, we were given index cards with the name of a street with the address range of a specific delivery zone printed on one side and the assigned zone printed on the reverse side. It was common to see postal clerks studying these cards at every opportunity: on buses, in the break room or restroom, and at the dinner table. The pressure to pass the examination was tremendous because passing determined your continued employment.

Within this arena of scheme study, there were also distribution assignments attached to working in the mail car on trains. I resisted the temptation of transferring even though the history of the colored Pullman porters was alive in our communities. The work schedules, consisting of ten- to twelve-hour workdays with six and seven days off, were enticing. I was informed that in earlier years processing mail on trains was one of the few jobs available for former slaves because it was extremely dangerous. The cars were wooden, and accidents often led to death or disability. The distribution of mail on trains was phased out several years after my initial employment, and the employees were reassigned to mail processing plants throughout the country. Slotting their seniority became a contentious issue, and I was glad that I had not opted to transfer.

The scheme proficiency test consisted of a distribution case in an isolated room under the watchful eye of an instructor. These instructors were cold, mean men who befriended no one. Their job was to test scheme knowledge, and they went about the task with determined efficiency. In the test, the instructor presented the employee with a package of one hundred cards with addresses on one side and no identification on the reverse side. The clerk was given two minutes to sort each of the cards in the appropriate bin in the distribution case and was required to be 95 percent accurate. The rate was later changed to 98 percent, which only raised the anxiety levels for postal employees. If you did not know the first five cards, nerves would take over and you were doomed. I was instructed to immediately rotate unknown cards to the back of the stack so I did not waste precious time attempting to recall the correct delivery zone. Failure to qualify after three attempts in thirty-day intervals led to automatic dismissal, which was a major cause of concern for me and my coworkers. There were employees who never mastered the trick of converting street addresses to zones, and after the third failure, they were automatically terminated. No grievances, no hardships, no discrimination complaints; that was the process, and it was accepted as a condition of employment.

After passing several scheme exams, I became comfortable enough with my ability to memorize street addresses and their destinations. However, I would delay the examination as long as possible. I began a routine of requesting extensions for each scheduled examination, a maximum of two. Then I would fail to report for the first two exams, accepting two automatic failures. After requesting the two extensions, I reported for the third examination and passed it with flying colors. This process added months to the qualifying period, but it also put added pressure on the final exam. The pressure of passing the test was so great that there was a story of a female employee in the Cleveland office who was so engrossed in studying up to the time of the actual exam that she reported for testing in her bathrobe.

Scheme study and testing was so effective that fifty-three years later I still recall the delivery zones of Cleveland, Ohio, distribution. Congress later amended the Fair Labor Standards Act to require compensation for scheme study, an amendment that was sponsored by a legislator from Missouri, Bill Clay, who would become a dear personal friend. Under the "suffer and permit" limitations in the legislation, the postal service was required to modify significantly the terms of scheme study, but at that time, you either passed the schemes in three attempts or found other employment. Later, automation through computerization dramatically reduced the requirement for scheme study.

Cancellation

To prevent stamp reuse, the postal employees placed ink marks on the stamps to indicate their prior use. The process was called "cancellation," and there was a separate operation devoted to cancelling the stamps prior to mail distribution. The mail handler passed each letter through a pinch point in the Marc mechanical cancellation machines, which disfigured the stamp with an ink blot. There was also an ink pad at each letter case so the clerk could manually disfigure the stamp on any letters that were missed on the cancellation machine. Prior to processing the letters on the cancellation machine, the letters had to be positioned in a tray with the stamps all facing down to the left of the operator.

The cancellation of stamps affixed to flats and parcels involved a different operation. The employee used a hammer-like device to strike alternately on an ink pad and the flat or parcel, physically placing a mark on each stamp. The employees assigned were skilled at positioning the mail item and disfiguring the stamp while in the process of retrieving the next item. Experienced employees, mostly substitute clerks, would develop a rhythm of striking the stamps and the ink pad in tandem; on my tour, Chico was the best. He was a tall, well-built, colored employee who was one of the most popular among the substitute employees. Chico was designated Captain of the Subs on Tour 3, and he cancelled flats with a flourish. He had a portable radio positioned near his perch and would cancel to the beat of the music.

In the course of distributing letters, there was ample opportunity to engage coworkers in conversation. Our conversations ranged from history, discrimination, sports, philosophy, and theater to, of course, girls. You name it; someone was an expert. As the youngest among these seasoned veterans, having turned twenty-one only months before, I was provided an education. I was accustomed to being the youngest among my peers. I was enrolled in the first grade at the age of four, so when I entered my senior year in high school, I had celebrated my sixteenth birthday only months before. During my military service, my fellow soldiers, many of whom had been drafted, were in their mid to late twenties while I had only recently turned seventeen. My mother was required to sign the enlistment papers and provide a birth certificate. When we went to the courthouse to retrieve my records, we were surprised to learn that at birth my name had been recorded as William Burrus Jr. My father's name was William Henry Burrus, so at that point mine was officially changed to include the middle name.

Substitute

We were instructed that substitute clerks were required to report to the swing room for assignment. The swing room was where we would wait—off the clock—for the call to begin work. It was adjacent to the cafeteria and had a Ping-Pong table that occupied our time while we waited for instructions. We spent the idle time playing cards (whist), talking, learning schemes, playing Ping-Pong, or just looking out the window. I was good at Ping-Pong, having played during my three-year tour in the army. There were days when subs spent more time playing Ping-Pong than performing paid work.

Over the ensuing months, this was the routine, and I was fortunate that my group was assigned to begin working within several hours of the posted hour. We were informed that our schedule would be posted on the work floor's overhead electronic bulletin board by group for the following day. The swing room with its electronic bulletin board looked like the train station.

The work routine would begin tour at 3:30 p.m. and, upon call by the supervisor, would be terminated after six hours without lunch or eight and a half hours (or longer) with lunch. The employment rules at the time were set exclusively by management, so they were made based on the conditions of the moment and the whims of the supervisor or other higher authority. There was no regularity to the workday for a substitute. It could range from one to twelve hours and one to seven days a week, depending on the manpower needed at a specific time.

The decision of whether or not to pack a lunch was important because of the uncertain length of the workday. One could choose to eat in the cafeteria on the fourth floor where the food was of modest price, but the quality depended upon the time of day. All employees were permitted to use the cafeteria, but as recently as 1941, seating in many post office cafeterias was determined by race, with coloreds limited to a designated area. Before an amendment to the Randolph Sheppard Act in 1974 that required the operations of all vending facilities on federal properties to be operated by the blind, the cafeteria was under employee control.

On one occasion, an audit revealed that funds in the Cleveland cafeteria were missing. To conceal the misappropriation, a burglar threw the safe from the fourth-floor cafeteria window, hoping it would break open and the financial loss could be attributed to the event. The plans were thwarted when the safe landed on the roof of a car parked below and remained intact. The burglars were never caught, but the manager resigned from his post.

Christmas Rush

The month of December was a special time in the post office. The influx of Christmas cards and packages overwhelmed the capacity of the regular workforce. All schedules were changed to twelve-hour days for a period of two weeks, and management hired hundreds of temporary workers: policeman, firemen, school teachers, and housewives who wanted to supplement their income. Women were permitted to work during the Christmas rush, but they were denied career employment for the balance of the year.

To work during the Christmas rush for temporary employment, one had to visit the local office of the congressperson and request a temporary Christmas appointment. The congressional office forwarded a list to the post office, and the prospective temporary employees would report for duty for the Christmas mail rush. The twelve-hour schedule for the regular workforce led to many deviations from normal behavior. Seeing a clerk sipping from a container of what appeared to be a soft drink but was in fact mixed with vodka, which had no smell and was undetectable by the supervisors, was not unusual.

Eventually I settled into a pattern of normalcy, living at the two-bedroom apartment of my sister—sharing one bedroom with her three-year-old son, Kevin—and working the night shift at the post office and engaging in social activities with my coworkers. My sister was an excellent cook, so I was well nourished. I fell into a routine of mail distribution that had no sense of completion. There was a mountain of mail at the beginning of each workday and a mountain of mail when the assigned tour was completed. There was never a visual sense of accomplishment.

CHAPTER 2

Making My Way

CONNECTIONS

Shortly after my initial employment, I married Claudette Vinson, a native of Steubenville, and soon became the father of two daughters, Valerie and Doni. Claudette's brother, Eddie "Pumpkin" Vinson, was an All-Big Ten tailback at the University of Iowa in 1954–55, so my marriage to his sister was a step up the social ladder.

Forest Evashevski, the football coach at the University of Iowa, had embarked on the bold experiment of recruiting colored high school players from small schools. He visited Steubenville Senior High School, which was across the Ohio River from Wheeling, and recruited Eddie Vinson, Calvin Jones, and Horace Gilliam from the racially mixed Steubenville High School. Each would earn All-American and Big Ten accolades, and Gilliam went on to a rewarding pro career. Calvin Jones, a defensive tackle and the only college football player ever to win the Outland trophy for three years, signed with a Canadian team. Tragically, the airplane on which he was a passenger disappeared and has never been found. Eddie received a pro offer from the Los Angeles

Rams, but the salary was so small that he elected to teach school and proceeded to become the mayor of Inglewood, California, and then a state assemblyman. My association with these legends in the Ohio Valley and the fact that I had been selected as all-state made me the resident expert on football issues among my coworkers.

New Assignment to Flats

After months of this routine among the same group of employees, almost exclusively men, I was informed that my assignment would be changed to working the "flats" on the third floor with a begin tour of 10:00 p.m. This change meant reporting to a different floor, among a different group of coworkers, and performing different tasks. Flats were distributed on the third floor of the main post office in an open area that was two blocks by one block. Windows lined the exterior walls. "Flats" were loosely defined as any mail matter that was too large to fit in a letter case but was not a parcel. The bins into which they were distributed were configured to accommodate large envelopes and magazines. The distribution followed the same scheme, so my limited experience in the letter section prepared me for the task. However, as a new employee to the flat section, I was assigned the more physical duty of removing full sacks from the iron racks that wheeled the flats to and away from the distribution cases.

There was no air-conditioning on the work floor, so instead we used fans to move the air when it was hot and opened the windows that lined the exterior walls by turning the handles and pivoting the windows inward. There was constant disagreement over were the hurricane fans should be directed. In the winter, there was uneven heating from the radiators, and some employees wore sweaters or coats while they worked. Strings dangled from florescent light fixtures attached to the thirty-foot ceiling. When working in a defined area, the worker pulled the string to begin work and upon completion of the shift—end tour—pulled the string to close down the station and save energy. The floor was wooden, and during idle time, some employees would stick knives into makeshift targets. If assigned to work the culling belt where letters were separated from flats and parcels, we were issued paring knives for cutting the string from bundles collected from the street mailboxes. While waiting for the arrival of unprocessed mail, we would make a circle on the wooden floor with the removed string and throw the knives at the target to pass the time. Throwing the knives became competitive over time, and the most demanding test was to throw the knife as close as possible to the challenger's shoe. I became pretty good.

We had to get approval to leave our work area to go to the restroom, which was near the vending machines and elevators. There were two sets of elevators, one to transport employees between floors and two elevators to transport mail. During a major dispatch, a mail handler was assigned to the freight elevators. His job was to load and deliver mail to the dock or to the floor of distribution. This was a cushy job reserved for senior mail handlers.

Entering this new work environment, I welcomed the escape from the torture device, and with my new responsibilities of "tying out" full sacks of distributed flat mail, I was free to move throughout the floor, interacting with other workers. Mail sacks were attached to a metal rack in a sequence matching the flat distribution case; upon filling a bin in the case, the clerk would remove the flats and deposit them in the racked sacks. Each mail sack had a row of grommets inserted into holes and swivel hooks attached to the mail racks that were placed into the holes, creating an opening to deposit mail. Technically it was a job assigned to the mail handlers; however, supervisors found it more productive to use substitute clerks because they could be used on distribution tasks and there was no grievance procedure to challenge work assignments.

A full No. 2 sack by rule was limited to sixty pounds. However, the rule was often violated because tying out full sacks slowed down productivity. It required stopping distribution, affixing a destination label in the pouch, removing the sack from the rack, and tying on its replacement. It was not unusual for a mail sack filled with flats to weigh seventy-five pounds or more. Being young and athletic, I welcomed the physical challenge. This new work assignment was filled with a different group of workers, all male with the exception of two females who were not required to tie out full sacks. After tying out the sacks, we stacked them on nutting trucks for transport to the dock for dispatch. At a given hour, the mail distributed for a specific Cleveland destination would be tied out (combined) and presented to the dock for transportation to the respective section of the city. I took great pride in my ability to remove the sacks from the racks at a fast pace, replace them quickly, and sequence the full trucks for dispatch to the docks. With experience, I was able to simultaneously maneuver three full nutting trucks, each loaded with twenty to thirty sacks.

All Hands on Deck

One Thursday night each month was especially challenging for the flat section. That was the night that the *Look* monthly magazines were delivered, and it was "all hands on deck"—everyone was required to participate in the flats distribution work. Each magazine weighed in the neighborhood of two pounds, and each distribution bin held twenty-five to thirty *Look* magazines. The weight restriction was generally ignored, and at the end of the shift we were physically spent. We took great pride in distributing and tying out all the magazines so the subscribers could enjoy their view of the world on Friday.

A similar "all hands on deck" call was made once each month in the letters section when the social security and welfare checks were processed for delivery. The call was that every check would be processed and transported to the assigned station for delivery the following day. The Social Security office would deliver millions of checks to post offices nationwide. Cleveland had approximately 750,000 citizens at that time, with a sizeable number of them receiving Social Security, retirement, or public assistance (for which checks were delivered at the same time), so there were hundreds of thousands of checks that had to be processed in a window of a few hours.

The checks and *Look* magazines would be received on the loading dock, brought to the appropriate work center for distribution, and sent back to the dock for transport to the delivery station. The entire window of time to perform the operation was dictated by when the checks arrived and the time of dispatch. If the checks were received late, there was less time to distribute the letters in time for dispatch to the delivery station. The clerks had to put everything on hold to "get out" the Social Security and welfare checks. We often heard stories of letter carriers in the process of delivering mail being followed down the street by agitated citizens demanding, "Where's my check?"

Once while working in the flats section, I noticed a glossy magazine titled *Life in the USSR*. As we often did with items of interest, I flipped through it, glancing at the contents. That was during the Cold War, and everything about Russia was suspect. I anticipated that the magazine would be a source of propaganda, but I was inquisitive and copied the ordering information. I subsequently placed an order for a subscription, and for several years I received copies of the magazine at my home, fully aware that it only showed the positive side of life in Russia—but that's fair game because we only showed the positive side of America. After several years, I cancelled the order and satisfied my quest for a more rounded view of the world through expanded TV coverage. I have never had an interest in Communism, but I am sure that the FBI developed a file on William Burrus.

In the center of the work floor was a table where damaged items were taken for repair. The activity was referred to as "rewrap" and was also considered a preferred assignment. This assignment was generally reserved for clerks, and we used tape and string to restore items close to their original condition. One Christmas Eve when I had volunteered to work rewrap, among the damaged items was a small parcel that needed repair. Because there would be no delivery on Christmas Day, we were operating with a skeleton crew. While repairing the damaged package, I noticed that it contained a diamond ring with a short letter expressing the wishes of the sender to become engaged. I inserted a note admonishing the sender for failing to insure the ring. After repair, the ring was appropriately dispatched, and a young lady most likely enjoyed a special moment.

Ronald "Smitty" Smith

I formed a new set of working relationships in the flats section, most notably with Ronald Smith, a fellow employee and mail handler who was approximately ten years my senior. Smitty, as he was called, was good-natured and streetwise. He moonlighted as a barber in Floyd's Barber Shop, and in short order he became my barber. The shop was always filled with customers and barbers who knew everything about every subject. In just a short time, they converted me to jazz music, and I became a fan of Charlie Parker, Miles Davis, and other jazz greats.

During my formative years in Wheeling, my choice of music had been rhythm and blues. I was not a very good dancer despite the lessons that I took in tap dancing, but I knew all of the latest songs and the artists. The local radio stations played country and western, so to satisfy my listening pleasure, I tuned to "Randy" from Nashville, Tennessee, late at night, concealing the radio under the sheets so I would not disturb my mother. My conversion to jazz was a new and exciting experience embellished by the mail-order record albums that were processed in the flats section. Capital

Records had initiated a sales campaign that included mail delivery of music albums customers selected monthly from a published list. The packaging was not sufficiently strong, and the rewrap table always had a few albums protruding from the boxes. I was able to keep abreast of the latest and more popular jazz albums. In addition, Smitty had a connection to a bootleg album distributor, and one night each month he would bring an armful of albums to the locker room for our inspection and sale. As a friend, I could negotiate a good price and would often leave work having spent less than ten dollars for three albums. In short order, I accumulated a collection of jazz music and could engage in meaningful conversation about The Modern Jazz Quartet, Billy Holiday, Stan Getz, and others. My sister Jane also developed a taste for jazz, and often we would compare notes on our favorite artists. We were especially fond of jazz vocalists Sarah Vaughn and Lorez Alexandria.

Smitty's hair was processed—you know, straightened with chemicals. It was the new fashion in the black male community, and I was tempted to try it, but I resisted and continued the Afro style that I felt was more consistent with the black militant movement of the times. On occasion, I would visit the barber shop on 120th and Superior Avenue just to engage in stimulating conversation. Smitty was the owner of a new black Cadillac, and it appeared that he knew everyone in town. At work, he and I became a team, tying out sacks—and we were the best.

Smitty later transferred to Los Angeles and, after working in the post office for several years, gained employment at a movie studio in Hollywood styling hair for actors, including Robert Conrad, who was quite popular at the time. On one occasion, while we visited the West Coast, he escorted Ethelda and me to a live viewing of *Challenge of the Stars*.

Working Two Jobs

To increase my standard of living, which was limited by the pitiful postal wage of $1.67 per hour, I began painting houses during the day and working at the post office at night. Painting the exterior of homes was a physical job. At the time, the twenty-foot ladders and walk boards were constructed from wood, and the paint was oil-based, resulting in my inhaling toxic fumes in extremely hot weather.

The professional way of exterior painting is to begin at the top and work one's way to ground level. We placed the ladders against the house at a distance of eighteen feet apart and attached the walk boards with jacks to the rung of the ladders near the top. This arrangement enabled us to paint the distance between the ladders before relocating the setup. Each time we moved to paint a different area, we had to carry the walk board and supporting jacks down the ladders, move the ladders, and carry the walk board and supporting jacks back up the ladders. To save time, we would move the ladders without collapsing them. I became experienced at repositioning the extended ladders (forty feet) from one location to another, which was an extreme balancing act.

This process was tiring, and after six to ten hours in the blazing sun, I needed rest before going on to my post office job. I often took advantage of the generous postal leave policy that credited four hours of sick leave and six hours of vacation leave for each two-week pay period. In combination, I was able to be absent periodically and receive full pay. Leave had to be used strategically because supervisors constantly reviewed it for patterns of abuse.

This secondary employment was not unusual at the time since women, including my new wife, had yet to enter the workforce in large numbers, so many of my male coworkers also had second jobs in a variety of occupations. Over the ensuing fifteen years before my attention was diverted exclusively to union affairs, I worked a second job as a house painter, a shipping clerk at a toy distribution warehouse, and a dispatcher at Pinkerton's Detective Agency. I supplemented my income, but I lost quality time with my children.

Party

The city of Cleveland is divided by the Cuyahoga River, which separates the east side from the west side; at that time, people of color were restricted to housing on the east side with boundaries generally from Thirtieth Street to Lee Road, a distance of approximately fifteen miles. Housing and entertainment on the west side was exclusively for whites, so when postal employees of different races left work, they went in their own directions, east or west. Cleveland did not have legal racial restrictions, but we knew where we were not welcome, so we would visit establishments that catered exclusively to people of color. We worked together and formed relationships, but in our personal time we gravitated to our own.

Life for Cleveland postal employees working the night shift had its own rhythms and customs. When our neighbors were going to work, we were ending our work day, so we socialized primarily with one another. On the morning after payday, we would spend hours in the bars, drinking and bonding with each other, dependent upon other obligations including secondary employment. We would visit a bar on Cedar Avenue that catered to colored postal employees and provided a check cashing service for a fee that included any amount on the check that was less than a full dollar. So if the payroll check was in the amount of $152.68, the tavern retained the sixty-eight cents as a check cashing fee. We would arrive at the bar directly from work at 8:00 a.m. and would often stay far into the day—and night—drinking and talking. On several such occasions after I got married, my wife voiced her displeasure, so I limited my frequency at the bar.

I never engaged in heavy drinking, and on the few occasions that I imbibed to the extent that I could feel it, I stopped to clear my head and recover full control. (I never became attached to marijuana for that reason, as I did not believe that I could control the level of intoxication.) One exception was a Cleveland Browns home game when the temperature was hovering near zero and

I drank much more than I could handle. My choice of drink at that time was 151 proof rum mixed with coke—not because it tasted good but because it was manly. After that occasion, I took stock and decided that alcohol—even mixed—did not please my taste buds, so I discontinued drinking hard alcohol except on rare occasions. My preference from that day to this has been wine in moderation.

During my childhood in Wheeling, the place to engage in public drinking was the pool hall that was located in the basement under Doc's drugstore and a movie theatre. The pool hall was dimly lit and served alcohol to the men who were on the edges of society, unemployed and of ill repute. Of the few restrictions placed on me by my father, at the top of the list was to stay out of the pool hall. Like any rebellious youth, I was inquisitive, and at the age of fourteen I was a regular, learning the game. By sixteen, I was competitive with all of the players except Fats, a smooth-dressing player who could make any shot, including the far rail into the side pocket, the toughest shot on the table. He was the king of 8- and 9-ball, and I wanted to be like Fats. I never developed my game enough to be competitive with him, but I could hold my own with the other players. I especially enjoyed the ritual of tapping the end of the pool stick on the floor after vanquishing an opponent and pronouncing for all to hear: "Rack."

Doc White's drugstore was the rendezvous point for young colored children. Doc was the patriarch of the colored community and, along with his partner, Doc Davis, was the co-owner of the drugstore. They sold sundries, and Doc White was known for scooping the exact amount of ice cream that would fit in the cone, pounding against the side of the container until all of the ice cream that would not fit had been removed. Each time I purchased an ice cream cone, I would plead with Doc to "give me some edges." Doc reserved the lower floor of his establishment as a gathering place for teenagers; it had a jukebox for dancing. I never learned the latest steps for fast dancing, so when I deposited my quarters,

I picked a slow number and loved getting close to the girls. That was as close as we would get to sex. Doc White served as the liaison between the city government and the colored community, organizing many social events, including picnics and late night boat rides. Prior to entering the army, I was a frequent visitor to Doc's and the pool hall, but I never adopted the unsavory habit of alcohol consumption.

Another favorite hangout after work was at the homes of fellow employees who held rent parties. They would prepare food—normally fried chicken or fish—serve drinks, and reserve one room for poker with the house taking a cut (10 percent) on each hand. These parties were very festive and often served as a rendezvous for couples to meet and plan their evening. The rent parties would often continue far into the evening. I did not frequent these events because I did not participate in excessive gambling or drinking. I did not think the expected winnings were worth the possible loss of my hard-earned money due to the hand of cards one was dealt. On the occasions that I did attend these functions, I would leave at a decent hour.

While in the military, I did not develop the habit of gambling but rather loaned money to the soldiers who did. The rate was 50 percent. I gave $10 for a $15 payment by the soldiers who lost their entire monthly checks in a matter of hours and needed money for basics until they received their next checks. The soldiers who did gamble and drink excessively would visit the closest city on paydays and frequent the bars reserved for the military. Some would return to the barracks with cases of beer that they would drink throughout the weekend. I never developed a taste for beer, and I did not understand why it was so popular as a drink of choice. I elected instead to visit the closest town and mingle with the townspeople. Visiting town was the way we met girls, many of whom adjusted their lives to center around the visiting soldiers.

Finding places for entertainment was challenging for colored soldiers stationed in the southern states because coloreds were not permitted to frequent many of the establishments. In addition, at the time of my service, the military drew many of the recruits from that slice of the population that had been exposed to racial divisions as a matter of law and custom; for them, racial separation was considered natural. When I was stationed in Texas for an extended period, the news was reported that a colored soldier had molested a white girl in Waco, so all of the bars prohibited colored soldiers. Therefore, we would often visit Villa Cuna, Mexico, for entertainment, which was over one hundred miles from the post.

To break the fatigue and monotony of military training, we relaxed through social gatherings fueled by alcohol, but the camaraderie that we developed while soldiering often disappeared when we engaged in recreational activities. The military had recently integrated with the deactivation of the last all-colored unit, 94th Engineer Battalion, in 1954, the year that I enlisted. The officers and top-ranking soldiers were predominately white; many were from the Deep South and had never interacted with people of a different color before entering the military, so the racial mixing created moments of discomfort. Many of the white recruits had not attended school or socialized with peers of a different race. They had been exposed to all of the prejudices produced by their environment, so interacting with coloreds as equals for the first time was a new experience for them—and me.

On occasion, a ranking white soldier would casually use a racist term with no intent of animosity; on the weekends after they extensively imbibed beer, we would find that we had more in common than we had envisioned. Thus, I evolved from my life in Wheeling, where I had no personal contact with white people with the exception of one family who lived in my community and my employers in various establishments. Soldiering was a unifying experience, but the struggle for racial equality was long from over.

CHAPTER 3

Struggle and Change

New Friends

My coworkers had a major influence in shaping the remainder of my life. Of the four to five thousand employees (when considering attrition) with whom I had the privilege of working directly during the early years of my postal employment, fewer than ten were women—colored women. Anne Thomas, one of the few women in the flats section, befriended me, and we developed a permanent friendship. Anne lived in my neighborhood on the east side, and prior to my purchasing a car, she would occasionally provide me transportation to and from work.

At the time, female postal employees were limited to wives of deceased veterans, so the workforce was overwhelmingly male. Colored men constituted perhaps 20 percent of the clerk workforce in Cleveland and were concentrated in the physical jobs. My older coworkers were a source of my education as many were college graduates who were unable to obtain other employment because discrimination was rampant in the post office and in society as a whole. My coworkers willingly shared their knowledge of the world, schooling me daily in subjects ranging from Shakespeare to world affairs.

Clarence Coles was the resident expert on literature, and he and I would share our knowledge of great works, including "Gunga Din," "The Rime of the Ancient Mariner," and other classics. Clarence displayed his talents as an actor at Karamu House, a historical African American theatre, and electrified us with his booming voice. Smitty, Banks, Maceo, and Freddie Green were war veterans and regaled us daily with their knowledge of the world. Ricks was near my age, but he was wild and crazy. He liked to challenge me in throwing the paring knife into a target on the floor. When the conversation turned to football, having been selected as an all-state football player among the colored schools in West Virginia and given my association with my All-Big-Ten brother-in-law, I thought that I knew everything. Although I was never a Cleveland Browns fan, during the Jim Brown years when the Cleveland Browns were perennial contenders for the championship, I was the "expert" on football issues in the daily discussions. I loved the game and played semipro with a local team when my work schedule could be adjusted.

Jimmy Shields, the owner of a gas station at the end of Parkwood Drive, became my best friend and confidant. I would spend hours in the station after work discussing personal and worldly issues with Jimmy and other regular customers. Jimmy and his brother, James, who had a gas station on 105th Avenue, had relocated to Cleveland from a rural area of Alabama, and they would tell me stories of oppression that I had not been exposed to in West Virginia. When I moved away from Cleveland, our relationship became distant, but whenever I returned to visit my children and grandchildren, the gas station on Parkwood Drive was a necessary stop on my itinerary.

While still in high school, I had developed the desire to dress well. Using my wages earned as the bank custodian, I purchased several tailor-made suits and matching dress hats. The hats caused minor disagreements with my mother when I used her cornmeal to clean them. The hats had color bands that matched my ties, and I favored Mr. "B" Billie Eckstine shirts with the rolled collar. After gaining employment and organizing my finances, my choice of dress was slacks and sweaters, and I assembled an impressive collection of fashionable attire.

Transportation

With the combined incomes from postal employment and painting houses, I was able to purchase a 1952 Ford convertible although I didn't have a driver's license at the time. My father did not own a car during my years at home, and when I was in high school and purchased a repossessed 1946 Packard from the bank where I was working, my school buddy Thomas Wallace served as my driver. While in the military working as the company supply clerk, I typed myself a military license even though I couldn't drive. Adriel Brown, a native of Warren, Ohio, befriended me. He was many years older than I, and during our travels, Adriel did all of the driving.

My relationship with Adriel developed when I was assigned to tanks at Fort Knox, Kentucky. Each tank had a crew of four members: the driver, the commander, the gunner, and the loader. The assignments were alphabetical, thus Adriel and I were assigned to the same crew, along with Brooks and Buckner. Brooks and Buckner were white, but we formed a bond that ignored any racial separation. After reassignment to Fort Hood, Texas, I lost track of Bill Buckner. I was informed that Brooks was murdered by a jealous husband in a domestic dispute. Adriel and I remained friends for the rest of our tours.

We were so close that together we purchased a 1948 Ford that served as transportation to nearby cities and Mexico for weekend entertainment. On one occasion, when the National Guard was satisfying their active service obligation, my commander requested volunteers to serve as drivers for the officers. I volunteered even though driving the stick-shift jeep was way beyond my skills.

After repeated excuses on my part when I lurched and stalled the jeep, the officer turned to me and said, "You cannot drive." I was still game, so when I used my leave to return to Wheeling, Adriel insisted that I drive the car even though I didn't have a civilian driver's license. On the trip from Fort Hood, Texas, to Wheeling, a distance of two thousand four hundred miles, I kept the car on the road and did not cause any accidents. By the time I returned to Texas, I could drive.

Females Enter the Workforce

I settled into a normal routine of working two jobs and engaged in family life as time would permit, but work at the post office was altered forever by the mass hiring of females. As mail processing began the transition to mechanization in the sixties, the post office hired scores of females, including my sister Billie Jane, as temporary workers who were assigned as monitors at the end of the rows of distribution cases. On a predetermined schedule, they were to instruct the distribution clerks in their row to extract the mail from a specific bin and place it on the moving belt under the cases. The mail would be inserted into trays and presented to the specific area for secondary distribution. Someone in higher management must have determined that this was a task more suited for women. During this period, the postal hiring policy included uniform testing for all applicants, but the results were separated by male and female registers, and males were given preference in hiring even if they had a lower score. A male applicant who tested at the minimum of 70 percent would be hired instead of a female who scored 98 percent.

Women were demanding equal rights, and President Kennedy signed the Equal Pay Act on June 10, 1963, striking down the dual pay systems that existed throughout the workforce. I have been unable to directly connect the Equal Pay Act to postal hiring of females, but it was during this time that females in the postal workforce dramatically increased. To illustrate the dearth of female employees, in 1965 there were 307 female letter carriers among the 125,000 total nationwide. Records show that in 1958 the Columbus, Ohio, Post Office had one female employee and Cincinnati had nineteen. Postal employment was a male-dominated bastion. It was many years before large numbers of females were hired in the Letter Carrier Craft, and when they were hired in later years, there was no uniform tailored to fit.

When females were first integrated into the postal workforce, among the many changes required was the need for separate restroom facilities. In the Cleveland office—which employed more than three thousand workers in a single facility consisting of three working floors—there was not a single female restroom. Until female restrooms were constructed, the newly hired females were required to exit the work floor and use the one restroom in the personnel section. This arrangement created problems since there were no female supervisors to monitor the female workers. It was common for employees who were working the night shift and needed someplace private to sleep to disappear for hours on end. The initial search for absent employees was in the restroom, but even after the construction of the women's restrooms, there were no female supervisors who could inspect the restrooms for missing female workers.

Supervision was so lax that some employees left the building while on the clock to visit a bar, to go shopping, or to see a movie. The system of employee control was such that after an employee "hit the clock" to begin tour, if he or she did not want to report for work the worker merely put the time card in his or her pocket or purse and left the building. If the time card was not in the rack, management assumed that the employee had not reported for work on that day even though he or she would be receiving wages.

Female temporary employees were employed in large numbers. They were hired as non-career employees, receiving no credit toward retirement and no access to the limited appeals process afforded career employees. When the women clocked in, the guys assembled around the hole that had been cut into the floor to accommodate the moving belt that transported mail between floors to check out the new hires at the time clock below.

Like me, the women entered the workforce with scant knowledge of the tasks to be performed, and many reported in high heels and fancy attire only to learn that they would have to remove mail bags from tractor trailers on the loading dock as part of their regular duties. The newly hired women were shocked to be given the least desirable assignments because they lacked seniority. The men were also in for a shock as many of them had never worked alongside women before.

The Struggle

During those early years of my postal employment, the civil rights movement had yet to grip the nation. Television had not permeated our society, so the brutality of discrimination was perceived as limited to isolated specific events, and the prejudices engrained over centuries were constantly present in daily work activities. The supervisors were white, and they brought to the task all the baggage of their environment.

The mixing of races in the Cleveland community differed from that in Wheeling, West Virginia, where I had been raised. There was limited interaction between the races in Wheeling. Following the Civil War, Jim Crow laws forced segregation in West Virginia, and I had to attend separate schools, use colored-only restrooms, drink from colored water fountains, and purchase hot dogs from the window of our favorite restaurant. Even the roller skating rink where we would go as children was segregated with colored use being restricted to Mondays.

Wheeling had a separate movie theater for coloreds, but it was shut down shortly after World War II because there were fewer than one thousand coloreds in the Ohio Valley on the West Virginia side. So for many years, there was no movie theatre in the city where we would be granted admittance. During the years that we were banned from the local theater, we traveled to Bridgeport, Ohio, a very small community at the foot of the bridge spanning the two states. My playmates and I would often walk the two-mile trip to see our favorite action heroes. Later, when we were permitted to attend the town's movie theater, we were restricted to balcony seating; we retaliated by throwing popcorn on the whites seated below.

Many of my classmates in high school worked at the whites-only country club and the bowling alley throughout the summer and occasionally during the school year. They would set pins, wait tables, wash dishes, and perform other servant tasks. My father never encouraged my employment at either of these establishments, but my friends told me stories about the income they earned, and the racial slurs they endured.

The Jim Crow laws legislated in West Virginia were not as restrictive as those in the Deep South. When my best friend, Donald, and I joined the army, we had to travel to South Carolina to begin training. We boarded the train at the Wheeling train station, and four white recruits boarded at the same time. We all sat together for the ride. There were six of us total—four white and two black. When the train arrived in southern West Virginia, the conductor informed us that Donald and I would be required to change cars as the one we were in was reserved for whites only. The four white recruits demanded to go the rear car with us so we could continue the trip together. My story was not exceptional; each of my colored coworkers had a similar story to tell, so discrimination within the post office was expected.

Describing to white people the demeaning and corrosive effect of public signs that restrict personal activity is extremely difficult. It is a stigma on one's self-worth in a society dominated by people of a different color. While I was never required to walk off the sidewalk when approached by a white person, I was aware that in many parts of the country that was the law, the violation of which could subject one to beatings by police officers.

In society at large, the 1950s ushered in the demand for equal rights for minorities, accelerated by the bus boycott in Montgomery, Alabama, and the arrival of television. As television became a standard in American homes, visual images of horrific events occurring thousands of miles away were projected daily in graphic detail and real time. Beginning with the election of John F. Kennedy as president, the dominance of white, Anglo-Saxon male rule was under attack. The acts of blatant discrimination that were ongoing in many parts of the country were exposed before a wide audience and became a constant subject of discussion among the colored postal workers. I was able to share my experiences in Wheeling, including the nights when my family sat on the front steps of our rented house and looked across the valley to the mountain on the Ohio side of the river. We watched Ku Klux Klan members in white sheets gyrate around a bonfire, expressing their determination to deny us equality.

While working in the flats section and at other assigned postal tasks that generally isolated colored employees, we discussed the atrocities, so every day there were new subjects to be explored while we performed our duties. We discussed the protracted struggle of the Pullman Porters, who had been transferred from the cotton fields to the plantations on rails; the murder of Emmett Till, a young boy who did not understand the rules of the racist South and was brutally murdered for whistling at a white girl; the campaign of George Wallace when he proclaimed "segregation forever"; President Eisenhower's conservative policies that deliberately ignored the abuses of basic human rights; a running total of the most recent hangings and burnings of young colored men; the bombing of the Montgomery church, which took the lives of four young, innocent children; racist courts that unfairly judged coloreds while then denying their right to serve on juries; and judges who despised your very existence while holding your life in their hands. We were never without rich material, but we restricted the discussion of racial issues to Tuesdays and Fridays.

On Mondays, we discussed sports, and during the Jim Brown years, we had much to discuss regarding the dominance of the Green Bay Packers.

On the designated days that we discussed racial issues, the conversations naturally turned to the atrocities imposed on people who looked like us. Many of my associates were college educated, with some substitute teaching experience in the public schools, and their voices added a historical context to the events of the day.

In the course of the discussions, I was assigned the task of researching the lynchings and executions of colored men and reported to our group that more than five thousand colored men and women had been lynched after the Civil War, and hundreds had been tried, found guilty, and electrocuted for alleged abuse against white women while hundreds of thousands of colored women had suffered rape with no penalties imposed on their assailants. The skin color of the slaves imported from Africa had been diluted through involuntary procreation with men of European descent to the extent that millions of human beings referred to as colored had skin color ranging from white to black. The rape of colored women was a constant occurrence. Even when convicted of such, few white men had been incarcerated and not one—not one—had been sentenced to death. Death for rape was reserved exclusively for colored men.

The 1931 saga of the Scottsboro boys in Alabama had exposed the extreme abuse of the legal system in convicting colored men sentencing them to death for imaginary sexual charges. Nine young black men ages twelve to twenty-one jumped a train looking for work. Some white boys who had been on the train but jumped off told police they were roughed up by a group of black boys. At the next stop, the white townspeople pressured two white women to allege rape. (Years later, one woman, Ruby Bates, testified that she had not been raped.) An all-white jury sentenced eight of the boys to death, sparing the twelve-year-old with life imprisonment. The boys received initial support from the Communist Party, and reluctantly the NAACP Defense League represented them. (The NAACP had a policy of avoiding rape cases because of their explosive nature.) The cases were tried in Scottsboro, Alabama, and remained in the judicial system for six years. After repeated findings of guilty and appeals, including to the Supreme Court, the boys were exonerated, but only after spending several years on death row. Apparently, although the former slaves were no longer considered property, in the warped minds of the oppressors, they still had no more claim to life than a pig or cow.

We identified the states where the intent to deny constitutional rights was paramount, noting that there were fewer than one dozen states that regularly engaged in the horrific practice of lynching young colored men for imagined violations—the southern way. Alabama, Georgia, Mississippi, and Florida led the way with an average of at least one lynching per month. On July 6, 1920, James Foster Spencer, a colored postal clerk working the mail car, was removed from the train and lynched just for fun. There was no prosecution. The lynching of colored men had been elevated to a spectator sport with concession stands and women and children in attendance.

We discussed the Thirteenth, Fourteenth, and Fifteenth Amendments to the Constitution and the deliberate actions by local and state governments to ignore them by continuing to deny rights to colored people. The area of the country known as the Bible Belt enforced Jim Crow laws that denied people of color every protection of life and liberty. There were stories of white families that engaged in the vicious abuse of these boys, families that claimed to have found religion but stored grotesque souvenirs of body parts ripped from the victims, hidden away as heirlooms of their disturbing acts of murder.

My colored coworkers who had relatives in Alabama and other southern states would share stories of the degrading practices that caused the Montgomery boycott. Racist bus drivers in major metropolitan cities, including Montgomery, preyed on colored women who used public transportation to get to their jobs as maids, cooks, and housekeepers in "whites only" neighborhoods across town. The drivers would regularly display their disdain by forcing colored adults to wait until white children had boarded and forcing them to enter the front door to pay but disembark and board through the rear door. Coloreds could not sit across the aisle from whites and were forced to stand beside empty "whites only" seats. The white bus drivers were permitted to carry guns and clubs under their seats to dispense vigilante justice to anyone who might object.

Martin Luther King Jr. received the credit for the success of the Montgomery bus boycott, but it was those women, led by Rosa Parks and Jo Ann Robinson, who were determined to stand up to the indignities and abuse. Rosa Parks has been elevated to iconic status for her courageous stand in the Montgomery bus boycott, but she began her quest for liberation as the NAACP investigator in the Recy Taylor rape by white vigilantes eleven years before. These women withstood the "get tough" policy of Mayor Gayle, who ordered fines and jail for women who refused the continued degradation of segregation on public buses. The women in Montgomery refrained from using public transportation for 381 days, ending on December 21, 1956, just fourteen months before I began postal employment.

We never denigrated to the point that we blamed an entire race of people for the misery imposed, but we observed that if there was justice, a "come to Jesus" movement would not come close to saving millions of ungodly people. Each of us brought our personal experiences to the discussions, and while the verbal exchanges and analyses did not result in anything tangible, they made for stimulating conversation. I was exposed to a range of experiences and opinions. I never became bitter, but I formed perspectives of the world and my place in it. Politics, world affairs, theater, and other subjects of choice received our attention with vigorous debate, but race was personal, and Tuesdays and Fridays were days that we all reported for duty.

Progress

We agonized and celebrated the slow and deliberate progress. We rejoiced when Thurgood Marshall and the NAACP secured miraculous legal victories, and we were hopeful when John F. Kennedy was elected president. We engaged in the campaigns of Louis and Carl Stokes as they broke the color barrier and were elected congressman and mayor. We followed the campaigns of Martin Luther King Jr. and absorbed the rhetoric of Malcolm X, Stokely Carmichael, Cassius Clay, Rap Brown, the Black Panthers, and others on the front lines of the battle for dignity and respect.

These events and the determination of the oppressed ignited the protests about racial discrimination. However, as of today, history has not adequately recorded the effect of this racial struggle on American white women. Colored men were being lynched and their women raped with impunity; the only solution was constitutional justice. In the congressional battle over civil rights, at the very last moment, the issue of equal rights for women was added to the Civil Rights Bill by Virginia Democrat Howard W. Smith, and the victory became one of equal rights for women regardless of race. As colored leaders blazed the trail, shedding their blood, white females rode the wave of progress without the pain and suffering associated with the fight for racial equality. While some white females were in the forefront of the struggle for equal rights, the bitter struggle was about race, not sex.

A Legal Victory

The unraveling of the Jim Crow laws, which were enacted after Reconstruction to keep colored "in their place" through separate but equal education, began with the unanimous Supreme Court decision in Sweatt v. Texas in June 1950. Heman Marion Sweatt was a Houston postal employee whose application to enter the Texas Law School was denied on the basis that coloreds were not admitted. Sweatt took the school to court and lost. He appealed the lower court's decision, and his case then was appealed to the Supreme Court where his attorney, Thurgood Marshall, was victorious.

The Sweatt victory was followed by the 1954 unanimous Supreme Court decision in Brown v. Board of Education that ruled in favor of desegregating schools although the implementation of the law was deferred for remedy until 1955, when under extreme pressure the court ruled that the decision would be carried out "with all deliberate speed." Thurgood Marshall was again the attorney, and he won the landmark case for equal education. After the decision was initially announced, President Eisenhower—with racist intent—requested that the court refrain from setting a deadline for compliance. He proposed to leave the time frame for compliance to each state, which meant that those in the Deep South could continue blatant discrimination and the denial of quality education to innocent colored children. As we performed our postal duties, my colored coworkers and I discussed these victories and setbacks and the changed landscape in those states that complied expeditiously as well as those like Virginia, which dismantled its entire public school system in defiance of the order to desegregate.

The subject of discrimination was a constant topic in our workplace interactions, and several of my associates even joined the freedom movement, engaging in the protests. One of my coworkers, Grady, volunteered for the lunch counter "sit-ins" in North Carolina and requested that I join him. I declined. He returned with tales of being spit on, shoved, and verbally abused. I am not sure how I would have reacted to the abuse, but I look back with regret. My excuse at the time was my family obligations, an excuse which will haunt me forever because the greatest thing I could have done for my children was fight for their freedom.

41

We were at rest from World War II and the Korean conflicts. During my service in the army, President Eisenhower had considered intervention in Vietnam at the time of the massacre at Dien Bien Phu. My unit, the 101st Airborne Division, was put on alert, but wise heads prevailed, and in the early sixties, Vietnam was no more than a place on the map. The economy was stagnant, and despite the stimulus from the construction of the interstate highway system, there were few new jobs. The new highway system would facilitate the exodus from cities and create a new suburban American culture. There was no hint that we were reaching the boiling point on domestic policy involving race. Resistance to government-sanctioned discrimination was building to a crescendo, and we as a nation were on the cusp of revolutionary change. These events were the backdrop that dominated those formative postal years that would shape my future.

During this period, I had been converted to full-time postal employment with forty hours of guaranteed work, but to supplement my income, I continued working a variety of other part-time jobs. I wanted to do more than exist. I wanted to get ahead and live the American dream.

Pride

The civil rights movement exploding on the American stage during the early years of my postal employment was a pivotal time for American society. The suburbs emerged as the new town centers, and schools and political influence gravitated from the central city. The Vietnam War divided the culture, and an entire generation was creating a new norm. The colored community was demanding equality, and the dynamic leaders Martin Luther King Jr., Thurgood Marshall, Malcolm X, Stokely Carmichael, Cassius Clay, and countless others were forcing change. Thurgood Marshall and Martin Luther King Jr. were the most effective and most dynamic civil rights leaders of the time, but it was Stokely

Carmichael who removed the stigma of color by convincing us to embrace a single noun as identification.

From the days of slavery through the Civil War, Reconstruction, and beyond, descendants of the African slaves were referred to as "negroes," niggers," "nigras," "coons," "darkies," and "coloreds" and were separated among their own by skin color. The use of the word "colored" to identify descendants of former African slaves was demeaning to an entire race of human beings in the use of a word that was intended to identify what they were not—"colored" was intended to identify "not white." The most demeaning and most often used name of reference was "nigger," and it included all of the hate and animosity built up over two hundred and fifty years. Prior to the Stokely campaign and the emergence of the Black Panthers, the use of the word "black" within the colored community was an invitation to fight, but Stokely was successful in achieving the full acceptance of the term as a universal reference. As a result of the movement led by Stokely, the various shades of brown that made up the colored community fell under a single identifying term: black.

On June 16, 1966, Stokely gave the historic "Black Power" speech in Greenwood, Mississippi, creating the slogan "Black is Beautiful" and transforming the identity of people of color. Two years later, black track athletes Tommie Smith and John Carlos raised their fists in defiance while standing on the 1968 Olympic awards stand. The demonstration was a magical moment, and despite the removal of their records by the Olympic Committee President Avery Brundridge, those athletes were truly heroes. Mr. Brundridge ignored the fact that the German competitors in the 1936 Olympic Games had given the Nazi salute from the winners' stand without repercussions. Tommie observed that if he won, he would be an American, but if he didn't, he was a Negro. The silver medalist, Peter Norman, a native Australian who was white, supported the demonstration by wearing a civil rights button but received no punishment. These brave athletes demonstrated on the world's stage that blacks were beautiful. Stokely was successful in convincing America—white and black—to use the universal term "black," and despite the hue of my skin color, I was a black postal employee demanding the basic rights of collective bargaining, which would bring dignity and respect.

CHAPTER 4

Preparation for Success

The Beginning of a Union Career

Months after my initial date of employment, I became aware of the presence of the National Alliance of Postal and Federal Employees (NAPFE), an organization established for the protection of colored people in government service. Its record was one of fighting to elevate black workers within the postal service, and it was responsible for aggressively fighting discrimination to break the colored ceiling. The Alliance had a proud history representing colored railway clerks who were denied admittance to the white union. After passage of the Equal Employment Opportunity Act, the Alliance was effective in representing employees in discrimination complaints but was denied full representation status in the union elections. Conflicts arose when employees filed grievances and Equal Employment Opportunity Commission (EEOC) complaints and the resolution violated the collective bargaining agreement. Years later, I negotiated the requirement for a union representative to be present during EEOC discussions when grievances had been filed.

Many of my friends, most notably Matt Smith, whom I deeply respected, were active in the Cleveland Alliance Chapter, and I was solicited to become a member. Despite strong personal feelings about equality, I was unable to rationalize how I could improve conditions for all employees by marginalizing myself in an organization without the right to bargain. If I had chosen the Alliance, I would never have had the opportunity to negotiate binding conditions of employment and to have a direct impact on the lives of all postal employees.

Colored employees had been permitted to join the United Federation of Postal Clerks (UFPC) in the early 1950s, shortly before my employment, but the UFPC Local 72 continued to be a white-dominated organization. It had progressed to the election of a colored man, Bill Crockett, to the position of president, and he served as the poster boy for colored postal employees. It was over a year from the date of my initial employment before I was even asked to become a union member, and feeling that the request was not sincere, I declined. Union membership at that time was more akin to joining a social club as they had no legal right to represent and expended union resources primarily in the political arena, currying favor with politicians. Dues were manually collected each payday, and union functions or activities were not widely advertised within my circle of acquaintances. At a later date, I did join the clerk's union, but continuing membership was dependent on regular biweekly cash payments. No one in my circle of acquaintances was an active member, so I often avoided the dues collector. Over time I was put on the non-active list.

National Postal Union (NPU)

The National Postal Union (NPU) was formed in 1959, the year after I began my postal career, when a group of dissidents in the clerks union that called themselves "Progressives" walked out of the UFPC National Convention in protest of the denial of "one man, one vote" in its election of officers. The UFPC's tradition was similar to that of most unions today. From its founding, it included delegate voting, which empowered small locals over the large locals that otherwise dominated the elections that were held at national conventions.

If the local was small (five to twenty-five members), it would get one delegate to vote at the convention where officers were elected. Large locals received the same allocation of votes (one vote for twenty-five members), so New York Local, for example, would be credited with 108 votes for its twenty-seven thousand members. But 181 locals with ten members each would be credited with 181 votes even though they only represented 1,810 members. Local unions were chartered with five or more members, so the composition of the union mirrored the country, which has many more small cities than large ones. (There is a post office with postal employees in every city.) After repeated efforts to modify the constitutional provisions to permit the vote for each member, the Progressives led by John MacKay walked out of the convention in protest. The leaders of the protest movement formed a new national union, NPU, selecting John MacKay as its first president. Many of the large locals representing clerk employees, including New York, Chicago, and Detroit, became a part of the newly formed union. The Cleveland Local continued affiliation with the UFPC.

Because I was outspoken in the daily discussions, I caught the attention of National Postal Union organizers, and my friend Anne Thomas invited me to meet with John R. Smith, who was a dynamic leader in the newly created union. He visited Cleveland from his home in Dayton, where he served as the local president. Over dinner he convinced me that I could serve as an agent for change and signed me up as a member. John's message of worker solidarity was not totally foreign to me. While living in Wheeling, I had limited exposure to the efforts of coal miners' and steel workers' unions. The husband of my friend Dorothy Smith, with whom I lived during my stay in Steubenville, was an employee of the Weirton steel mill, and he enjoyed six weeks of vacation time, which the union had negotiated. The United Auto Workers

(UAW) had negotiated similar provisions, and both were fighting the forty-hour workweek. I was soon an advocate for change in the post office.

John became my mentor, and for many years to come when my career within the union needed a boost, John Smith was there. John was and is a role model. We share a love of poetry, specifically the words of Frederick Douglass. Later in our careers, we both included excerpts from Douglass in our public speeches. Here are some inspiring words Frederick Douglass delivered on August 3, 1857, in Canandaigua, New York:

> If there is no Struggle there is not Progress.

> Those who profess to favor freedom and yet depreciate agitation are men who want crops without plowing up the ground; they want rain without thunder and lightning. They want the ocean without the awful roar of its many waters.

> This struggle may be a moral one or it may be a physical one, but it must be a struggle. Power concedes nothing without a demand. It never did and it never will. Find out just what any people will quietly submit to and you have found out the exact measure of injustice and wrong which will be imposed upon them and these will continue till they are resisted with either words or blows, or with both. The limits of tyrants are prescribed by the endurance of those whom they oppress. In the light of these ideas, Negroes will be hunted at the North and held and flogged at the South so long as they submit to those devilish outrages and make no resistance, either moral or physical. Men may not get all they pay for in this world, but they must certainly pay for all they get. If we ever get free

from the oppressions and wrongs heaped upon us, we must pay for their removal. We must do this by labor, by suffering, by sacrifice, and if needs be, by our lives and the lives of others."

I had been taught to love poetry by my high school English teacher, Mrs. Thomas, who loved the written word, and by my stepmother, who hung a copy of Rudyard Kipling's masterpiece "If" on the kitchen wall of our home and required that I memorize it and be tested regularly:

If you can keep your head when all about you
are losing theirs and blaming it on you,
If you can trust yourself when all men doubt you,
but make allowance for their doubting too;
if you can wait and not be tired by waiting,
Or being lied about, don't deal in lies,
Or being hated, don't give way to hating,
And yet don't look too good, nor talk too wise:
If you can dream – and not make dreams your master;
If you can think – and not make thoughts your aim;
If you can meet with Triumph and Disaster
And treat those two impostors just the same;
If you can bear to hear the truth you've spoken Twisted
by knaves to make a trap for fools,
Or watch the things you gave your life to, broken,
And stoop and build 'em up with worn-out tools:
If you can make one heap of all your winnings
And risk it on one turn of pitch-and-toss,
And lose, and start again at your beginnings
And never breathe a word about your loss;
If you can force your heart and nerve and sinew
To serve your turn long after they are gone,
And so hold on when there is nothing in you

Except the Will which says to them: 'Hold on!'
If you can talk with crowds and keep your virtue,
Or walk with Kings – nor lose the common touch,
if neither foes nor loving friends can hurt you,
If all men count with you, but none too much;
If you can fill the unforgiving minute
With sixty seconds' worth of distance run,
Yours is the Earth and everything that's in it,
And – which is more – you'll be a Man, my son!

This poem captures the essence of reaching beyond the natural instincts of living with low expectations of one's capabilities and sends the message that great things are possible. John and I would often cite passages from Dougluss' speech and Kipling's poem in our speeches, and without exception they would be well received.

After signing up as a member of the Cleveland Local, I began attending local meetings and understanding the rules of engagement. Within our council of NPU members, we envisioned changes such as increased wages, longer vacations, expanded seniority rights, a grievance procedure, and more, and we spent countless hours strategizing the means of achieving these goals.

During my membership in NPU, Dave Silvergleid served as the national president and George Wade was the local president. Dave was a model of professionalism. Many years later when I was serving as national president, anytime Dave was in Washington, he and his wife, Dottie, would stop by the office to say hello. Entertaining Dave, who had been the president thirty years before when I had been a member with no portfolio, was weird. I was entertaining him in the very position that he had held.

Progress

As we progressed through the 1960s, the postal unions had sporadic success in convincing legislators to address the many needs of the post office and its employees. Until the Postal Reform

Act of 1971, all postal funds were appropriated by Congress, so union efforts to improve conditions of employment were within the political arena. I joined with my fellow union members in repeated rallies, including a trip to Washington for a candlelight vigil around the White House. For that event, my group of NPU activists traveled from Cleveland by train, and the trip created great memories. In 1967, our efforts led to the upgrade of all postal employees (PL 90-206) and distribution clerks from Grade 4 to Grade 5. It brought a meager $321 a year pay increase, which served to temporarily dampen our cry for more. In our continuous struggle to improve conditions of employment, the unions succeeded in achieving legislation that provided free life insurance for postal employees. The post office began making contributions to health care premiums, but wages were so low that in many communities postal employees with families qualified for welfare. Our only means of protest was lobbying, so after I joined the union, trips to Washington became routine; it was our only means of appeal.

The presidential election of 1960 was a time of hope with the candidacy of Senator John F. Kennedy. Everyone that I knew supported his campaign. We were optimistic of significant change if he was successful. The unions had petitioned Congress for legislation granting collective bargaining rights, and we believed that with the Kennedy election we would achieve that objective. I could never determine if the unfolding of events affecting postal employment after his election was strategic or coincidental. Senator Kennedy had supported the Rhodes–Johnson Bill of Reform, but after the election, instead of sponsoring the bill, he appointed a task force to study federal employee relations. We were extremely disappointed, but the task force recommended the issuance of an executive order, and President Kennedy signed Executive Order (EO) 10988 on January 17, 1962. Through its provisions, we entered the era of collective bargaining. It did not represent the full range of bargaining, but the seed had been sown by the executive order of 1962. That was the beginning. This legislation was then followed by the Nixon EO 11491, which was superseded by the postal reform of 1970 following the illegal strike.

John F. Kennedy's election was a topic of deep discussion. We discussed his religion, which was a big deal because it was the first time a Catholic had been elected to president. His beliefs did not strike a chord with me because I was not aligned to any particular religious faith. I had attended Catholic school, but I had not been required to join the Catholic Church. When I was young, I attended a Methodist church and had been baptized in a Baptist church. Over the years, though, I had drifted away and did not regularly attend services. Today, I occasionally accompany my wife, who is a member of her brother's Baptist church.

We discussed Kennedy's politics and the invasion of Cuba, a country of people who also had African roots. During the height of the slavery trade, many Africans were shipped to Cuba as slaves to harvest sugar cane, so we had much in common. In our daily discussions, we reserved Wednesdays for politics, and we expressed our impatience with the political parties that championed issues that we did not relate to. We viewed the political process as a means of removing the societal limitations that denied fundamental decency and the fulfillment of the American dream for African Americans. We wanted the Constitution to have real meaning to us as citizens of our country. Since I had not been exposed to politics during my early years, the debates were stimulating and led to many heated discussions. I was not supportive of any political party and had not engaged in or heard political dialogue at home, so more often than not I listened while my older coworkers discussed the issues.

I concluded that our society had completed a period that was dominated by American heroes—Franklin Roosevelt, Dwight Eisenhower, and Douglas McCarthy—each of whom thought of colored people as inferior human beings. They were confirmed racists, but America worshiped them. The expectation was that Kennedy would deliver, but prejudice and control was ingrained in American society, and his political support was not so sufficient that he could initiate civil rights legislation and be reelected. His party, the Democratic Party, was dominant in the Jim Crow states, and they resisted any and all legislation intended to afford civil rights to all.

After the election, President Kennedy kept his promise and opened the door of collective bargaining, but his contribution to the struggle for racial equality was found wanting at the time. I recall not knowing how to react to his assassination in 1963 because he had promised so much in delivering equality, but at the time of his untimely death, very little had changed. The Kennedy election raised the hopes of the colored community. We believed that he would champion civil rights and the yoke of slavery would be removed forever, but we were met with disappointment. Throughout the South, evil white vigilantes continued to lynch young colored boys with impunity, and Jim Crow was still the law of many states.

The Kennedy presidency did usher in a shift of political allegiance in the black community, many voting for a Democrat for the first time since the Emancipation Proclamation signed by Abraham Lincoln as a desperate act to end the Civil War. In 1960, the Republican Party made a calculated decision to appease the lingering racial divide and supported candidate Nixon's Southern Strategy, which was a pact with the devil. Richard Nixon and the Republican Party waged a campaign to appeal to forces that opposed equality for African Americans, and the message resonated in the black community. This appeal to the racist elements of the Republican Party is pronounced in the primary elections where the radicals dominate the voter turnout and the candidates must appeal to the absolute worst.

The Beginning of Bargaining

With the implementation of the Kennedy Executive Order 10988, representation elections took place in each postal installation from June 1 to July 15, 1962, and employees selected the union that would represent their interest. The United Federation of Postal Clerks (UFPC) and the Letter Carriers emerged as the dominant unions. The National Postal Union (NPU) stood for the principle of one postal union representing all postal employees, but failing to convince others of our philosophy, we were successful only in selective offices and crafts. The "one union" approach was enticing for many postal employees who demanded a voice in their employment, but our fight against tradition and long-held associations proved too much of a challenge.

A core group of us NPU supporters in the Cleveland office met monthly in the bar on Cedar Avenue to conduct union business and discuss strategy for expanding our rolls. We were believers throughout the 1960s. George Wade, Anne Thomas, Tim and Bob Callahan, and Bill Harris were part of this group, and they supported me throughout my career in the Cleveland office, helping me develop as a leader. We printed flyers and distributed them, along with incentives for new members, to employees in front of the main post office.

Following the executive order, we were positioned to represent custodial employees within the consultation process. Bargaining under the executive order was clumsy at best, but it was a start. Each craft group of employees was given the right to vote for representation, selecting the union that would negotiate their contract terms and represent their interests. The union with the highest number of votes was granted formal recognition with the responsibility and the right to consultation, bringing employees' concerns to management's attention. This was not a formal grievance procedure, and it did not culminate in binding arbitration. Our means of appeal of management decisions was to the Civil Service Appeals and Review Board and was a laborious process that was not binding. The elections resulted in the designation of specific unions with formal and informal bargaining rights. The NPU embarked on national and local organizing drives to build its membership and expand its official consultation rights. It was competitive in many large cities as the dominant clerks union because it did not have the baggage of other unions' "whites only" heritage. In most offices, NPU was selected for informal bargaining rights and was entitled to be present when disputes were under discussion, but it could not make any decisions. This process was far short of legal collective bargaining, but it was a beginning.

Preparation for Success

Throughout my formative years, my father wanted to expand my skills and prepare me for adulthood. He explored numerous activities for me, including typing, piano lessons, and dance. I was even assigned to accompany a distant relative to his job of shoe shining in a waterfront hotel. Within minutes, I felt that it was degrading to shine the shoes of white customers who insisted that I use separate "facilities." I knew that it would not be a permanent occupation, but the experience helped me later when I was shining my boots as a soldier. I would spend entire weekends making my footwear the shiniest in the battalion. Sometimes, as a joke, I would shine only one boot of a fellow soldier who had the cruddiest boots in the unit. When he stood in formation on Monday morning, his one shiny boot made the other look even worse.

My father's efforts to find my talents were not productive. The one skill for which I developed dexterity was typing. I was enrolled in a class dominated by girls and my hands were oversized, so adjusting to the keyboard was a challenge. This effort to identify my skills meant I had to spend many summer days looking out the window, wishing that I could do what the other kids were doing: playing stickball or shooting marbles.

My father wanted me to achieve a quality education, so he enrolled me in the colored Catholic school when I entered the seventh grade. The Catholic school was reserved for colored children from grades one through twelve—all in the same building. The experience was positive, but I could not understand why the colored boys and girls were integrated in our school while, just four blocks away, the main Catholic school was reserved for white boys only. After two years, I appealed to my father that I wanted to transfer back to the colored school because they had a football team. When I notified Principal Anne Marie that I would be leaving, she informed me that it was their plan to send me to Notre Dame University upon graduation, which was enticing, but I wanted to play football.

I was a good student in each of the many schools that I attended. In Columbus, Bellaire, Bridgeport, and Toledo, Ohio, the classes were integrated, but Lincoln High School in Wheeling, West Virginia, was for colored students only. Of all my many teachers, my colored teachers in high school English and math were outstanding. They knew their subjects and had a passion for teaching. Mrs. Thomas, my English teacher, had a love for Shakespeare, Browning, and other literary giants, and she required us to memorize the classics. She taught Booker T. Washington and Frederick Douglass, and, without expressing a preference, she permitted the students to determine their opposite approaches to the advancement of colored people. I gravitated toward Douglass, who rejected the premise that our fate was to serve a so-called dominant race. In math, Mr. Shannon knew his subject better than any teacher throughout my schooling. He taught basic math, algebra, and trigonometry.

Near the end of my senior year, having been first or second in every class that I took throughout high school, everyone assumed that I would be either valedictorian or salutatorian, and far in advance Mrs. Thomas had begun preparing me for the graduation speech required of the top two students. I was required to stay after school to compose a speech and commit it to memory. The top three students in each class were awarded a monetary prize bestowed by a benefactor named Stiefel, a wealthy magnate who bequeathed a sum in his will to the top students in each graduating class.

As graduation neared, an unfortunate event occurred in the final week of my schooling. A teacher said something to me that I thought was inappropriate, and I responded in kind. Two days later, when report cards were distributed, my grades were adjusted, and I was tied for salutatorian with two other students who had been ranked below me. The prize was going to be divided between the three of us. I suspected that it was a conspiracy brought on by my conflict with the teacher only days before, and I informed the administration that I would not deliver the speech on graduation night. They responded by threatening to discuss the matter with my father, who, in a hastily called meeting, informed them that he would defend his son. They must have had a change of heart because I was certified as the salutatorian and received the $100 Stiefel prize dedicated for second place. My friend Donald Turner was awarded first place and received the $125 prize.

Donald and I had formed a close relationship at the time of his transfer to Lincoln High School, which was the only high school for colored students within a fifty-mile radius of Wheeling. I lived in the community, but Donald was bused daily from the small town of Wellsburg, West Virginia, sixteen miles away. I established an innocent romantic relationship with Donald's younger sister Barbara, and she was the magnet that attracted me back to Steubenville after my army service. During the graduation ceremony, midway through his speech, Donald forgot his words and stood in front of the microphone struggling to recall. I sat through the ordeal in nervous anticipation. After Donald concluded, I made my presentation without a glitch. My father had requested that I reference the "sands of time," and while I do not recall the specific text of the speech, I inserted the phrase and caught my father's eye as I delivered it. He looked on from his front row seat with pride.

At each stage of my education and military service, I tested well, and while in the army, I was offered the opportunity to attend officer training school or to be schooled at an academy that focused on China, language, and history. I rejected each of these offers because I wanted to be in control. I wanted to be in a position to decide. A general approached me in formation once and asked me if I intended to reenlist, to which I responded, "No, sir. When my time is up, I'm getting as far away as I can."

While serving in the army, I received basic training in the 101st Airborne Division in Fort Jackson, South Carolina, and the Fourth Armored Division in Fort Hood, Texas, for advanced training. I did not find the role of soldiering to be consistent with my ambitions, so I secured a job in the army supply room and enhanced my typing skills. I later used this training to secure the postal assignment of a tool and parts clerk.

When entering the military, recruits are tested for a variety of purposes, but one voluntary test I took was to determine if I qualified to be trained as an officer. When the results were posted on the open bulletin board, a white soldier ten years my senior was amazed that I had achieved a score some ten points higher than he did and had qualified for officer training. He did not know me but assumed that a person of color did not have the intelligence to score higher than he. My schoolteachers would have been proud. However, the officers program required a commitment to reenlist, and I had already made up my mind to leave military life and stretch my wings.

Change of Assignment

My father's efforts to expand my skills were paying dividends. Applying the typing training that I had received in high school and the assignment as a supply clerk in the army, I transferred from the Clerk Craft to the Maintenance Craft as a tool and parts clerk working the day shift from 9:00 a.m. to 5:30 p.m. I was relieved of the responsibility of being tested on schemes, so the time that had been devoted to scheme study was converted to personal activities. The assignment was in the penthouse of the main post office, and I was the only employee on the entire floor. In this new assignment, I had the time and opportunity to immerse myself in union issues. However, due to the shift change, I had to change my part-time employment from painting houses during the day to working at a toy distribution warehouse and later at Pinkerton Detective Agency as a dispatcher at night.

I had little knowledge of postal building materials and tools, but the mechanics took me under their wings, and in a short time I was proficient. Among the duties and responsibilities was the ordering of soap, toilet paper, and paper towels. I gave special attention to these necessities because these were absolute essentials for a three-thousand-person operation. I was later consolidated with maintenance supply on the second floor as a supply clerk responsible for processing equipment. I took advantage of the freedom associated with these assignments as I prepared for a role as a union representative.

In 1972, I was first elected to serve as vice president of the NPU Cleveland Chapter and participated in consultation meetings under the executive order, where I honed my skills of representation. We met monthly for union meetings in a reserved room in the bar on Cedar Avenue. Normally fifteen to twenty activists would be in attendance. In the application of our newly achieved representative status, we primarily discussed with postal management the terms of vacation scheduling and seniority. Many of the provisions that were negotiated survive to this day, and the process prepared me for later years when I was charged with negotiating terms of employment nationwide. The Pittsburgh Local was particularly effective in negotiating provisions under the executive order, and I learned much from the styles of the NPU Cleveland Local leader George Wade and John Richards of Pittsburgh.

All Men Are Created Equal

These experiences served as the background for the events that would follow and have a profound impact on me and our country. President Kennedy and Martin Luther King Jr. were assassinated, and President Johnson sponsored civil rights and voters' rights legislation that would change America forever. At work, we discussed at length the long road we had traveled, observing that on March 6, 1857, in a 7:2 majority decision, the Supreme Court of the United States had ruled in Dred Scott v. Sanford that former slaves or their descendants could not be citizens of the United States. They could be free, as I have record of my great-great-great-grandfather William Burrus, but as decided in this Supreme Court decision, he and all of his descendants were unable to be citizens of the United States of America. The Supreme Court decision written by Chief Justice Roger B. Taney (Maryland) read in part:

> The words "people of the United States" and "citizens" are synonymous terms, and mean the same thing. They both describe the political body who . . . form the sovereignty, and who hold the power and conduct the Government through their representatives. The question before us is, whether the class of persons described in the plea in abatement [people of African ancestry] compose a portion of this people, and are constituent members of this sovereignty? We think they are not, and they are not included and were not intended to be included under the word "citizens" in the Constitution, and can therefore claim none of the rights and privileges which that instrument provides for and secures to citizens of the United States. . . .
>
> [The] legislation and histories of the times, and the language used in the Declaration of Independence, show, that neither the class of persons who had been

imported as slaves, nor their descendants, whether they had become free or not, where then acknowledged as a part of people, nor intended to be included in the general words used in that memorable instrument.

This decision put things in perspective.

Although Abraham Lincoln freed the slaves when he issued the Emancipation Proclamation, freedom lasted less than one generation, replaced with state by state Jim Crow legislation, which, in many ways, was as controlling as slavery. The Dred Scott decision denying citizenship was overturned by the Thirteenth, Fourteenth, and Fifteenth Amendments and the Civil Rights Act of 1865, but the southern states responded by implementing the Black Codes, which were legal means to reinstitute slavery by another name. These southern states had structured their economies and culture around free labor, and they didn't intend to give that up without a fight. Black citizens continued to be denied voting and civil rights until Lyndon B. Johnson succeeded in passing the Civil Rights Act of 1964 and the Voting Rights Act of 1965.

This disenfranchisement was not limited to the South; New Jersey and Illinois joined with the southern states in legislating barriers to equality. In Mississippi in 1960, only 5 percent of eligible blacks were registered to vote. The freedoms now enjoyed by black Americans come not from the original words of the Constitution that had been in place for 180 years but from the decency and courage of President Lyndon B. Johnson, a native of the South. These are the vehicles that gave us freedom, and their adoption had ripple effects. The most astonishing was the abrupt realignment of the American political structure, where the southern states had been solid supporters of the Democratic Party. These states had initiated the Civil War, causing the most casualties of any armed conflict before or since, under the banner of the Democratic Party. But in the space of the signing of Public Law 88-352 and 42 USC § 1973, they became the most ardent supporters—now referred to as the "base"—of the Republican Party. They would have you believe that "conservative values" are the defining issue, but history records otherwise.

One cannot imagine my personal relief and that of my black coworkers when on July 2, 1964, the laws of the country proclaimed that discrimination was illegal. Even those of us who had lived in states that had eliminated discriminating laws, black Americans had continued to experience second-class status. Many of my black coworkers used their vacations to travel to the birthplace of their parents and other relatives in the South. They would return to work with countless stories of denied admittance to hotels to rest from the long drives and the need to pack food and refreshment for the journey because they might not be welcomed at restaurants en route. Now this would end. Finally, the words of the Constitution had meaning.

After eighty-three days of filibuster, on July 2, 1964, we witnessed the beginning of the end of legal state-sponsored terrorism against people of color by sheriffs, police officers, and just mean people in the enforcement of Jim Crow laws. The struggle would continue for many years in many parts of the country, but now we had legal status as full citizens of the country. We had been subjected to untold levels of terror intended to keep us "in our place," but now such actions would be illegal and the words "all men are created equal" applied to us.

Perspective

The happenings of that period had a profound impact on what we would become as a nation. The growing protest against the Vietnam War led by young people who rejected the norm; the Civil Rights struggle; the assassinations of John and Bobby Kennedy, Martin Luther King, and Malcolm X—all these events created dynamics that would forever change our society. However, to put things in perspective, the 1960s were not just about protest and assassinations: We walked on the moon. There was hope for a better future.

CHAPTER 5

First Contract, 1971

Strike

Within the context of these events, postal employees were demanding equal pay and a voice. After repeated false starts, Congress was considering legislation to address our concerns. One of the most prevalent subjects in our daily workplace discussions during that period was the pending bill to address the sorry state of postal wages. Congress promised significant wage increases. At the time, the starting salary was $6,200 a year, and the top pay after twenty-one years was $8,400 a year. After torturous delay, the offer of a 5.4 percent increase was considered an insult and rejected by the rank and file after Congress had approved a 41 percent pay raise for themselves.

The postal strike that followed had its genesis in the suspension of 56 Bronx New York letter carriers, 16 Bronx New York clerks (some records indicate 53 letter carries and 13 clerks), and 16 letter carriers from Throggs Neck who staged a sick-out on July 1, 1969, in reaction to President Nixon's announcement of the meager pay increase. The following day, the "sick" clerks and carriers were issued two-week suspensions without pay.

While the congressional legislation was reaching the contentious stage, the New York letter carriers, egged on by dissident leader Vince Sombrotto, who was not a steward or an officer, led the demand for compensation for the suspended letter carriers. When the suspended workers returned to work, the New York Clerks Union reimbursed its members for the lost pay. Furious over the lingering back pay issue and the congressional pay proposal, the New York Letter Carriers demanded a vote to strike.

At a tumultuous meeting on March 17, 1970, by a margin of five hundred votes (1,555:1,055), the dissidents prevailed in the vote to strike. The letter carriers unions voted to strike, but the first employees to withhold their labor were the clerks who were the earliest to arrive at the offices and refused to cross the letter carriers' picket lines. This decision by the clerks, who were the single largest group of postal employees in New York with twenty-seven thousand members, went against the wishes of the local union leaders. There was much at stake, and there was no historic precedent of workers striking against the government of the United States. The leaders could be jailed, and huge fines could be imposed on the unions and the elected officials.

Following the letter carriers' vote, the clerks union scheduled a hastily called meeting. New York President Moe Biller had serious, legitimate concerns about the government's response to a strike of postal employees and insisted that a referendum vote be conducted of all of the members before deciding the issue. Militant members egged on an already agitated group, which then erupted, forcing Moe to exit from the back of the stage. Events spiraled out of control as the combination of the letter carriers' strike and the clerks' refusal to cross the picket line stopped mail services. The local leaders of the New York Clerks Union endorsed the sentiment of the irate members and on Saturday, March 21, announced that the union was on strike. Although the clerks had already refused to work for a few days, on March 21 the strike was official.

This illegal walkout was without an elected leader at the national level. National presidents Stu Filbey and Jim Rademaker were frantically attempting to quell the uprising, and the New York Local presidents, Biller and Johnson, had been overcome by a militant membership. The Mail Handlers, Rural Letter Carriers, Maintenance, Motor Vehicle, and Special Delivery Unions never engaged in the illegal walkout although their members at the local level were swept up in the activities. These strange circumstances resulted in the stoppage of mail services nationwide, with more than two hundred thousand postal employees joining the walkout.

Throughout the strike, there was frantic maneuvering behind the scenes between the White House, the American Federation of Labor (AFL), and the national union presidents. Secretary of Labor William Usery urged the union presidents to order a return to work with a promise of negotiations, but the defiant local leaders refused to do so unless the government was offering more than promises.

In Cleveland, the local NPU chapter was monitoring events in New York, and upon hearing of the strike, we agitated for local job action. In a hastily called meeting, I was a vocal supporter of the strike and spoke passionately in favor of joining our New York brothers by shutting down the Cleveland facility. An emergency meeting was called by the president of Local 72, Nick Lucci, to which the members of all the unions, including NPU, were invited. The sentiment to strike was overwhelming, and on the evening of March 19, 1970, the employees of the Cleveland office went on strike.

The strike lasted for eight days with different cities beginning at different times. Hundreds of millions of letters backlogged the system. The entire mail system came to a screeching halt. It was at that point that President Nixon resorted to mobilizing the National Guard, but it was not possible for soldiers unfamiliar with the postal distribution schemes to separate mail for home delivery. As they arrived in their jeeps in full military attire with weapons and all, we taunted them with derisive chants of being ill-equipped to do our jobs. I asked if they intended to shoot the mail. This attempt at intervention lasted just one day until the superiors concluded that mail distribution could only be performed by professionals. After the military failed in their feeble efforts to process the backlog of mail, President Nixon was forced to seriously consider satisfying the unions' demands.

Not every employee in the Cleveland office voluntarily refused to work. A hardcore group of strikers stood at each of the entrances to the main office and the truck loading dock to ensure that employees did not sneak in without notice. We carried hastily made signs and chanted our grievances. Many of the clerks who worked in personnel and considered themselves different from those of us in processing attempted to bypass the striking workers, but we blocked every entrance. There were many heated exchanges.

The government increased the pressure by fining the unions and elected union officials $1,000 for the first day, $2,000 for the second day, and progressively increasing amounts for subsequent days. Union appeals of the fines were unsuccessful. Finally, on March 22, 1970, President Nixon, in a televised address, promised to begin negotiations. On March 24, an agreement was announced by the union presidents for a 12 percent pay raise retroactive to October 1969, health benefits, compression of the pay scale, collective bargaining rights, and amnesty. While the union presidents only had a verbal agreement from the federal government and the local presidents and members could not confirm the details, mounting pressure on the New York Locals pushed Gus Johnson and Moe Biller to recommend that their members return to work. On March 25, 1970, the strike ended. However, all eyes were on New York; even though employees in some cities had returned to work, the strike was not officially over until New York employees declared it over.

In the final agreement completed one month after the employees returned to work, the 12 percent pay increase that had been promised to end the strike was reduced to 6 percent, and pay was retroactive to December instead of the promised October retroactive date. Amnesty was a key feature in the final agreement, and not a single employee who participated in the illegal walkout suffered discipline.

The strike coincided with an emergency medical condition of my youngest daughter, Kristy, who was five. She had been taken to the doctor on several occasions for a dangerously high temperature. On the first day of the strike, we took her to the emergency room, where we were told that unless her appendix was removed immediately she would not survive. She was operated on and was doing well enough that I could divide my time between the hospital and the picket line. As they wheeled my baby into the operating room, in a weakened state she looked at me and said, "Daddy, I didn't cry." My daughter survived, and we stopped mail service in Cleveland.

For clarity, the details of the 1970 postal strike were
- The strike began on March 18, 1970, started by New York Letter Carriers.
- The New York Manhattan Bronx Local officially joined the strike on March 21, 1970.
- Over two hundred thousand postal employees nationwide participated in the strike.
- The strike ended on March 25, 1970.
- Congress approved a 6 percent pay increase as a return to work.
- The Postal Reform Act (Public Law 91-375) was signed into law on August 12, 1970, including an 8 percent pay increase.
- The first contract was finalized on July 20, 1971, including five $250 wage increases over the two-year duration and one $300 lump sum payment.

Bargaining

Following the strike, as the unions prepared to negotiate the first collective bargaining agreement, Postmaster General Blount issued a "gag order" prohibiting postal employees from contacting Congress on postal issues. He wanted to curb the limited momentum that the unions had achieved politically in lobbying for postal reform. In response, Congressman Billy Ford of Michigan, a true friend of postal employees, included an amendment to the Postal Reform Act that would deny salary to any postal official who enforced the ban. In January 1971, the presidents of the APWU, Letter Carriers, Rural Letter Carriers, and Crafts and Mail Handlers Unions formed the joint bargaining committee Council of American Postal Employees (CAPE) and engaged in bargaining for the first time in the history of the United States Postal Office.

At the end of the first official bargaining period, the parties were at an impasse with no agreements on any issues. The disputes were referred to a fact-finding panel, which, over the course of forty-five days, concluded that it was unable to make substantive recommendations on the issues. With the threat of arbitration looming, crisis bargaining ensued. On July 20, 1971, an agreement was reached that included decent pay raises, partial cost-of-living adjustments, no layoffs, a multi-step grievance procedure, and the foundation for collective bargaining.

Filbey and the other union presidents achieved in the first round of bargaining a solid foundation for better wages, worker rights, and procedures. In the design of the grievance procedure, the negotiators assumed that volume would be contained by the process, but in the years to come, they were proven to have been overly optimistic. The volume overwhelmed the process, and it was necessary to rewrite that section of the contract in subsequent negotiations.

A major shortcoming of the initial agreement from the union's perspective was the right of local management to challenge the conditions of employment that had been negotiated at the local level under the executive order. Following the Kennedy executive order, the locals had proceeded to negotiate the use of leave and wash up based on seniority, and many locals—most notably the Pittsburgh and New York Locals—had negotiated extensive provisions. The 1971 contract permitted local management to challenge existing local contracts Local Memorandum of Understanding (LMOU) provisions. When an agreement could not be reached, they could declare an impasse and discontinue honoring the provisions while awaiting arbitration. This issue dominated internal union discussions until years later when I was able to successfully curb management's authority to challenge previously agreed to conditions.

All of the passion associated with the assassinations, the war, and the civil rights struggle were mixed in the boiling pot of unrest among postal employees. In the strike, we had angrily duplicated the scenes we had witnessed involving civil unrest over the decade. It was during this period that I first gave thought to a position of union leadership as a career.

Merger

On July 1, 1971, the United Federation of Postal Clerks (UFPC) merged with four postal unions—the National Postal, General Service Maintenance Employees, Motor Vehicle Employees, and Special Delivery Messengers Unions—to create the American Postal Workers Union (APWU). The strategy was to merge with each of the four independent unions separately to create the APWU constitution and send it to the members for a plebiscite vote. The vote for the merged constitution was overwhelming, and APWU was formed.

Each union, with the exception of NPU, had a long and proud history with a full range of officers that had to be merged into the new union. At the time of the merger, eight of the nine top positions were filled by officers of the craft unions. Executive

Vice President Dave Silvergleid, the former president of NPU, was the sole exception. The merger was successful because President Filbey was committed to the principles of the CIO and had entered discussions with President Joseph Beirne of the Communications Workers of America (CWA) about the possibilities of the merger with all postal unions and the CWA. These discussions eroded when the Letter Carriers President, Jim Rademaker, expressed concern about turning over significant assets to a merged union, and the Mail Handlers were being courted by the Labors International Union (LIUNA). The Rural Letter Carriers never expressed an interest. President Filbey paid a steep price in the creation of the American Postal Workers Union. He accommodated too many officers with the belief that the numbers could be corrected in short order. Filbey's optimism that the top-heavy officer structure could be corrected quickly has been unfounded. Forty years after the merger, despite numerous talks of reorganization—including a special convention called exclusively to address the officers' structure—instead of reducing officers, today we have more officers and fewer members than at the time of the merger.

Following the merger at the national level, each local and state organization, where they existed, were mandated to merge. I was assigned to represent the NPU Local in merger discussions and participated with the other Cleveland local unions. There was little difficulty merging the craft unions (Clerk, Maintenance, Motor Vehicle, and Special Delivery) as each former local president was automatically added to the executive board with the clerk president designated as general president. The only contentious issue was what their salaries would be. The meetings were tense because the NPU Local had been engaged in continuous efforts to convince members of the other unions to accept the one union philosophy and join NPU. We had members of all of the crafts and demanded appropriate representation in the new union as we were the second largest union of those merging. Having completed negotiations on the placement of the craft presidents and having resolved the issue of salaries, the local negotiators representing maintenance, motor vehicle, and special delivery were merely bystanders in the debate between NPU and UFPC (clerks) on appropriate representation.

The UFPC Local 72 was six times the size of NPU with approximately 1,800 members. At the time of the merger, it was the second or third largest local in UFPC, so the officers were accustomed to having political clout. Lee Ikner, vice president of Local 72, was the chief spokesman, and he possessed a dominant personality and was determined to have his way. At one session, the debate between us became so intense that he gathered his material and left the building. I considered the encounter a victory because we were meeting in the offices of Local 72, so he in fact had evacuated his own building and I was left to lock up.

The clerks union was demanding a sizeable majority on the local executive board, and after repeated unsuccessful meetings, I made my final offer, proposing that the number of representatives from the clerks union and NPU be determined by applying a percentage of the number of members brought to the merged union to the number of newly created executive board positions. My final offer was rejected. I did not seek a position in the merged local for myself. We reached an impasse, making it necessary for President Filbey to come to Cleveland and determine the makeup of the executive board. His decision followed my pattern, so I and the NPU membership were satisfied.

The Ohio State union also engaged in the merger, and as a result of the exposure I had received as an activist, I was designated a member of the State Merger Committee. In that capacity, I was involved in the writing of the Ohio state constitution and was appointed state director of research and education. We did not make the same mistake as the national union in retaining too many officer positions. Specific positions were identified to be eliminated after two years, including state director of research and education. However, while serving in the position, I traveled throughout the state, teaching the new collective bargaining agreement and meeting union members. Tom Ewell, the Ohio State president, and I formed a connection, and he served as a mentor during those formative years. Tom was an unsuccessful candidate in the 1972 APWU election of officers. We lost a good man, and he went on to serve as an elected official in the Akron city government.

1972 Convention

Shortly after the merger was completed, APWU held its first convention in New Orleans. I was selected as a delegate of the newly formed local union, and since this was the first convention that I attended, I did not know what to expect. The convention began with outbursts by a cadre of former UFPC officers who were hell-bent on unraveling the merger. To disrupt the proceedings, they offered repeated resolutions from the floor microphones with the intent of cancelling the merger and returning the former unions to their original state as craft unions. I do not recall their justification, but they were demanding that the merger be dissolved and we convene as a clerks union.

Filbey was equally determined that the merger would survive, and we got through the New Orleans convention as a single union. Communications Workers of America (CWA) President Joe Beirne was a guest speaker, and he spoke about the positives of taking the next step toward the merger of the entire communications sector. Presidents Bierne and Filbey were men with vision, and they could see beyond the petty differences. Having recently completed the partial merger within the postal service, the convention delegates were not in a mood to consider additional mergers. The convention did succeed in establishing the Rank-and-File Bargaining Committee with authority to supervise the negotiation process. I was not familiar with the convention rules and did not fully understand the proceedings.

My most vivid memory of that first convention is the phone call that I received in my suite shortly after our arrival in New Orleans. Before the 1972 convention, I wanted to upgrade my car and negotiated a deal for a brand-new, metallic-blue 1972 Cadillac Coupe Deville. I selected all the options from a book, and the dealer delivered to me an absolutely gorgeous machine. The car was less than two months old when I drove it to New Orleans. Upon arrival at the hotel, I presented the keys to the attendant. The phone call to my room was to request my return to the front desk to attend to "something about my car."

After securing permanent employment at the post office—supplemented by my part-time employment—I had purchased a series of automobiles. The first was a 1952 Ford Convertible that I bought in 1960 and kept until I purchased a 1962 Ford Convertible, which was my pride and joy. It must have been the shiniest car in Cleveland because I washed and waxed it every day that it did not rain or snow. I kept the '62 Convertible until 1968 when my father offered me his 1966 canary-yellow Thunderbird at a reduced price. It was a beautiful machine with a black vinyl top. I loved that car and repeated the regular washing and waxing regimen. One could determine if I had reported to work by looking in front of the postal employees' entrance. My car, with the license plate WHB 2, would be parked at the meters. When circumstances permitted, I would go to the meters and deposit coins. Sometimes that was not possible, and I must have received over fifty tickets, which were still unpaid by the time I left Cleveland. I hope there is a statute of limitations.

Upon arriving at the front of the hotel, I could see damage to the entire driver's side. My brand-new car was dented. I was outraged and wanted my new car in the same shape as when I parked it. The following day I drove to the local Cadillac dealer to determine the extent of the damage. While the dealer assured me he could repair it without an exorbitant cost, I was totally dissatisfied and wanted a new car, which the hotel would not agree to.

The attendant never explained what happened, but it did not take a genius to reach a conclusion. The theft deterrent system that I had installed was a non-active telephone mounted on the console that completed an electric circuit when it was on the cradle. In the midst of turning past a parking column, out of curiosity the driver must have removed the phone, causing the motor to cut off, and the loss of power steering made the attendant scrape the driver's side on the column. The hotel paid for the repair after my return to Cleveland, but it never looked the same to me, so I traded it in two years later. This horrible experience tarnished my opportunity to fully enjoy the 1972 convention.

During the convention, I was involved in the first picket by APWU Convention delegates. The picketing was initiated by the New York Local under the leadership of Moe Biller. Most of the convention delegates took part. When questioned about whether a permit would be necessary for the picket, John O'Donnell, Moe's attorney, replied, "If you're going to picket, forget the police permit and go ahead and picket." The illegal protest was against Farah Clothing Company. O'Donnell forged a telegram from the Amalgamated Clothing and Textile Workers Union requesting APWU to join in picketing. He gave the fake telegram to President Filbey, putting him in a position of assisting a fellow union. President Filbey led the demonstration but never knew that the telegram was a forgery.

Throughout the convention, I keenly observed President Filbey, who was masterful in the use of Robert's Rules of Order, and I received my first introduction to the art of chairing a democratic organization. His selection of the speakers at the microphones and his responses to disruptive questions were masterful. I took mental notes of how to control assemblies and how to be an effective leader.

CHAPTER 6

Preparing to Lead

I became a member of the local chapter of the A. Philip Randolph Institute, which was led by Berthina Palmer, a dynamic woman who took me under her wing and demonstrated the aspects of leadership, and had been elevated to the position of vice president of the local NPU union. But at the time, I was considering other employment. I had taken the test for the Bratenhall Police Department and Lincoln Electric Company, which paid a huge bonus at the end of each year. Both employers paid better than the post office, and the financial challenge and sixteen-hour workdays had strained my family life and caused the dissolution of my first marriage. Claudette returned to Steubenville with our daughters, Valerie and Doni. I had remarried—to Janice Reid, one of the women from the initial groups of female postal employees—and was blessed with two more lovely daughters, Kimberly and Kristy, so the choice of employment was an issue to be decided carefully. After much thought and consideration, I elected to continue postal employment and see where it would lead. I decided to attend Toastmaster's Speaker's Academy in

Cleveland to improve my speaking skills. During the exercises, we had to write an essay explaining why we had enrolled in the training, and after much consideration, I ended my paper with the objective of being president of the union.

At the post office, working alone in the penthouse, I filled mechanics' supply orders. Because the work was not continuous, there were periods of downtime, which provided ample opportunity to read the APWU contract and learn the procedures. I had so much available time that I was able to read the entire Employee Labor Relations Manual (ELM). I was certified as a steward and circulated among employees, processing grievances or attending to union issues.

Recognition

As an activist with some national recognition, I was called to Washington as one of five members selected to interview for the vacant representative-at-large position in the Maintenance Craft. As a condition of the merger, Moe Biller had insisted that the position be established and awarded to NPU. Since Moe had demanded that the position be created, I knew he would be influential in the selection, so I was not optimistic of my chances. As expected, a New York officer, Zolton Grossman, the director of Maintenance Craft New York, was selected. Zolton served in that position for four years until defeated by Jim Lindberg. Jim and his wife, Ginger, became close friends, and we continue to communicate after his retirement.

When Zolton assumed the position, there were no defined duties for him to perform, so he never relocated to Washington. When Jim took over the position, he followed suit and remained in Dallas. Years later, I initiated the policy that all national officers had to be located in the Washington office. This mandate met with some resistance, but Jim willingly relocated and served out his career in the Washington area.

Inclusion

The inclusion of African Americans in national-level APWU positions was a subject of continuous discussions among the black union activists, and we petitioned President Filbey to make such appointments. Monroe Crable, president of the General Service Maintenance Employees, and Leon Hawkins, vice president of the National Federation of Motor Vehicle Employees, had been black officers at the time of the merger. Crable was defeated by Dick Wevedau after the merger. Leon continued to serve, but he was not a general officer with authority beyond his craft, and we demanded a presence beyond these token positions.

The presidents of many of the major locals were *men* of color, and we wanted to take the next step. Women had yet to break the glass ceiling; none held a leadership position. We had created an organization titled the Committee of Concern under the guidance of Tommy Briscoe, president of the Chicago Local, and Ivory Tillman, vice president of the Detroit Local. You had to know Tommy Briscoe to fully appreciate his dynamic personality. Tommy smoked a cigar and often carried a gun, and he ruled the Chicago Local with an iron fist. Tommy always had something to say in his gruff authoritarian voice. He scheduled a meeting in Chicago to discuss our issues and invited President Filbey to address us.

Filbey consented and entered the room from the back of the stage and went to the podium where he proceeded to berate us for not being more aggressive in convincing members of the National Alliance, a black organization, to join our ranks. I bolted to the floor microphone to refute his assertion, but upon completion of his remarks, Filbey disappeared behind the curtain and left the hall. Refusing to be denied a response to such distasteful remarks, I presented my speech to an empty lectern. I responded, "How dare you come before the black leaders of APWU and blame us for your record of excluding African Americans from decision-making positions. We have shown our loyalty by providing leadership at the local level, but despite our contributions, you deny us inclusion in Washington. You blame the victims, and we demand relief through the appointment of African Americans at the national level." My remarks were received with applause, but Filbey had left the hall.

Shortly after the Chicago meeting, Los Angeles President Lorenzo Stephens and Atlanta President Wallace Baldwin were rotated in and out of APWU headquarters, but the Committee of Concern was not satisfied; we chided them for fetching coffee for the white officers. Appropriate representation at the national level was an issue until Lorenzo Stephens was appointed to the newly established position of human relations officer.

Several months after the appointment, the national Human Relations Committee was established, and I was designated as one of approximately twenty members. A meeting was called in Washington, and I was exposed to activists from throughout the country. Over the course of a week, we established the goals of the committee and its relationship within the union.

Ethelda

Upon my return to Cleveland, I made an appointment with Nick Lucci, the local president, to encourage him to fulfill the objectives of the Human Relations Committee by getting the local involved in community projects. The union office was on the second floor above a clothing store. As I entered the office, I was met by the most beautiful woman I had ever seen. I am talking about Sophia Loren beauty. She had her hair pulled back and looked like an Indian princess. I was grateful that the president kept me waiting for twenty minutes so we could engage in small talk while I smoked a cigarette. Sooner than I wanted, the president admitted me into his office and tolerated my presentation, promising "to consider it." He terminated the discussions after ten minutes, but I was not extremely disappointed because the sooner I left his office, the sooner I would be in the presence of his secretary. I was so smitten that I walked out without my cigarettes. A week later, I used them as an excuse to return to the office. She informed me that she had kept them in her desk for several days and then threw them out. I would buy thousands of packs of cigarettes in the coming years, and the secretary, Ethelda, would become my wife.

Death of My Father

On December 25, 1972, my world changed. My family was celebrating Christmas at my sister Billie Jane's home. We had just completed the gift exchange and our meal and were relaxing in her living room. Mother and her husband, Frank, had come from Detroit so we could spend Christmas Day together as a family, and all were in a festive mood. Around 7:00 p.m. the phone rang, and Jane excused herself to answer it. Within a few seconds, I could hear a muffled cry from the hallway, and when I investigated, she informed me that Daddy had died. He and his lady friend had spent the holiday in Atlanta and were returning to Detroit by plane. As he approached the ticket counter to check a package, he wrote his name and died. Emergency personnel were summoned, but it was too late; our father had passed. Earlier in the day, I had suggested that we call our father and wish him a merry Christmas. My sister reminded me that he was going to Atlanta for the day with a friend and would not be home until late.

I guess it was appropriate that our mother was present when we received the news, but from the day that she had left her family, it had been our father who was the guiding force protecting his children. He was a kind and gentle man who did not drink or use profanity. Instead he created the word "radnon." He never explained its origins, but in every instance when a curse word was expected or deserved, he would say, "Radnon." Our father would not wear a mustache because he said that only colored men wore facial hair. He was not a Bible thumper; the source of his gentle nature resided in his character. He never called me William or Bill. Instead he called me a variety of nicknames, including Doc, Son, and Butch. My sisters, stepmother, and mother referred to me as Buster or Pete, names adopted by my associates and friends. I followed my father's example, calling my daughters Sweetheart or Baby. I only refer to them by their legal names when I am upset.

In 1943, our father had been drafted to support the war effort even though he was a single father with two young children. I do not know if the Wheeling draft board placed an extra focus on black men to meet their quota, but our father was thirty-six years old and was the sole supporter of two children, ages six and nine. When he asked what he should do with his children, the board responded that "it was his problem." I don't know if a personal relationship existed prior to the draft board notice, but my father immediately pursued Blanche Pugh. I remember meeting her on an outing at the local park. I was dressed in my sailor's suit and was floating a stick in the wading pool. When I fell in, she retrieved me. Within weeks they were married. Blanche Pugh was a native of Mobile, Alabama, and she had a two-year-old daughter named Effie. Like many other blacks, she had come to live with her cousins in Wheeling to escape from the brutal racism of the South.

With her marriage to our father, Blanche and Effie became our family. Blanche, or Mother as I would soon call her, became our caretaker, and she taught me the necessary skills to be a man. During the early years when our father was in the military, the four of us relocated to Columbus and then Toledo, Ohio, and lived in a number of situations that were far from ideal. On one occasion when our quarters consisted of a single room, Mother insisted that the females sleep together in the one bed, and I slept in a small area near the hot water tank with blankets but no bed. After repeatedly losing socks, we began to suspect that the culprit was a rat. Mother set a giant trap and within hours, a rat the size of a small cat was struggling to return through a hole with the trap clamped around its neck. Mother finished it off with a broom.

When I was seven years old, we relocated back to Wheeling to live in a house with Mother's cousins, the Savage family. Laverne Savage was a year younger than Jane, so we had much in common and spent several years of our childhood playing together. We occupied the lower floor of a two-story house that was built on a steep hill. One night, the driver of an automobile lost control and careened off the road above, lodging in the rear of the house. Nobody was hurt, but we had real concerns that the impact had damaged the supports of the house and that it would collapse. We exited the house and stood in the street in the middle of the night and watched as the car was removed without further damage to the house. The authorities determined that it was safe, and we continued living there for an additional two years. In the next house where we lived, I had my own private bedroom adjacent to the kitchen, so it was necessary that the room was always kept presentable.

One day the Savage family literally saved my life. I had stolen my mother's coin bank and was spending the money on childish things. Freddie Miles, a neighborhood friend, awoke me early in the morning to inform me that our playmates had found where I had stashed the bounty. My mother overheard him and found out what I had done. The beating that followed was serious, and but for the intervention of the Savage family, it would have continued. The whuppin' must have worked because I haven't stolen anything since.

I was six years old when my father entered the service, and like other children during the war, I pictured him bravely killing Japanese just like in the news reels shown at the movie theaters. After his discharge, I questioned him about his service, and he informed me that the military did not permit colored sailors to use guns; he had been used in the only occupation available, as a cook. After his discharge from the navy, Dad went to school in Columbus and qualified to be a beautician, and he and my stepmother were certified as hairstylists. They opened a salon with an attached newsstand to support the family. However, there were not enough colored customers in the Wheeling area to support the enterprise, so my father was constantly searching for better employment.

Mother taught me cleanliness—I was required to make up the bed every day—personal hygiene, and the importance of an education. She hung a copy of the poem "If" on the kitchen wall and required that I memorize it. I learned how to wash clothes while helping Mother do the laundry of rich white families. I learned the right way to starch and iron a white dress shirt, leaving no creases and reserving the collar for last. This was years before spray starch, and the starch was spread on the clothes as they were ironed. At the age of twelve, I was assigned to wash and sterilize the combs and brushes in the family beauty salon. Mother would inspect them with a microscope to ensure that they were spotless. For several years, we had an icebox to store perishable foods. It was my job to empty the water and meet the ice man as he drove through the neighborhood. She taught me the process of canning foods: peeling peaches and apples, boiling them, sterilizing the jars, and canning them for storage in the coal cellar. In the absence of our father, which was quite often, Mother and Effie became family.

Years later, after many family experiences and Jane's departure for college, our father went to Detroit for employment, and Effie and I formed a special relationship. She was five years younger than I. I was filled with pride later when my baby sister became a reporter for the Cleveland *Call & Post*, the paper that focused on events in the colored community, and then she married a doctor and moved to Philadelphia. I was fifteen when my father left for Detroit seeking employment in the auto industry. I became the man of the house, and he turned over to me the job of the sole custodian at the bank in Fulton, West Virginia. I would ride my bicycle or catch the bus to make the five-mile trip from my home before school, unlock the bank, and perform the cleaning that I had not completed the previous day after school. During football season, I juggled the activities of school, work, and football, performing successfully at each task.

The football team traveled by school bus to play the other colored schools in West Virginia. After the away games, we often spent the night in the homes of residents in the city, but for one game, I did not have any toiletries because I was not sure that a scheduling conflict with the bank could be resolved. Arrangements were made to replace me for the following day, so the bus picked me up from my job at the bank on the way and I boarded to the cheers of my teammates.

In the winter of 1972, as I participated in the funeral arrangements for the single most important human being in my life, I reflected back on the lifetime of events and experiences that we had shared. Thousands of memories flittered through my mind, including the funeral of my grandmother's husband when I was two or three years old. My father escorted me down the aisle of the dimly lit room to pay respect. He lifted me up to view the body, and I thought he was going to place me in the casket. Fear engulfed me, and the firm hands of my father lowered me to the floor and provided the security that I was loved.

Several years before his death, to fulfill our mutual desire to spend quality time together, we scheduled a trip to his birthplace in Bells Chapel, Kentucky, so that I could see where he lived prior to coming to Wheeling. I had been told the story of how my grandfather traveled to Wheeling to seek employment in the coal mines and how, after establishing himself, he had sent for his two sons who had been left behind on the jointly owned farm with their uncles in Kentucky. After several years working in the mines, my grandfather was injured in a cave-in and lived out his life in Wheeling disabled and under the care of my father.

In researching my family tree, I successfully traced the Burrus family to 1806, to my great-great-great-grandfather William Burrus, who was born in Virginia. At the time of the census, he was a free man of African descent sixty-five years before the Civil War. He and his wife, Mary, had three children: Sarah, William, and Mary. The trip to Bells Chapel was intended to rekindle the relationship with our ancestors with the hope that we would bring honor to their name. I drove from Cleveland to Wheeling, where we met to make the drive to Kentucky. It was raining, and we were tired. We were engaged in a meaningless discussion to stay awake when my father made a reference to "niggers." I was appalled. I had never heard my father use such an offensive term, and I exploded. I never used the word in jest or anger, and I was offended that my father had used it in my presence. I told him that every time he used the word, he was insulting me in the general negative reference. We survived the moment, and by the time that we arrived in Bells Chapel, our relationship was back to normal. I met cousins who told stories about the time when my father lived among them. I often wonder how different my life would have been if my grandfather could have raised his family on the farm that he and his brothers owned.

My father was aware of my union involvement at the time and had informed Willie Bryant, a Detroit maintenance employee who was a candidate for national office on several occasions, that his son in Cleveland would be president "of that *radnon* union." On the eve of the beginning of my career as a union official, I lost my biggest supporter, my father. He died at the age of sixty-five, never enjoying retirement or a life of leisure. Years after I began postal employment, he acquired work as a postal custodian, then went to school and qualified as a postal maintenance mechanic. The Thanksgiving before his passing, my family spent the weekend at his house, during which time he talked about his pending retirement. From the day that our mother left, his primary objective was taking care of his children;

through the stays in foster homes to the constant moving from city to city, Daddy was always there for comfort and support for Jane and me. Our father was absent more than he was present, but no man has ever made a greater impact on his offspring than our father—William Henry Burrus Sr.

CHAPTER 7

The Contract of 1973

1973 Contract

In the years immediately following the successful negotiations in 1971, the union activists geared up for the next round of bargaining. We were determined to correct many objectionable contractual features. In the 1973 negotiations, the union presidents succeeded in including new provisions in Article 19 that placed some restrictions on management's right to change handbooks and manuals. Language was also agreed upon to restrict management's right to perform bargaining unit work, and the schedule for full-time employees was set at forty hours per week.

Having survived the 1970 strike, we approached the negotiations with militancy but were surprised and relieved that agreement had been reached prior to the expiration of the ninety-day period of bargaining. The contract included generous pay increases and an uncapped cost-of-living adjustment (COLA), replacing the $160 limit applied in the initial contract. Specific items were identified for local negotiations, resolving, in part, the debacle from the 1971 negotiations, and it was agreed that the postal service would pay the full cost of life insurance. All of the unions, National Association of Letter Carriers (NALC), Mail Handlers, the Crafts, and the Rural Carriers, negotiated under the banner of the Coordinated Bargaining Committee (CBC), and since the agreement met the expectations of the membership, it was ratified with a comfortable margin.

The Election

During this period, I continued to work two jobs while considering leaving postal employment, provided the right opportunity came along. However, my involvement with the union solidified my commitment to the postal service, so I stopped looking for permanent employment elsewhere and instead searched for opportunities within the postal service. I considered the possibility of entering postal management but rejected it as a career because there was just one postmaster general. It was highly unlikely that in the time frame of the 1960s and 1970s I could project that an African American would achieve that position, and I wanted to be in charge. A colored American postal employee had succeeded in achieving a high-ranking position in the Russian postal system, but that was during the period when the Russians were attempting to export Communism and scores of black intellectuals were enticed by the promises of equal treatment. In 1932, Homer Smith, a colored mail clerk in Minneapolis, went to Moscow to advise the Russians on improving their postal services, but after fourteen years, he became disillusioned with Communism and returned to the United States.

As I continued to evaluate my opportunities, there were periods when I worked seven days a week, and my off days at one job were workdays at the other. I saw my children between jobs, and when I went to sleep, their mother instructed them not to disturb me because "Daddy is tired."

In 1973, while attending a local union meeting, I engaged in the discussions on an agenda item with the objective of making a point. My presentation must have resonated with others because after the meeting, while I was mingling, a well-intentioned member approached me and suggested that I be a candidate for Research and Education in the coming local union elections. He was being gratuitous, but to his surprise, I responded that I intended to be a candidate for president.

As the local union election neared, I began talking to my closest friends from the former NPU local about a possible campaign for the presidency. Anne Thomas was my biggest supporter and friend, but my circle of committed allies also included Tim and Bob Callahan and Bill Harris. We spent hours in my living room plotting strategy and estimating resources. I was nominated for president, but a serious error occurred in the process. Candidates were required to mail a certified letter to the chairman of the Elections Committee confirming acceptance of the nomination. I thought I had mailed the letter, but the day prior to the deadline, the president called to inform me that my letter had not been received. There was not sufficient time to mail and deliver a certified letter, so in near panic, I asked if I could hand-deliver it; he consented.

I began my candidacy with many handicaps, not the least of which was that I was an African American with an Afro trying to unseat a president of Italian descent in a union dominated by white males. In addition, I was assigned to the Maintenance Craft, which comprised less than 20 percent of the members in the union; I had been a member of the National Postal Union at the time of the merger that had been finalized only three years before; and I had never held executive office in the dominant union.

My election committee printed two-foot-by-four-foot posters with my picture and campaign slogan printed on them and nailed at least twenty of them to the fence bordering the sidewalk immediately across from the post office. The mail handler in charge of postal printing provided me a listing of every employee in the APWU Crafts, with their addresses. We had to convert them to written addresses because we had to conceal the unique markings on the postal brass mailing plates. We sent a mailing to each member on the list.

As a fundraiser, the committee planed a ladies' fashion show. They secured a lounge in a bar, new outfits on loan for the models, tickets, and all of the other necessities for a first-class affair. They prepared invitations and distributed them, and to my surprise and appreciation, Doug Holbrook, the president of the Detroit Local, one of the most progressive locals in the union, and his entire executive board were in attendance. The show was a smashing success. The feedback that I received on the work floor indicated that I would be competitive. It was generally assumed that a candidate had to be in the dominant Clerk Craft and I was assigned to the Maintenance Craft, but I had been an employee for sixteen years and was well known throughout the office. On the day that the Election Committee counted the ballots, I was returning from a training seminar in Dayton, Ohio, in a car driven by Matt Davis, a Cleveland coworker who would later become a national officer. Matt was a fast driver, but the trip took what seemed to be forever.

During my stay in Dayton, I had been engaged in discussion with Jim Williams, a vice president who had a national presence and was the most knowledgeable person in the union on Article 12's excessing. Jim was well respected by everyone, and I was flattered later when he asked me about my chances in the election. To his astonishment, I responded that I had won.

The experiences that I had in the army and in the postal service to that time prepared me for my life to follow. I had always been able to pay the bills and put food on the table, but I knew that I had the intellect, the fortitude, and the desire to do something big and to make a difference. The presidency of the Cleveland Local was a window to my future.

Jane, My Sister

Upon our return to Cleveland, Matt drove directly to the bar where the votes were being counted. I immediately sought out my sister, Jane, who had achieved postal employment several years after me and was my election observer. Jane was three years older than I and had a strong personality. Our mother left when I was a young child, and in the years prior to my father's remarriage, we were shuttled from one foster home to another as our father, whom we adored, spent evenings at his place of employment as a butler, chauffer, and general handyman. He was unable to see us on a regular basis.

Because of my father's continual search for better employment, we moved so much that by the time I entered the third grade it was the fifth school I had attended in the fourth city. I started my schooling at an early age. I vividly recall the apprehension in the adults' voices as they prepared me for enrollment in kindergarten and questioned whether or not I would be admitted when I was only three years old. I was accepted, and the state provided free babysitting services. When I was in the second grade, we were living in Toledo, Ohio, and Jane was my chaperone to and from school. One special occasion, Jane had to leave school early, but before she departed she instructed me on the directions home: "Go straight to the corner and turn right where the billy goat is in the enclosed yard." After school, I followed her directions, but on that day the goat was not in the yard, so I continued to go straight. After walking several miles, even I, who was born with the absolute worst sense of direction, realized that something was amiss. It was getting dark, and I was terribly afraid. I retraced my steps and finally found the fence on the corner but still no billy goat. I turned anyway and saw the police who had been dispatched to find me and my sister, Jane.

Jane was the one constant in my life, and until I reached the age of fourteen when she went away to college, I do not remember

91

a single day when she was not there to support her little brother. To her coworkers, she was known by her first name, Billie, but our family consisted of William Sr., William Jr., and Billie Jane, so to separate her from the other Bills in the family, I called her Jane. Billie, the union member, was my election observer, but Jane, the human being, was my sister.

I Won

Jane informed me that the officials had been counting for several hours and it was close, but I was holding my own. After several more hours passed, she told me that they had completed the count but that Josia, the elections chairman, would not release the results. He was a strong supporter of Nicki Lucci, the incumbent president, so we were suspicious. I protested that after more than six hours of counting, the results should be posted.

After an additional hour from the time of my complaint, the results were finally posted, and I had won by twelve votes out of almost two thousand that had been cast. The chairman announced that the results were not official and a recount was necessary. After two more agonizing hours, a tearful chairman posted the final count: I had won by seven votes. I was later informed by one of the tellers that each time that they counted, they would shave a couple of votes, but not wanting to bring attention to themselves, they limited it to one or two votes. As a result, with each recount, the margin of victory declined from twelve votes to the final margin of seven votes. Despite the shenanigans, I had won.

After a night of celebration, I went home and reflected on my achievement. From the hills of West Virginia, I had climbed the mountain. I was president-elect of the Cleveland Local, American Postal Workers Union.

The following day while at work, I received a call from Josia, who informed me that it was his intention to count the ballots again. He was a heavy drinker and had imbibed excessively the night before and ended up begging the forgiveness of the defeated president for "letting him down." I had watched him place the ballots in the trunk of his car and drive away to "places unknown." There was no way that I was going to permit another recount, so I had my attorney intervene. The ballots were not recounted, and I was declared the official winner.

During the several weeks between the counting and the installation, I packed my personal possessions at the post office and completed the necessary paperwork to discontinue postal employment and begin a new career. One day when I was breaking for lunch, I was crossing the street and heard my name being called. Bill Childress, a local union officer who was a strong supporter of the defeated president, was escorting Nicki Lucci's gorgeous secretary across the street. He wanted to introduce her to the new president. I was wearing the most garish red bell-bottom trousers, which were in style at that time in Cleveland, and an Afro. Childress did not know about my earlier visit to the office. We exchanged brief pleasantries. I later learned that Ethelda was informed that I intended to replace her upon assuming office, which was the craziest idea in the world. I had absolutely no intention of missing the opportunity to work in the same confines as this goddess.

I had a lot of work to do, and I welcomed the challenge. Representing the interest of three thousand workers was the task before me, and I looked forward to confronting postal management and demanding better conditions for employees of the Cleveland office. Postal employment was rapidly changing. Since the Postal Reform Act in 1970, the managers were applying a more businesslike approach to the service. It was necessary that the union also change, and I had ideas of what we could do to elevate postal employment to a worthwhile career.

PART TWO:

Working for Change

CHAPTER 8

President of the Local

In celebration of my victory, the installation of officers was the crowning achievement of my efforts to find my place in the world. From my early childhood, I yearned to be in a position to decide. I was astute enough to know that the human race was composed of those who decided and those who conformed. I wanted to be a part of the former group. I had no road map to get there, but now *I could taste the wind.*

Inauguration day came. I was filled with pride and satisfaction. I awoke knowing that by day's end I would be an installed officer with the opportunity to impact lives. My wife, Janice, who had supported me in my struggles and tolerated my sixteen-hour-long workdays for so long, shared in my sense of accomplishment. Our two children, Kimberly and Kristy, were too young to appreciate the magnitude of my achievement, but they knew that something important had happened and that they were a part of it. My daughters from my first marriage, Valerie Jean and Doni Mari, were living in Steubenville, where their mother had relocated after the dissolution of our marriage. They spent each summer with me in Cleveland. Since the inauguration was during the school year, they were unable to share the pride of the moment with us.

The installation of officers was a formal affair. The time passed slowly while we waited to drive to the hotel where the ceremonies would be performed. Thousands of thoughts flittered through my mind as I focused on the speech that would begin my career.

The affair was attended by over three hundred union members, and President Stu Filbey was the keynote speaker. He came from Washington with a speech praising the leadership of the outgoing president. I do not believe that he mentioned my name once throughout his entire thirty-minute address. An uninformed attendee would have believed that Nick Lucci had been reelected. I did not focus on minor issues; my speech was one of deep feeling and focused on our collective struggle. It was well received.

The Cleveland Local APWU represented three thousand members. The perception among the members was that the union leadership was stuck in the past. I was determined to establish a new level of representation and set about initiating changes. The former officers had rented office space and had a full-time secretary from the additional revenue received from the merger, but President Lucci had absolutely no concept of running an office. There was no copy machine, only one telephone line, and no computer, and the membership list was kept on mimeographed brass plates. The secretary was beautiful, but the entire filing system was a mess. My first challenge was to bring the office into the twentieth century.

During my presidency, we had our moments of success and failures, but we definitely broke new ground. In representing the employees, we expanded seniority rights and leave usage, initiated training programs, became involved in the community, and created a budget. The union purchased an office building where we conducted monthly meetings. We also reserved space in the union hall for scheme training. Perhaps what everyone remembers the most, though, was the annual Christmas party that I initiated for the members. It lasted all night to ensure that employees on all tours could participate. It was free to every member of the local, and hundreds came as the office was only two blocks from the postal facility. We provided unlimited drink, food, and music. In later years, after the union purchased a union hall several miles away, members still made the trip and truly enjoyed the festivities.

Leadership

My relationships with the officers and members of the Cleveland Local were positive with only a few instances of major conflict. The approval of LWOP (leave without pay) for union activities was an issue of constant attention but never erupted into public disagreements. We successfully made major amendments to the local constitution, and I succeeded in helping Bill Harris get elected as the Ohio State vice president.

I served as the Cleveland Local president for seven years and was unopposed in my final election. In the final local election, Bill Childress petitioned to run against me but was ruled ineligible because he had not attended the minimum number of constitutionally required meetings. The Labor Department paid special attention to this constitutional requirement, overturning several high profile elections due to meeting rules. I was willing to waive the meeting requirement, but Richard Butler, an executive board member of the local, was adamant and convinced the board to exclude Childress's candidacy. My subsequent election to national office would make the issue moot.

Elections Committee

Several months after assuming the presidency of the Cleveland Local, I was appointed to the National Elections Committee by Pat Nilan, director of legislation. I reported to Washington along with approximately twenty others from locals throughout the country. We were housed at the International Inn on Thomas Circle several blocks from APWU headquarters; the hotel had seen better days. The ballots were counted several miles away on Rhode Island Avenue, so we were bused in groups from the hotel to the ballot counting location.

Roland Smallwood, president of the Mount Vernon, New York Local was designated chairman, and we began two weeks of service that reminded me of my early days of postal employment. The building where the ballots were counted was under renovation, which it sorely needed. A plaque adorning the entrance of the building recorded a construction date in the 1800s, and it looked and smelled its age.

In the ballot counting room, there were twenty to thirty tables. The Merkle Printing Company employees were paired up at each table, and under the watchful eye of a member of the Elections Committee, one called out the intent of the voter to the counting partner. Any markings that were not clear would be referred to a special table for disposition. The Elections Committee members' role was to clarify the intent of the voter when there was a question and to deliver all material not related to the election count to the chairman. You would be surprised at some of the messages members submitted, with or without the ballot.

Because the number of votes (91,000) was higher than expected (61,000), the counters and the committee members were called upon to work around the clock, seven days a week until the count was completed. We drew lots to determine the shift assignments, and unluckily, I drew the graveyard shift, which meant working all night. We rotated shifts after several days so that each member of the committee got a dose of working all night. This was a great relief, but in the transition, my group was forced to work sixteen straight hours. Filbey won the election handily, and when the last vote was counted and we presented our report, I left Washington on the first thing smoking, vowing never to return.

Battle at the Bulk

As I was assuming a leadership role in Cleveland, events were unfolding throughout the union. In January 1974, New York's postal management officials had modified the schedules of over one thousand bulk mail center (BMC) employees. The employees had been enticed to the newly established bulk operation because of its daytime schedules. Without consulting the union, management changed the schedules to 4:00 p.m. to midnight. In an effort to compete in the package industry, the postal service had constructed twenty-one facilities exclusively to process parcels and store mail bags. It was reported that the construction company owned by Postmaster General Bailer was awarded the construction contract for several of the facilities. Whether this was true or not, I'm not sure, but there was great union resistance to their staffing. The New York facility was in a remote location with no public transportation available at midnight.

When management was staffing the newly opened BMCs, the maintenance employees were assigned first, and the president of the Maintenance Craft, Dick Wevodau, convinced the newly assigned employees to file for union charters. In some circumstances, BMCs were constructed in areas where APWU locals already existed, but New York was an exception, and the newly assigned employees were members of the New York Local. The employees subjected to this scheduling change were members of the largest APWU local, and Moe Biller was the president. Moe had a reputation as a fighter, having been the most visible union leader during the 1970 strike. He went ballistic when management unilaterally changed the schedules. In protest, the employees were instructed by the union to report to work on the original schedule; upon arrival, the workers found that management had locked the entrance gates. Litigation followed, and a New York judge ordered arbitration to settle the scheduling dispute. The threat of arbitration led to a mutual agreement between the union and local management that employees with seniority would not be involuntarily assigned to the late tour. Even though it was a local issue, over the course of a year, Moe elevated the issue to national discussions, and at every meeting where activists were assembled, the issue became a major subject on the agenda.

New Standards for Leave

At the time I assumed the Cleveland presidency, the postal labor relations department was in the process of becoming professional in employment policies. They assigned a cadre of highly qualified central region labor representatives—Jim Helquist, Jim Holmes, Roger Stone, and Jim Stanton—who were smart and aggressive, and they initiated new positions on contract interpretations. Prior to the Postal Reform Act, the postal leave policies and procedures were established and governed by the Civil Service Board of Appeals. The board had established that discipline could not be imposed for absences approved by supervisors. Thus a supervisor's approval for payment of an absence would negate discipline for a day in question. The central region, however, devised a novel argument at the time that the discipline would be imposed not for missing work but for "failure to maintain a regular work schedule." In a series of regional arbitrations, arbitrators supported the new position, and employees became subject to disciplinary action for absences that were approved.

We could not win this issue at the local level because of arbitral precedent, and I was surprised and disappointed that the national union did not take this issue to the Civil Service Commission or national arbitration. In later years, when I was a national officer, the commission modified its position that was still applicable to veterans, but arbitration precedent had been well established. I will be forever disappointed that this issue of such magnitude was adversely modified without a greater level of objection.

These new postal leave policy changes were a major challenge. Annual leave is advanced at the beginning of each year and employees earn four hours of sick leave for each eighty regular hours of work, so until the leave is exhausted, employees who are absent do not suffer a loss of pay. The adjustment in the policy was applied to employees who had become comfortable with reporting off because they "didn't feel well" or had an alleged emergency because there was no threat of discipline. Following the changes, the number of disciplinary grievances exploded, and a disproportional amount of time was devoted to defending employees because of attendance-related infractions.

In response to the dramatic increase in discipline from the new attendance policies, the local Letter Carriers Union, Branch 40—whose president, Harold Lowe, lived on the same street as I in Cleveland Heights—responded with a policy of grieving every letter of warning related to attendance issues. The Pittsburgh Local under John Richards developed a computer program that was the first in the union to initiate grievances en masse.

In the Cleveland office, I initiated training programs for the stewards and officers to better prepare them for the increased workload. I also developed a professional relationship with June Kirk, one of the first black females to be elevated to management in labor relations, and we were in constant communication on labor issues. Lee Ikner was the vice president of the previous Cleveland APWU Local administration. He was unopposed after the merger and continued in the office. Ikner and I had clashed in the merger discussions, and our relationship was precarious. Within six months of the new term of office, he accepted a promotion to management in labor relations. For the balance of my service in Cleveland, he served as a management official discussing grievances, many of which were attendance related.

Learning to Arbitrate

In response to the significant increase in grievances generated by the new leave policy, the national union began permitting local officers to arbitrate their own cases. As president of the Cleveland

Local, I arbitrated many cases, gaining valuable experience in understanding the process of arbitration. I had observed a number of advocates and thought that I fully understood the procedures, but when you are at the table and the pressure is on, it is not quite as easy as it looks. Leo Persails, who would oppose me in later elections, was one of the best APWU advocates, using his dogged determination as an asset.

In my first case, I showed my inexperience by objecting to the opening statement by my opponent, Jim Helquist, who was the postal service representative. The case was about two employees who left the building on the clock and visited the bar across the street. One employee had pleaded guilty; I was defending the grievant who denied the allegation. I lost that case, but I learned invaluable lessons, including the importance of having necessary documentation. The greatest problem in grievance processing at the time was stewards who would send grievances to the regional level with just the papers of appeal and no supporting documentation.

With more experience, I became a skilled advocate and successfully resolved many grievances. However, my experiences in arbitration were not all positive. One case stands out in particular. An employee was convicted for receipt of pornographic material at his home. The story was reported in the news media, and the postal service issued a removal based on his conviction. I presented the case that the situation was not employment related as the news media had not identified him as a postal employee. The arbitrator denied the grievance and included in his award "that his [the arbitrator's] religion would not permit granting the grievance." Several weeks after receiving the award, the grievant committed suicide.

Honored

During my presidency, I was honored by Congressman Louis Stokes's presence at several local union meetings and social events. Congressman Stokes and his brother, Cleveland Mayor Carl Stokes, were legends in the Cleveland colored community. The established political machine was determined to deny the African American community representation in Congress and city government, but Louis and Carl Stokes broke the color barrier and lifted us to heights we only dreamed of in the past.

CHAPTER 9

Expanded Duties

Meeting with Filbey

During this period, I had the occasion to travel to APWU headquarters in Washington to discuss issues of importance; prior to my return to Cleveland, I visited President Filbey's office to pay my respects. I was seated in the waiting area and after a respectable time was ushered into his office. We shook hands, and I was seated across from his desk, where we sat in silence for almost ten minutes. When the situation reached the stage of being uncomfortable, I rose to excuse myself. Stu extended his hand and said, "Upon your return to Cleveland, would you express my best wishes to President Burrus?" I departed without informing him that I was President Burrus, the officer whom he had installed after praising the defeated president.

As I consider the Chicago speech and the installation, I do not know what to conclude. I had never heard an accusation that President Filbey harbored any racial feelings—and did not conclude such from our personal encounters—but prior to assuming national office, Stu was the last president of the all-white Baltimore Local and, like many others, he was a victim of his times. However, my memories of Stu are honorable, and I think of him as the right president at the right time. His legacy should be that he was a good man.

Appointment

While serving as president of the Cleveland Local, I received a call from Dick Wevodau, president of Maintenance Craft, inquiring if I would accept an appointment as national vice president of the Cincinnati Division Maintenance Craft. My immediate response was that I was extremely busy as president of the local and chairman of the Presidents' Conference and would have to think it over. I then called John Smith, my mentor in Dayton, and requested his opinion. John advised me to accept the position and offered his assistance if I needed it. I returned the call to Dick and began my services as vice president of Maintenance Craft to the Cincinnati division. The duties involved processing step 2Bs (a step 2 appeal involving discipline disputes), reviewing contract disputes, and arbitrating unresolved maintenance cases. These duties placed additional demands on my time, but I had been conditioned by the many years of sixteen-hour days.

I had a number of memorable cases, but one that stands out is a step 2B grievance I was processing that contested a fourteen-day suspension for an employee at the Cincinnati BMC who refused to wear a hard hat in the performance of duties. The file indicated that the grievant had received the appropriate training and was disciplined before for the same infraction. I telephoned the grievant to understand his justification for the repeated refusal. At the end of the review, I concluded that I could not prevail in arbitration, so I settled the case for five days back pay and mailed a copy of the resolve to the grievant. Several days later, I received a call from the grievant informing me that the back pay that I secured "was just enough for me to sue your ass." Gary Kloepfer never sued me, but he did go on to become the national at-large representative for Maintenance

Craft and a dear friend. When I announced my retirement at the 2009 All-Craft Conference, I held a private meeting the evening prior with my closest advisors, and Gary Kloepfer was included.

Another memorable arbitration case while I was serving as Maintenance vice president involved the subject of "snow leave." Over the years, the union had lost a series of cases involving employees who were forced to use their leave when major storms prevented them from reporting. In the mid-1970s, management labor representatives in the central region prepared a map with pins showing the home locations of employees who reported and those who did not. Arbitrators were convinced that employees who did not report to work and lived in the same communities as those who reported did not meet the requirements for administrative leave. The union did not prevail whenever the snow map was allowed as evidence.

When I was scheduled to arbitrate the Cincinnati snow grievance, I knew that I would have to face the map, so I elected to challenge its admission by appealing to the arbitrator that I was entitled to cross-examine each employee represented by a pin to determine where they departed from on the day in question, the type of vehicle they drove—four-wheel or two-wheel drive—conditions of the roads on their route, distance of the commute, local authority instructions, and so forth. The arbitrator granted my motion, but because his schedule would not permit the laborious examination of hundreds of employees, he disallowed the snow map and granted the grievance. From that date forward, the snow map has not been an effective exhibit to decide snow leave on the basis of statistical evidence.

In the wider Cleveland labor community, I became immersed in the Cleveland Central Labor Body and was a founding member of a dissident group that attempted to wrest power from the long entrenched incumbents. We were unsuccessful, but I was exposed to dynamic local leaders who taught me the fire necessary to represent the interest of workers. Officers of the Local Steel Workers Union were particularly impressive.

1974 and 1975 Conventions

The 1974 National Convention was a total waste of time and money. We argued over the rules regarding the number of votes required to call the roll. New York and Philadelphia brought large delegations to the conventions. One hundred or more delegates were lined up in rows with a captain at the end with a walkie-talkie to receive Moe Biller and Al Rosen's instructions on how to vote. However, even the largest delegation's vote was diluted by the hundreds of small locals that, when combined, could prevent a two-thirds majority. The solution was to cast votes for every member, and the only way of achieving that was through a roll call. We also argued over a New York–sponsored resolution: "No Contract, No Work." The subject of restructuring was presented by my friend, Detroit President Doug Holbrook, who chaired the Constitution Committee and presented a thorough and balanced review of the officer's structure, offering appropriate modifications. The report was rejected by the delegates. After we failed to achieve agreement on restructuring, I am not sure if President Filbey had predetermined to request approval for a special convention the following year in Kansas City, but he presented the proposal and it was approved. It was the one success from the convention.

The 1975 Kansas City special convention unfolded no differently than the previous convention, with no group able to muster the two-thirds majority for change. Ranny Erskine, the president of Tampa Local, chaired the Constitution Committee. He presented a package of changes for restructuring the officers' structure, but it met with the same fate. After four days of disagreeing over the positions that should be eliminated, we left without making any progress in restructuring. The parliamentarian had advised President Filbey that the way to proceed was to have each resolution be decided by majority vote, and after completion of all the constitutional resolutions on restructuring, have a two-thirds vote on the package. It was impossible to overcome the resentment built up on each vote and achieve a two-thirds vote at the end. The factions that had been in the minority on the individual votes prevented adoption of the package when the bar was raised to the two-thirds requirement at the end. Filbey would have been better served to have required two-thirds on each resolution as it was presented—maybe then we would have achieved something.

1975 Contract

The National Association of Letter Carriers, the Mail Handlers, and the American Postal Workers Union continued in joint bargaining, and the 1975 contract negotiations proceeded without the threat of a major disruption. The negotiators achieved limitations on management's right to use prior discipline in the filing of charges. They also phased out the "public policy employees" (workers appointed through congressional referrals who were outside the limitations of the contract) and limited the use of casuals. An agreement was also reached that casuals could not be used in lieu of career employees. This language was applied to a ruling that required the payment of hundreds of millions of dollars to career employees who had been supplanted by casuals.

Presidents' Conference

The local presidents had become impatient with activities at the national level as the local leaders continued to attempt to find a consensus on restructuring the constitution to eliminate the excess of national officers acquired through the merger. The local presidents met in Pittsburgh and formed the Local Presidents' Conference. John Richards was elected as the initial chairman by acclamation, and we began meeting regularly to share experiences and form alliances. The Presidents' Conference formed a committee of five presidents to meet with a delegation of resident national officers to discuss restructuring, and we met in Chicago. The intent was to reach an agreement on an outline of a new structure that would be a starting point for deliberations at the next convention. After several hours of discussions, the national officers informed us that they did not speak for the administration, so we terminated the discussions and prepared for the battles ahead. The Local Presidents' Conference was expanded to include state presidents, and it served as a forum for the exchange of information. I succeeded John as chairman, and the supporting presidents included Moe, John Richards, Phil Fleming, Doug Holbrook, and Ivory Tillman of Detroit; John Numair, Wallace Baldwin, and Archie Salisbury of Dallas; Doug Seaman and Chris Cooper of Columbus; Jack and John Panzeca of Cincinnati; Dave Leonard of Michigan; and dozens of others whose names escape me.

1976 Convention

As we approached the 1976 National Convention, I was firmly established as the Cleveland president, having won the initial election and the rerun held in 1975. The Labor Board was notorious in requiring elections to be rerun for the flimsiest of reasons. In the Cleveland case, they determined that the defeated president had used a faulty mailing list, so even though he was responsible for the list, his error provided him a second opportunity to win. I prevailed again and proceeded to initiate changes in the local.

One of these changes involved the transportation to the convention city of Las Vegas. This year was the first occasion that the convention would be held in this glamorous venue, and everyone looked forward to the experience. I discovered that the cost of chartering a flight would be cheaper than buying individual tickets for twenty-five delegates, and combined with family members and companions, we would have sufficient numbers to make chartering cost-effective. I discussed the idea of delegates throughout the state joining with us with the APWU State President, Bill Tullos. Bill agreed, and we planned the trip, originating in Cleveland with a stop in Columbus before heading west to Las Vegas.

We filled the plane and enjoyed champagne and light snacks on the six-and-a-half-hour flight. The trip permitted the delegates from the state the opportunity to bond and relieve the competition that was on regular display between Cleveland and Cincinnati. At one state meeting when the Committee on Political Action (COPA) solicitation was made, before Cincinnati made its pledge, I promised that Cleveland would raise one dollar more than the Cincinnati Local. By the time we returned home from the Las Vegas convention, the local members from throughout the state had established relationships that transcended our competition. To date, no APWU local or state union has arranged similar transportation even though, of the twenty national conventions held, eighteen were in warm weather cities requiring most delegates to travel via air.

The Las Vegas venue promised to be exciting, as the city was evolving into a major gambling resort. The Cleveland delegation was housed in the Aladdin Hotel and Casino that, in 1976, was located at the end of the strip. The convention delegates were consumed with trying to win their fortune at the gaming tables and the slot machines, although most of them lost more than they could afford. I developed a system of playing the slot machines that reduced our risk. Forming a group of four Cleveland delegates, we pooled $100 apiece and changed it into quarters. This totaled 1,600 quarters, so at 2 quarters per pull, we would have 800 chances at hitting the jackpot. We selected by lottery the order we would play, and then each day one of the members of our group would deposit the entire amount into a quarter slot machine, stopping after eight hundred pulls (or however many pulls would exhaust the original amount) and passing on the winnings to be used by the next delegate on the following day. During those years, the slot machines returned about 80 percent of the monies deposited, with frequent winnings in small amounts. The theory was that each team member would expose the entire amount, but if he did not successfully hit the jackpot, the balance of small winnings would be handed over to the next player in line. The system was working as expected until the third day when Richard Butler broke the rules and deposited winnings in the machine to extend his playing time. He lost, and the stash was reduced dramatically. We ended the effort with losses of approximately 50 percent of the initial investment, but the original $400 investment was spread over five days between four of us.

The convention was turning into a disaster. Dave Johnson, the general executive vice president who had named the convention "The Now Convention," was losing control. The delegates were out of hand, and Chester Parrish, who was serving as secretary treasurer, assumed the chair. The disruptions continued, and President Filbey, who was not present at the convention due to ill health, was summoned from Washington and arrived in a wheelchair. Still, nothing of substance was resolved.

Death of a Giant—Francis S. Filbey (1917–1977)

On May 17, 1977, President Filbey succumbed to his deteriorating medical condition and passed. Filbey had a long history as a labor leader. He had served with distinction as the president of the Baltimore AFL-CIO and as president of the Baltimore Local UFPC, although during the period of his presidency the local did not accept colored employees as members. I never had the opportunity to develop a personal relationship with him, but my observation was that he was a man of character and dignity. The Wednesday night meetings in his office when he would open his private bar and entertain the resident officers were legendary. He liked big cigars and could never be found without one protruding from his mouth. Without Filbey, it would have been an additional generation or more before the merger and the creation of APWU.

He was a visionary and a man for his times. We lost a good unionist in Filbey. I attended the funeral and was not prepared for the cultural ritual practiced by his family. The family was in one room receiving mourners and Filbey's remains were in another. I expressed my condolences to the family and noted that we had lost a great leader.

The Selection

After President Filbey's passing, it became necessary to select his replacement. Dave Johnson was the general executive vice president, but there was no automatic succession, so a meeting of the executive board was called. Important matters in the local kept me from attending the proceedings to replace Filbey, so I requested that Richard Butler, Cleveland president of Special Delivery Craft, go to Washington in my stead. I wanted to have a firsthand account of the events and asked Richard to keep me updated by the hour. After not hearing from him for some time, I frantically contacted APWU headquarters to have someone instruct Richard to contact me immediately. My request worked, and within an hour, I had a report that there were four candidates for president: Pat Nilan, Ted Valliere, Emmett Andrews, and Chester Parrish. None received the required majority vote from the forty-nine-member executive board, so backroom bartering was underway. Several hours later, Richard called to inform me that Emmett Andrews had been selected as the second national president of APWU with the support of Moe Biller and his allies on the executive board.

Emmett began a turbulent presidency for which he was ill equipped. He had served as the director of industrial relations and in several other national union positions and was known as a fighter, but his personality and thought process were not conducive for leadership of a large, raucous union. His personal limitations and the events of the time conspired to make the following three years among the most difficult in the union's history.

Less than one year after Emmett assumed the presidency, the election of national officers was held. Moe transferred his support to a challenger from New York, John Napurano, a perennial candidate who was supported by the Cleveland Local. Emmett won, but his relationship with Moe never recovered. In just a matter of time, Moe offered his candidacy for president of the union.

CHAPTER 10

Top of the Mountain

1978 Negotiations

As we reached the 1978 national negotiations, the mood within the APWU was negative and expectations were running high. Veterans of the 1970 strike were banging the drums, demanding more or else. "No Contract, No Work" was the cry of the militants who could not prevail in adopting a convention resolution, and they threatened to carry their demands to the streets.

Negotiations were scheduled for joint bargaining with the Letter Carriers and the Mail Handlers. The Rural Carriers had elected to bargain separately. Throughout the process, reports from the bargaining table were not promising. Unlike the 1973 and 1975 negotiations where postal management was more flexible, in 1978, management was resisting significant change. It was reported that the 1975 negotiations were completed so early that President Filbey took a trip to Russia during the bargaining window, which usually lasted thirteen weeks, and returned just in time to affix his signature to the final agreement.

As the deadline to finalize the negotiations approached, reports from the 1978 sessions were negative. President

Emmett Andrews found himself in a subordinate position in the negotiations. He was dwarfed by the presence of Joe Vacca of the Letter Carriers, who had been a major player in the 1970s, and Jim LaPenta, who was a legend within the postal community after having worked both sides of postal reform, representing the Mail Handlers. These union negotiators towered above Emmett in experience and knowledge of how to work the system.

The final agreement left unchanged the provisions of Article 19, which permitted the employer to make changes midterm, included a total rewrite of the grievance arbitration process, and included "discussions" as the first step of disciplinary action but provided that they could not be grieved. What the agreement will be remembered for, however, was the cap to the cost-of-living adjustments (COLA) at $160 per measuring period. In general, the cap did not represent a pay reduction based on historic inflation adjustments, with the exception of one COLA, but if the existing uncapped formula was considered bad for management, it must have been good for the union. While none of the rank-and-file leaders had independent actuarial projections that would cause the $160 cap to lead to significantly reduced wages, we knew that inflationary uncertainty had been shifted from the employer to employees.

The local presidents were outraged. As the chairman of the Presidents' Conference at the time, I was thrust onto the stage by this explosive issue. I called a meeting of the Cleveland membership, and the crowd was so large I had to install speakers in the parking lot. The membership was engaged, and I would not again experience a union meeting so well attended. It is certain that the strike of 1970 and the noise emanating from opinion makers penetrated the consciousness of inactive members, and they attended in droves to hear my message.

After the local meeting, I traveled to New York to discuss strategy with Moe and to hold a hastily called Presidents' Conference. We met for approximately four hours in an attempt to draft a statement reflecting our position. Everyone assembled knew that the New York Local would have to back up any threat of action. Like the 1970 strike, New York and Wall Street were the keys. The financial industry depended on the billions of dollars that the postal service delivered daily. Stopping the mail would have serious economic consequences and was our leverage. In the meeting of the presidents, we wanted to draft a statement to present to the media reflecting our determination. Archie Salisbury, the president of the Dallas Local, wanted to be helpful. He attempted to record Moe's instructions, but each time that he went to the mike to offer a motion reflecting our intended action, Moe would take exception. Finally a motion was declared demanding that negotiations be renewed, and it was adopted. Moe and I then exited the meeting room to conduct a press conference.

As we entered the room of assembled reporters, I was overwhelmed by all the microphones thrust in my direction to record my every word. The press had been napping when the work stoppage had occurred in 1970, and they were intent on spreading the news in case the post office closed again. Despite the circus-like atmosphere, I read the prepared statement, and Moe and I alternated responding to questions. I was clearly in over my head, but we didn't make any major gaffes, and I escaped New York with renewed determination to defeat ratification of the tentative agreement.

Denver Convention

Within weeks of the signing of the 1978 tentative agreement, the APWU National Convention was held in Denver, Colorado. The delegates arrived in high spirits, and as a preview of things to come, a delegate exploded a firecracker in the lobby of the Hilton. On the opening day of the convention, the New York delegation and some others who shared their disdain for the negotiated agreement staged a protest around the perimeter of the convention floor. As President Emmett Andrews attempted to open the convention, he was met with a cacophony of boos, drowning out his effort to speak. Each time he approached the microphone, the booing would commence until he was seated. In exasperation, Emmett made an upward gesture to the assembly with the middle finger of his right hand, and a delegate recorded the image with a camera. This picture would be used extensively by those opposed to the contract in the weeks to follow.

The Denver Convention faced a number of issues, including the lingering demand of amnesty for the APWU members who had participated in a wildcat strike. Kenny Leiner, a union dissident in the New York Local, had been a thorn in Moe's side since a cadre of trained professionals (known as the Outlaws) integrated postal unions with the intent of radicalizing the postal labor movement. At the time of the 1970 strike, the Outlaws had created havoc at every New York Local meeting. Kenny and his supporters had staged a walkout at the New York Bulk Mail Center, and two hundred employees were summarily fired. The postal service was prepared to crush any repeat of the 1970 action, and the striking employees were used as an example.

President Emmett Andrews became entwined with the issue when he expelled Kenny Leiner from the national executive board after he lost the appeal of his discharge. Emmett concluded that since Kenny was no longer a postal employee, he was ineligible to hold union office. Moe championed Kenny's return to the executive board under the pro-union line that management cannot determine the officers of the union through their employment decisions and demanded that Kenny be reinstated. Amnesty was a major issue at the convention.

Later, while I was serving as executive vice president, Kenny Leiner introduced me to the idea of fasting and eating only broiled oranges, which released a chemical that burned fat and cleansed the system. I began a regimen of fasting for five days once a year. The objective was not to lose weight even though I was constantly five to ten pounds above my ideal weight. I wanted to test my willpower and stamina. I continued the novel diet for four or five years and proved to myself that I had sufficient willpower to succeed.

The prime issue at the convention was the rejection of the tentative agreement. After repeated interruptions of the convention proceedings, I offered a resolution: *The delegates go on record as totally rejecting the tentative agreement.*

I spoke in support of the resolution; after debate, it was referred to a roll-call vote, and I had to explain the application of Robert's Rules to a vote when the assembly rejects an action. In that situation, a yes vote was to support the resolution that condemned the contract. The Cleveland delegation voted 123:0 to reject the contract, and the total vote count was 8,507:1,639, which was a relief to those of us who had labored for its defeat. I then rose to offer a second motion that was drafted on the convention floor by me and Paul Harvey, a delegate from Houston, Texas:

If a majority of the membership voting for a national Contract rejects a tentative agreement, the APWU Negotiators shall inform the USPS, demanding to reopen negotiations. If the negotiations are not opened within five days after the vote is tallied, the General President shall be mandated to call a nationwide strike. Such negotiations shall terminate no longer than sixteen days after negotiations begin. If such negotiations do not result in a tentative agreement which improves substantially on the initial agreement, the General President shall be mandated to a nationwide strike within five days.

The motion passed overwhelmingly, and later in the convention, I asked the chairman if the resolve would be printed in the constitution since it had clearly achieved the required two-thirds majority in its adoption. This question was a bluff on my part in that many resolutions receive a two-thirds majority when voted on and are not placed in the constitution. To be presented as a constitutional amendment, the resolution must be advertised as such. He replied that it would be placed in the constitution, where it continued until a recent convention. I got away with the maneuver, and our resolve was recorded in the public domain. The convention debate on the resolution reflected the clear disapproval of the artificial cap on COLA and the determination of the delegates to defeat the tentative agreement.

At the conclusion of the second day of the convention, I dined with friends, and on my return to the hotel, I came face to face with President Andrews, who was walking with his assistant, Annie. Both of them had apparently had too much to drink and were walking unsteadily, and they were unaware of my presence. At a time when President Andrews should have been strategizing about ways to resolve the major issue of contract rejection, he had found the time to engage in excessive drinking with his girlfriend.

During the convention discussions, the delegates took President Andrews to task for not consulting the Rank-and-File Bargaining Committee in selecting the members of the committee to supervise the ballot counting. I rushed to the microphone to set the record straight because I was the chairman of the Rank-and-File Committee, and President Andrews had called me for input. I had declined because I did not want to be implicated in any way if the contract was ratified. The motion passed overwhelmingly because the question was called for before I could clarify the issue.

I had been elected as chairman of the forty-nine-member constitutional Rank-and-File Committee serving with Gerry Monzillo and John Richards. We had been called to vote on whether or not to recommend ratification of the tentative agreement. The vote on the committee had been seriously contested as President

Andrews removed the members from the meeting room one at a time to lobby them for their vote, but Gerry, myself, and others who opposed ratification held a majority together, and the final vote was for rejection by a vote of 29:15.

Despite the decision of the committee, President Andrews decided to submit the tentative agreement for membership ratification. John Richards, president of the Pittsburgh Local, later filed an emergency lawsuit in federal court that was denied in a widely distributed decision, and ratification proceeded. The national constitution was later changed to provide that a Rank-and-File Committee decision to reject a tentative agreement would block the ratification process.

An equally divisive issue occurred on the final day of the convention as the delegates voted to select the site for the following convention (1980). The competing cities were Honolulu, Detroit, and Los Angeles. Up to that point, all of the conventions had been held in warm weather cities, and locals in the East and Midwest rallied to support Detroit. The administration clearly favored Honolulu and convinced Los Angeles President, Glen Givens, to submit his local as a spoiler. The voice vote was inconclusive, so a standing vote was called for. That Detroit had prevailed was clear, but President Andrews solicited a roll-call vote.

Nothing is more destructive to convention proceedings than a roll call when there is a long delay while the tellers determine the voting strength of each local and a representative of each local goes to the microphone, one local at a time, to cast the local's vote. In the midst of the four-hour process, Givens, an Andrews supporter, announced that his local was withdrawing from consideration. When LA withdrew, President Andrews allowed members to recast their votes. Such action was clearly a violation of Robert's Rules as the roll call was limited to confirming the results of the standing vote and a motion to withdraw was out of order. President Andrews ignored my objection, and we proceeded with the roll call between Detroit and Honolulu. Despite the shenanigans, Detroit won, and we ended the convention on that note. However, we were informed by the Denver Hilton Hotel that we were not welcome to return to their facility.

Despite the focus on the tentative agreement, the delegates approved the automatic succession of the vice president in the event that the president became incapacitated in order to prevent the repeat of events such as those surrounding the death of President Filbey. However, the most memorable moment of the 1978 Denver National Convention was the dynamic speech delivered by Congressman Bill Clay of Missouri. He regaled the delegates, who listened with rapt attention, with a prophetic speech about the continuing assault on working people and received a standing ovation when he said with ringing clarity,

> Let me say this to you: Your time has arrived. One hundred fifty years ago, it was the time of the Indians. Seventy-five years ago, it was the time of the Irish. Thirty years ago, it was the time of the Communist and fellow travelers. Twenty years ago, it was the time of the Blacks. Ten years ago, it was the students. Today you postal and Federal employees are the new Niggers in this society, and don't you forget it.

The speech was met with thunderous applause. I am privileged to still have a copy of the speech, and it adorns a prominent spot in my library.

Vote No

As we returned to our locals, the so-called progressives were determined to defeat the agreement. We worked tirelessly to get out the vote, and when the dust had settled, we won. As chairman of the Presidents' Conference, I was present in Washington during the ballot counting, which was performed by an independent organization using mechanized equipment. The referendum had been placed on $3'' \times 5''$ cards that had a punch-out tab to record yes or no. The process of tabulation was not as laborious as the election of officers. Throughout the counting, the noes were the majority, but it was close.

The 1978 tentative agreement was rejected by the APWU membership. In short order, the Letter Carriers and Mail Handlers followed suit, and the tentative agreement was soundly rejected and ultimately referred to arbitration.

Binding Arbitration

Consistent with the convention resolution and failed ratification, President Andrews demanded that the postal service return to the bargaining table, but the postmaster general refused, insisting that the law required fact-finding, mediation, and binding arbitration. Eight hours before the deadline of the convention resolution, federal mediator Wayne Horvitz drafted a process to achieve an agreement. The procedure required fifteen days of bargaining, and if an agreement was not reached, binding arbitration would commence. The negotiations were uneventful as postal management refused to budge on the COLA issue, so the Federal Mediation and Conciliation Service (FMCS) selected Professor James Healy from Harvard Business School to serve as the arbitrator.

On September 15, 1978, Arbitrator Healy issued his award, which removed the cap on COLA, increased wages by 3 percent, and modified the no-layoff provisions. Employees on the rolls effective July 15, 1978, were protected for life, but all future employees were required to work six consecutive years before achieving no-layoff protection. Prior to that decision, no-layoff had been absolute for all employees for the duration of the agreements.

This decision was a huge victory for those of us who refused to accept an artificial cap on the cost-of-living adjustments, and every employee from September 15, 1978, to date has benefited significantly. I played a major role in that achievement and hold it among my highest accomplishments.

Following rejection of the tentative agreement and receipt of the Healy award, President Andrews elected to submit the binding award for a second ratification, and it passed. No one knows what he would have done if the membership had rejected the award.

The first few months following receipt of the arbitration award, including the new grievance procedure, we were immersed in training. Since the enactment of postal reorganization in 1971, grievances flooded Washington, and the backlog was insurmountable. It had been replaced by a process designed to resolve grievances closer to the location of the dispute. Arbitration panels were established and hundreds of arbitrators were employed to address the newly negotiated system.

Contract interpretation and enforcement were my forte, and I absorbed the changes through constant study and seminars to better apply our new rights to our employment decisions. I attended many training sessions, becoming knowledgeable about the new steps of appeal. At one training session, it was pointed out that we could grieve "the color of the supervisor's tie," which captured the mind-set of many activists.

Campaign for Office

A meeting of the Presidents' Conference was scheduled to discuss the new contractual provisions. We were basking in our success of defeating the tentative agreement and looking for other opportunities to make our mark. As expected, Moe announced his candidacy for president after having lost his wife, Annie, who was a New York native and never wanted to relocate. For the first time in its brief history, the Presidents' Conference voted to support candidates. Moe was supported unanimously for president as was John Richards for industrial relations director. A friend nominated me for director of research and education and I received the support of the conference, but immediately prior to the close of the nominations process and without my knowledge, Joe Anthony, vice president of the Pittsburgh Local and a friend, nominated me for the position of executive vice president. I was nominated for both positions and had to make a choice.

Following the meeting, I met with Moe, John Richards, and Joe Anthony, and they counseled me to be a candidate for vice president, informing me that they wanted a team of new top officers in the administration. When I hesitated, they did not understand why I would be satisfied with a non-executive position. Mike Zullo, vice president of the Brooklyn Local and friend of the conference, was also a candidate for director of research and education, so if I ran for that position, the support of the Presidents' Conference would be divided. Moe, John Richards, and I met with the resident of the Brooklyn Local, Russ Romano, along with Mike Zullo to discuss a combined ticket. The meeting did not result in a positive conclusion. I was left with a decision concerning the position I would select for my candidacy. Moe impressed upon me that he would prefer that I select the position of vice president, and I concurred. Thus the Biller–Burrus–Richards team was formed.

To plan the election campaign, Richards and I traveled to New York to meet with Moe and his advisors. We planned an aggressive national campaign consisting of the slogan "Leadership Team" and a national mailing to the home of every member. This strategy was a marked difference from the campaigns previously waged in the merged unions. Before the merger, all of the other merging unions had delegate voting and only the NPU had the one member, one vote constitutional provision; after the merger and a new constitution requiring the vote of each member, the traditional means of soliciting local and state presidents would not work. We intended to go directly to the members, and we planned to have a war chest to do it. We agreed that John Richards and I would each raise $10,000, and Moe would raise the balance. In 1979, $10,000 was a lot of money, amounting to approximately 40 percent of my annual salary after deductions. Moe committed to raising the balance (about $40,000) from contributions from associates and friends, including a public relations executive of Middle Eastern heritage, Robert Armao, who was well connected and had served as the public relations director for Nelson Rockefeller and the Shah of Iran.

Upon my return to Cleveland, I formed a committee of close personal friends to plan the efforts. My key supporters were Anne Thomas, the Callahan brothers, Bill Harris, and Loretta Huckabee. We did every imaginable fundraiser, even some that were probably illegal. Loretta was particularly helpful, planning an affair with food and music held at the union hall. Ethelda seasoned the meats, I grilled them, and Loretta collected the fees, served drinks, and was the general host of an event that attracted hundreds of members and their families.

Tim Callahan and Bill Harris developed an idea to manufacture buttons with the pictures of Biller, Burrus, and Richards on them. They purchased a button-making machine and produced thousands of buttons to be sold at the national convention in Detroit. Hours before our departure from Cleveland for the Detroit Convention, they showed me a sample button that included our pictures and the slogan "We Need a New Deck." The idea was that the members did not need the cards (officers) to be reshuffled; they needed a brand-new team of leaders. To my great consternation, the button showed Richards and me in full view with Moe wedged into the corner. Moe was the leader of the ticket, and I was aghast that the button would show him in a less than dominant position. Upon my arrival in Detroit, I immediately showed Moe the buttons. To my great relief, he consented to their distribution, indicating that the pictures were acceptable.

The Biller–Burrus–Richards team campaign material adorned the convention hall and included a large banner hung from the wall. We campaigned vigorously throughout the convention, maximizing the positives of each candidate. I had my strengths on full display; Moe was almost a folk hero from his stature gained from the 1970 strike; and there was no better candidate than John Richards to point out the weaknesses of the opponents. John had been a candidate for director of industrial relations in the prior national election and was a seasoned veteran. He had an innate ability to hone in on the issues. We knew most of the local presidents from our service as chairmen of the Presidents' Conference, so we were in our comfort zone at the 1980 Detroit National Convention.

Besides the election campaigning, other important resolutions decided by the convention were the reduction of the executive board and the lengthening of the term of office from two to three years. The national field officers waged panic-stricken opposition to the reduction of the executive board. The coalition of progressives had not previously focused on this issue, so we had not prepared a convention strategy, but we were able to rally the troops and prevailed in reducing the board from forty-eight to fourteen. The lengthening of the term of office from two years to three also received the necessary two-thirds support without serious opposition.

The 1980 National Convention will be remembered for many achievements but the most enduring will be the inclusion of POWER (Post Office Women for Equal Rights) in the APWU constitution. The debate over this issue elevated Josie McMillan to the ranks of leadership within the union; from the Detroit Convention forward, there was never a more dynamic and influential spokesperson in APWU.

The female activists had met in St. Louis in 1979 to develop a strategy to form an organization representing their interests. At that time, there was only one female national officer, Nelda Chock of Hawaii. There were no resident female officers. Just as the African Americans had fought for inclusion in the 1970s, the

'80s was the decade for women.

Josie went on to become the president of the New York Local and electrify assemblies with her knowledge, determination, and leadership. Joyce Robinson stepped forward to become the first female resident national officer and a dear friend and supporter. Sharon Stone, Barbara Protho, Sonya Leggett, Princella Vogel, and a host of other trailblazers rose from the action taken at the 1980 National Convention and proceeded to make major contributions.

Moe and I held a meeting with Josie and others the evening prior to the vote, which was not assured because there was plenty of opposition to POWER constitutional recognition. We debated the language of the resolution, and despite my plea for moderation, the women demanded more. I favored a general reference in the constitution, believing that the delegates would not approve POWER as an integral part of the union. Josie demanded full recognition or bust.

During the debate on POWER, I marveled at the floor organization of the female delegates. They had commandeered every microphone, and at the conclusion of their speaking in favor of the resolution, they called for the question. The chair could not accept the call for the question, but the vote was called anyway, and the female delegates speaking in favor far outnumbered those opposed. The required two-thirds majority was achieved. From that date forward, female APWU members competed on a level playing field when vying for leadership positions, and the results have been a more representative leadership, all thanks to those bold women at the 1980 National Convention.

The Biller team left the convention buoyed by the reception we had received. Dave Johnson, who was the incumbent executive vice president, was running for president, so there was no incumbent for the position that I was seeking. In the election that followed, the candidates for our respective offices were

President	Vice President	Industrial Relations
Emmett Andrews	John Wright	Forest "Frosty" Newman
David "Dave" Johnson	Don Silvestri	John P. Richards
Moe Biller	William "Bill" Burrus	Richard N. Masiello
Ted Valliere	Don Johnson	
	Jim Bryan	

Everyone assumes that the top ballot placement has an advantage, but neither Biller, Richards, nor I drew such placement. Biller drew third place on the ballot, I drew third, and Richards drew second. More than 107,000 ballots were returned and counted, the highest in the history of the union elections.

In my race, Don Silvestri and Don Johnson considered themselves the front runners. Each had calculated that I would win the large locals but that the margins would be close enough that their expected popularity in the small locals would carry them to victory.

Ted Valliere believed similarly that his strength in small locals would offset the New York vote for president. Emmett and Frosty had the advantage of incumbency, and each believed that he would win.

The Election for National Office

The process was slow and agonizing. Liz Powell, a friend and officer, was present at the ballot counting and telephoned results to the New York office. We remained in our respective cities throughout the ballot counting, so the New York office communicated the latest results to me by phone. It was harrowing to await the next phone call, so I engaged in waxing my car to pass the time. The first reports were that all three of us were leading, but the sample was too small to draw any conclusions. On the third day of the count, the margins had increased sufficiently, and we allowed optimism to invade our thoughts. By the fifth day, it was clear that we would be winners, and we could breathe a sigh of relief. I could stop waxing the car and think about the moment and what changes were in store. The final count had Biller winning by a margin of 19,000 votes, Burrus by 15,000, and Richards by 9,000. In votes cast, Richards led the trio with 48,000, Biller had 45,000, and I had 39,900. We had won, and my car had three new coats of wax. Biller, Richards, and I had been members of NPU prior to the merger, and now we were filling three of the top four positions in APWU. The fourth position, that of secretary treasurer, was occupied by Chester Parrish, formerly of the Motor Vehicle Craft, so the dominant union at the time of the merger, UFPC, did not have an officer in the administrative positions. Moe's election marked the first occasion that a sitting president had been defeated.

In our victory, between the three of us we had replaced six incumbent resident officers in Washington, DC. Ben Evans, an ally, had defeated the incumbent, John Dubay, as director of the health plan, so in total, seven resident officers had been defeated. Our victory was truly revolutionary, and we were prepared to take the union in new directions. Our thoughts turned to having an extravagant occasion for a new beginning, and we began to plan the first formal installation of APWU officers.

Saying Good-Bye

Twenty-two years had passed since I first walked through the doors to begin a postal career. As I was leaving Cleveland to assume the position of executive vice president at national headquarters, I had mixed emotions. I was leaving the employees who gave me my start. I had formed many friendships and associations among the tens of thousands of employees who had come and gone.

These were people who knew me personally and had shared many experiences, good and bad. During my final months, the majestic five-story building where I had spent my entire career was being replaced with a sprawling one-story structure that had none of the character of the one where opportunities had been nurtured.

Over the final months of my presidency, I was engaged in reviewing the allocation of space in the new building, including the locker rooms, the cafeteria, and the stewards' room. The new building was not very attractive, and there was no natural light from outside. The inside of the building had sodium-vapor lighting that affected my equilibrium, so I limited my visits. One positive was that the new building had employee parking. Parking had become a major issue within the union as employees' wages had increased and more employees could afford to purchase private transportation. I left before the final move was completed, but I am sure that the veterans had a small case of nostalgia. The old building had been the place of employment for hundreds of thousands of postal workers, and it contained many, many memories—good and bad. Since my departure, I have stayed in the hotel that is a part of the terminal complex adjacent to the Post Office building and have looked out the window, remembering.

I recall those years in Cleveland with fondness. The employees of the Cleveland office gave me a chance to prove my abilities, and I shall be forever grateful. I formed special relationships with many, including Art Rucker, who tested my intellect; Beverly Shealy, who was a strong supporter and friend; Joyce Williams; Velma Chism; Howard Dizard; Al Parker and Joe Reid; David Pringle "Neighbor" and Bill Childress, who tested me at every union meeting; Robert Webster, a strong union man whom Ethelda and I still stay in touch with via Christmas cards; Chuck Davis, a true friend with whom I shared many secrets; Charles and Mr. Nance; Doc Edwards; Joyce Williams; Robert

Butler; Richard Walker, who looked good in his clothes; Matt Smith, who beat me badly at Ping-Pong on my own table and was a friend; John Lynn; Ted Cook; Paul Tirabassi; Willie Griffin; Wesley Green; Jackie Bettis; Jim Lightner; Bill Kaminski; Connie Pierson; Johnnie Ganther (Arrington); special friends Richard Butler, Frank Bates, Anne Thomas, Tim and Robert Callahan, Bill Harris, Steve Kinkaid, Jim Wathen, Charles Walton, John Cahill, Bill Kaminski, Vi Ward, Roland Carter, Dial Hewlett (whose son is now a friend), and Theresa Derosa (who counted the money); and many others who supported me and made everything to follow possible.

Prior to the installation of officers, each member of the Biller–Burrus–Richards team agreed to host the other two at our respective final local meetings. Biller and Richards traveled to Cleveland, Richards and I traveled to New York, and Moe and I went to Pittsburgh. Biller and I had celebratory final meetings. There were gifts and acknowledgments of our contributions. Richards's final meeting was more subdued. At the time, I chalked the low-key atmosphere up to culture differences. It was months later, well into our first term, that Moe and I learned that Richards's meeting was not John's last as president of the Pittsburgh Local. He and the local membership had determined that he would continue as local president while serving as director of industrial relations in Washington, DC. This decision later became an issue of discussion leading to a convention resolution that failed to achieve the two-thirds majority.

I Had Climbed the Mountain

On a personal level, my election to general executive vice president was the answer to my wildest dreams. From the place of my birth in West Virginia and a troubled early childhood, I had climbed the mountain to become the second highest ranking officer in the largest postal union in the world. My election also represented the first time in history that an African American was elected by the membership to such a lofty union position. Labor unions have been in the forefront of racial progress, but they had vigorously opposed people of color in top positions within their ranks. In fact, it was not until the late 1960s that all unions in the AFL were required to accept African Americans as members. The Building Trade Craft Unions were particularly resistant. My brother-in-law was qualified as a licensed electrician, but in the 1970s the Cleveland Electricians Local would not accept him as a member; thus he was denied employment on union jobs. The record shows that even the unions that are overwhelmingly populated with people of color are constitutionally structured to restrict leadership positions to white males. Several people of color have been elected to high positions in unions, but their elections have not been by direct vote of the membership. The election of black officers in other unions had been achieved through delegate voting that involves the delegates voting on behalf of members. This process obviously is not a true reflection of the intent of every member. Our union includes members in every community throughout the country, and each member is empowered to vote. Whatever racial divisions exist nationwide, they exist in our union, so for me to achieve a majority for the second highest office was amazing. In this election, 107,000 postal union members had cast their votes, and I had won. It was time for a celebration, and we began to plan the event.

Everyone who achieves success in life can point to the support received from family, friends, and associates, and my ascension to the presidency could not have been accomplished without the confidence that many had in my ability to perform. The employees and fellow officers of the Cleveland office gave me a start and supported me over my career. I also received the unqualified endorsement of many throughout the country who invested in me the mantle of leadership. Mike Gunther, president of Carbondale, Illinois, and state president, was a supporter and friend, and I shall forever be grateful for his confidence in my abilities.

Urgent Meeting on FLSA

Officially Moe and I were eligible to assume office one month before the constitutional changeover because the Labor Department had ruled on complaints from the prior election and decided the case with a remedy that the president and vice president would assume office in October 1980. We did not want a separate installation, so we deferred the official swearing in until we were joined by the other officers.

Prior to the swearing-in ceremony and relocation to Washington, I decided to spend some time at a rustic resort with friends to unwind from the campaign. The log cabins didn't have televisions, but they did have phones. On the second day, I received a call from Moe, requesting my attendance at a meeting in Washington on the following day. I packed my belongings and drove hurriedly back to Cleveland—some fifty miles or so—to pack and secure a plane reservation for the trip. When I arrived at the hotel, Moe informed me that the Labor Department had requested a meeting with officers of the APWU to discuss the application of the Fair Labor Standard Act (FLSA) to the postal service. The defeated President Emmett Andrews, upon learning of his loss, had left Washington to return to his native state of California, and the Labor Department wanted to meet with officers who could decide.

In 1938, Congress passed the Fair Labor Standard Act, which in 1974 was amended to apply to the postal service. An ingenious young attorney, Gerald Feder, who had been staff counsel for the congressional committee that passed the amendment, brought a lawsuit on behalf of a postal employee alleging that the required scheme study was compensable under the law, and therefore back pay was due for time spent studying. The postal service had modified their regulations in response to the amendment to cover future liability when the postal service could make the transition to automated processing, making scheme study unnecessary, but it didn't cover past liabilities. The court decision was in favor of the postal employee, and the question was the application of the decision to hundreds of thousands of clerical employees and how much compensation they should receive. The Feder lawsuit opened the floodgates, and the postal service and the Labor Department wanted to contain the damage and forestall thousands of expected future lawsuits. At the time, probably three hundred thousand postal employees were subject to scheme training and each scheme required hundreds of hours of study, so the possible liability was enormous. Since Moe was the president-elect, he was asked to be in attendance. My participation was requested by Moe because of my extensive understanding of the scheme study rules.

Moe had never been a detail-oriented union official who studied the contract and the related rules, so he relied on my knowledge of the recently promulgated X118B Handbook for guidance in the discussions. My free time in the penthouse had afforded me the opportunity to study postal rules and familiarize myself with this particular issue. In total, there were probably twelve to fifteen of us in the small meeting room, including Vince Sombrotto, Jim LaPenta, Moe, myself, the Labor Department representatives, postal service officials, and various attorneys.

The subject of the meeting was the amount of back pay owed postal employees for FLSA violations and what would be the provisions governing "suffer and permit" going forward. The discussions were often heated, but the postal service offered $500 million as settlement. This sum was beyond my wildest imagination, but I rejected it. As a condition of the settlement, the postal service was demanding two additional years of grace before they began paying for scheme study. So for this kingly sum in real dollars, the postal service was offering relief from liability for the years that they had violated the law plus two additional years. I rejected the offer summarily as being insufficient to compensate for past and future liability. I was aware that the postal service had to cut off the spigot, so we promised to meet after the officers' installation to continue discussions. I returned to Cleveland to wrap up my service as president and to familiarize my successor, Vice President Frank Bates, with pending issues.

We did not consider the possibility of Ronald Reagan defeating Jimmy Carter and selecting a new secretary of labor who might apply different standards to the law, but that was what happened. In short order, President Regan made his selection, and, without notice to the union, the new secretary of labor resolved the USPS violations of FLSA. The settlement sanctioned a minimum retroactive formula for past violations and a partial waiver into the future. The labor official who was a part of our meeting, Karen Claus, did not call the union to alert us that further discussions were underway, and we learned of the settlement via news releases from the Labor Department.

When the final settlement was reached, I expected a political backlash within APWU, but it never materialized. Clearly I had rejected a settlement in an amount that was mind-boggling. Even though it had been the right call, in politics the right thing can be used against you, and that number would resonate. The Mail Handlers Union wrote an editorial in their magazine, but the story did not have legs, and it quickly became a part of history. I had swung for the fence and missed, but I learned a lesson that would follow me throughout the balance of my career.

PART THREE:

Making a Difference

CHAPTER 11

Settling In

Assuming Office

The installation of officers was magnificent. The New York Local did most of the planning, and they did a masterful job. Sonja Leggett, a local officer, displayed her talents in full. The event was held at the L'Enfant Hotel on Capitol Hill, and locals from around the country sent buses of members and their families to be a part of history. APWU had never held a formal installation for national officers, and we were preparing for a brand-new beginning. The dress code was formal, and postal employees were determined to show off their finest.

The Cleveland Local sent three buses of supporters, and when they arrived in Washington, they felt like celebrities honoring their hometown hero. New York must have sent ten buses, and a large contingency arrived from Pittsburgh. The evening was a huge celebration of our victory. When I arrived in Washington, I needed directions to New Jersey Avenue on Capitol Hill, where the installation would be held. New Jersey Avenue is located in different sections of the city, and it is not continuous, so each person from whom I asked directions would point me to a different section. It took me almost as long to find the hotel as it took to drive from Cleveland, but I finally arrived and prepared to begin a new phase in my life.

After the extended workdays and failure to communicate at home, my marriage to Janice experienced difficulties, and my relocation to Washington served as a mutual agreement of separation. A childhood friend and football teammate, Tom Wallace, had relocated to Washington much earlier, and each time that I visited the city, he and his wife, Shirley, graciously opened their home to me. Upon winning the election, I contacted him about available living quarters in the community, and he told me about an apartment complex in College Park, Maryland. When I packed my bags and relocated, I was scheduled to meet Tom so he could take me to the apartment. Being unfamiliar with the area, I became lost in a circle where we were parked on opposite sides waiting for the other to arrive. We finally connected, and he escorted me to the rental office where I secured a decent place to call home in my new assignment.

The unfurnished apartment required my immediate attention. Ethelda traveled to Washington, and we engaged in a buying spree, shopping for furniture, sheets, blankets, dishes, and all the things one needs to furnish living quarters. The first night that we spent in the new apartment we slept in our clothes on a mattress with no sheets or blankets. At the time, the APWU national office did not provide any assistance for newly elected officers arriving from distant places. As soon as I settled, I was determined to initiate policy so that those who followed would not face the same sense of being lost. Officers who relocated had to find a place to live, map out the travel to and from the office, secure new doctors and a dentist, new schools for children, and so on. Starting over in a strange city was terribly confusing for a forty-four-year-old man. After completing the furnishing, Ethelda returned to Cleveland to continue her employment as secretary at the union office.

The following day, Moe and I went to the APWU union office on Fourteenth Street. Having previously visited on a number of occasions, we found it to be the one familiar place in the city. It was located in the heart of the red-light district, surrounded by girlie shows, fast-food restaurants, and bars. Our reputations had preceded us, and the employees were apprehensive. With a shift in three of the top officer positions, we had dramatically changed the dynamics of the headquarters office, and the employees were uncertain as to how we would administer the union's affairs, thinking, *What evil changes will be imposed by these self-proclaimed militants?* The defeated officers had long since departed, so there was no orderly transition showing us "where the jewels were buried." John Morgan and Kenny Wilson, the incumbent director and assistant director, respectively, in the Clerk Craft, welcomed us with open arms. John retired several years after our arrival, but for many years Kenny was a valuable source of information on work-related subjects about the history of contractual provisions. He was also the chief turtle in a loosely defined organization of postal employees.

Michelle Cochran was the secretary to the office of vice president, and upon introduction, I inquired about the numerous half-filled boxes in her area. She informed me that she had been told that I was bringing my secretary from Cleveland to take her place. I assured her that I had no such intentions, and she could continue in her position if she chose to do so. The office in general was stuck in the nineteenth century: no computers, an antiquated telephone system, old furniture, small work spaces, disorganized filing systems, and generally horrible working conditions. That our challenge would not merely be with the postal service but with developing an operation that would enhance our efforts was clear.

The vice president's office was not decorated to my taste, so I brought in an interior decorator, Atrie, and she assisted Michelle and me in changing the furniture and the wall coverings. Pat

Nilan, legislative director, was using President Filbey's old desk. He agreed to let me use it, and after being refurbished, it was a masterful piece of furniture that dominated my office. The president's office was stuck in a corner, and Moe refused to occupy it. He wanted to be accessible to the members. After he convinced Motor Vehicle President Leon Hawkins to switch offices, work began immediately on refurbishing the new president's office.

While workers were renovating Moe's office, he needed a place to work. Since my office was nearly finished, we agreed that he and I would share the same desk until he could move into his office. He worked on one side and I worked on the other. The renovation of the president's office took approximately three months, and during that period, we administered the union's affairs under those weird arrangements.

Moe

I met Moe through our association as local presidents, and we formed a bond as agents for change. When we were both at the same meetings, we communicated on issues of mutual concern, finding that we shared many of the same values and objectives. He could be described as a liberal and continually supported the advancement of minorities.

We assumed office with the confidence that we could lead postal employees to new heights. Moe was unquestionably the highest profile leader within the union, having served as president of the New York Local through the 1970 strike. With twenty-seven thousand members, the New York Local was by far the largest in the union. The second largest local, Philadelphia, had seven thousand members. Upon assuming the presidency in 1980, he had celebrated his sixty-fifth birthday only days before, having declined the earlier opportunity to be a candidate for national office because of his ties to New York and his family. After the death of his wife Annie and the maturity of his sons, Stephen and Michael, he was prepared to offer his service on the national stage.

It is difficult to describe a complex human being with any degree of accuracy. Although Moe's later marriage to Collee Farris did not end well, she filled a void in his life and provided stability and helped shape him. Deep down, Moe was a kind man who was considerate of others. He was gregarious, smart, aggressive, and dedicated to improving the lives of postal employees. Any deficiencies in his record were not the result of lack of concern or effort.

Moe willingly shared authority, and over the years, we worked as a team through periods of agreement and disagreement. Our collective goal was to improve conditions for postal employees. Moe did have a mean streak that surfaced in his interaction with some associates, but he was not a mean man. He truly walked with kings while keeping the common touch. It was a privilege to serve the membership under the presidency of Moe Biller.

Safety

Our initial confrontation with postal management occurred due to the tragic death of Michael McDermott, a New York BMC Mail Handler who was sucked into a conveyor belt. No one else was present to provide assistance. The safety hazards of the conveyor belts were well known, and Michael McDermott's death was avoidable. We could not bring him back, but I was determined that such a tragedy would not be repeated. I attended countless meetings and wrote about it extensively, and his death reminded me of the huge responsibilities we had assumed.

Having had little training in safety, I turned to Jerry Fabian, a national business agent from Minneapolis, for assistance. Jerry was extremely knowledgeable in many fields of representation, and over the next fifteen years, we worked together to address many important safety issues. We achieved unprecedented success in moderating postal policy in a number of areas. When Jerry and I were addressing safety issues, the Postal Service was embarking on a major program of converting the processing system from a mechanized to an automated system—and with each new piece of equipment came many hazards. The letter sorting machines (LSMs) in particular posed serious safety hazards. The LSMs were configured with twelve consoles per machine to sort letters. Operators sat before keyboards and had to repeatedly press a combination of keys to sort letters as they were positioned mechanically before them. The assignment required significant skill and dexterity but also involved repetitious movement. When contracting to purchase the letter sorting machines from a German manufacturer, the postal service was made aware of safety issues, but because the LSM was intended as a temporary bridge between manual and automated sortation, postal management chose to ignore the hazards. In the process, thousands of postal employees suffered permanent injuries.

Carpal tunnel syndrome and tendonitis were the most debilitating injuries and the most common among the thousands of employees suffering from the effects of the LSMs. Many were affected for life. I took it personally that postal officials did not share my concern. The official postal strategy was to contest each claim for workers' compensation, forcing employees to fight for financial compensation. Even Congress got into the act, proposing to amend the regulation that injured employees would have to use their leave if they wanted compensation. I authored a pocket manual that described the symptoms, exercises, and other steps to be taken by machine operators to avoid injury. Together Jerry and I were responsible for reducing the risk by modifying the length of time for each key assignment, reducing the number of key strokes the employees had to execute, providing better chairs, and implementing other interventions that helped, but we were never successful in making operating LSMs completely safe work assignments. Perhaps our most significant achievement was the total modification of the keying and feeding operation of the BMC parcel keying stations. In an unprecedented agreement, postal management permitted the union to redesign the equipment to reduce exposure to injury. I only wish that we had been granted similar authority on other important safety matters.

One of the ways Jerry and I succeeded in making employee safety a truly joint process was by convincing management's safety representatives to convene a safety meeting in Detroit at the UAW/GM joint Safety Training Center. The automobile companies and their unions are extremely devoted to safety in their day-to-day operations, and they constructed a facility dedicated to employee safety. The center is over fifty thousand square feet and was devoted exclusively to safety, funded through an employer contribution for each employee work hour. We were successful in initiating numerous safety initiatives, but we had a long way to go to get where we wanted to be.

Representation

Early in the new administration, Postmaster General (PMG) Bill Bolger banned radio headsets and tennis shoes. These changes were a rebuff to the younger generation and a reaction to the Vietnam protests that divided the generations. Bolger had visited a processing plant and observed employees dressed in a manner that he was not familiar with. He was a career postal employee, and despite the working conditions in mail processing, the senior workers of previous generations were accustomed to a formal dress code of dress shirts and ties. Having spent his professional career in a bureaucracy, Bolger was unprepared to witness mail processing by casually dressed young workers.

I immediately demanded an audience with the PMG and impressed upon him that such attire was the norm for the new generation and they should not have to conform to the lifestyle with which he was familiar. The new generation was comfortable in jeans, T-shirts, and tennis shoes, and their source of diversion from the boring activities involved in postal work came through radio headsets providing the latest music fad that he did not understand. The stated excuse for banning sneakers and headsets was safety concerns. He alleged that employees would not be sufficiently aware of their surroundings and they would not have protection against rolling equipment. Bull!

After meeting with labor officials, we were able to agree to standards on footwear (allowing tennis shoes), the use of headsets in certain situations, and T-shirts that did not contain offensive language. As expected, some of the young people pushed the envelope, and one young woman in particular came dressed in a T-shirt that was two sizes too small to cover her ample bosom. The previous generation had begrudgingly surrendered. I was off and running, having been baptized into my advocacy on behalf of postal employees at the national level.

Later I had the opportunity to engage Bill Bolger when he championed ECOM, the novel concept of the postal service partnering with electronic communications. The basic idea was that a message would be transmitted electronically between twenty-five postal facilities, and at the destination post office it would be converted to hard copy and delivered by the letter carrier. When the operation was abruptly phased out in four years, I was able to retain the pay grade for the employees. Twenty years later, several of them expressed their appreciation to me for preserving the higher grade even though they were assigned to level 5 activities. In the 2006 negotiations, I was successful in gaining an upgrade for all APWU-represented employees, including the ECOM operators. These employees were converted to level 8 even though the assignments had been abolished twenty years before.

While Moe, Richards, and I were dedicated to specific duties, we did whatever necessary to defend the rights of the employees. While I was responsible for the APWU field operation and overseeing the regional coordinators, craft residents, and safety, I never considered my responsibilities to be limited by any artificial designation. If postal employees were denied a right or if an injustice had been imposed, I considered it my responsibility to address the issue even if it was outside my assigned duties. I have been accused of being a "loner," and perhaps that's true, but I have repeatedly been disappointed by those who fail to undertake a task just because it wasn't assigned to them or they were not included in the efforts of others.

John Richards settled into his new role as the director of industrial relations with gusto. He had an entire functional operation charged with the soul of a labor union: grievance activity. The relationship between Moe and John later deteriorated, but my respect for John was unaffected. He was smart and aggressive and was a veteran when it came to contractual battles with postal management. He also brought his gorgeous sailboat to ply the waters of the Chesapeake Bay for relaxation. We were prepared to initiate a new era of labor relations.

Our interaction with postal management was challenging because the top labor official, Jim Gildea, was old school. As the vice president of postal labor relations, Jim was the union's contact, so we interacted with him regularly. He had previously been a lieutenant of George Meany, president of the AFL, and had switched employers following postal reform. He had played a central role in postal reform from the labor side and had transferred to postal management to staff the newly created USPS Labor Relations Department.

Any large unionized employer requires a labor official who is strong enough to repel the excesses of operations that want to push the envelope in the name of production. Labor contracts place limits on the rights of the employer, and the role of the postal labor chief is to draw the line. The union needs someone with a straight enough spine to interpret the contract irrespective of its application. When disputes arise, time is the ally of the employer because deferrals to arbitration give them breathing space to continue excesses. While retroactive compensation serves as a partial deterrent to management, the money comes from another budget, so operations is off the hook. It is difficult to find a labor official who can stand up to the heavy hand of operations. Jim Gildea was a backslapper, and he was not sufficiently principled to call the shots and deal with the fallout. Tom Fritz, Sheri Cagnoli, Bill Downes, Tony Veglianti, Jim Hillquist, and Doug Tulino were chief postal management contacts during my career who were willing to make the hard calls, and as a result, we were able to resolve many issues of disagreement.

Settling In

As we entered office, the tasks before us were daunting. The issues demanding immediate attention were modernizing the office so that we could perform our tasks efficiently, instilling a sense of unity among the officers, enforcing the contract, hiring a whole new cadre of professionals, planning for the future, and balancing the books.

Moe brought new staff to Washington, which included an executive assistant to organize his staff, a new public relations expert, a new law firm, and a new printing company. Danny Frank was the public relations manager in New York. He was effective but had a few screws loose. It was Danny Frank who rented a monkey to illustrate the APWU's position. He chartered a plane to fly a streamer saying that postal management was unfair, and he hung a sheet out of the hotel window with an anti-management message. If we wanted the unconventional, we went to Danny Frank. He was unable to relocate, so Moe secured the services of Danny Driscoll, a staff member of defeated Congressman Jerry Ambro of New York, to serve as the director of communications.

The previous law firm was discharged, and Darryl Anderson was hired to represent APWU. He very quickly expanded his firm to include Art Luby, Susan Catler, and Anton Hajjar. Marnette Rice, a bargaining unit employee, was elevated to staff and put in charge of Moe's flow of paperwork. Dottie Campbell was brought from Moe's New York office and soon became the "mother hen" of the president's office. Changes were underway—and quickly.

Joe Anthony, a trusted confidant of John Richards, came to Washington briefly, but I assume that he and Richards decided it would best if Joe served in the home local, so he returned and John secured other staff.

Annie had been President Andrews's right hand and was the daughter of Roy Halbeck, the previous president of the Clerk Union. She expressed that she wanted to continue employment with the new administration, but she had developed a personal relationship with Emmett, and Moe determined that it would be difficult to continue her employment under his presidency. He did consent to permit her the task of converting the convention tapes to a written record, but after four months of delay, she was informed that her services were no longer needed.

As a New York native, Moe was particularly fond of tabloids, so shortly after assuming office, he changed the monthly APWU magazine to a tabloid. We also began a review of the APWU emblem, a shield with a mail bag, which had been adopted from the UFPC. We did not anticipate the significant level of opposition that this simple change would generate, but nevertheless, after the dust settled, APWU had a new emblem that was more in keeping with a progressive union. After repeated public disagreement with activists who resisted change, we negotiated a final solution, and it was agreed to insert the U for "union," so instead of "APW" as Moe and I preferred, the emblem became APWU.

Steps had to be taken to generate income greater than expenses. Moe elected to impose an assessment of $2.05 per member, per month, which was approved by the executive board, but within six months after our inauguration, Secretary Treasurer Chester Parrish announced his retirement, and Moe selected Doug Holbrook as his replacement. With Doug's appointment, the top four positions in the APWU were filled by NPU local presidents from New York, Cleveland, Detroit, and Pittsburgh— all locals that were committed to one postal union and the democratic principle of one member, one vote. The selection of

Doug Holbrook for secretary treasurer paid many dividends over the years to come. He and his wife, Jackie, became dear personal friends, and his service as secretary treasurer was irreplaceable. Doug's son, Kevin, later wired the sound system in our new house. He is a carbon copy of his parents, a wonderful young man. Doug was always professional. He had a calm personality and often served as a voice of reason in the administration and as the bridge between Moe and me. From the Detroit Local, Doug brought with him Phil Tabbita, Judy Beard, and Katherine Speck, each of whom have made major contributions to APWU.

Having completed the administration changes, we were well on our way to a functioning union. One unexpected occurrence was the decision by Merkle Press to close its printing operations. We were left with the choice of selecting Delancy Printing or Kelly Press. Choosing a printer was a major decision as the union's entire mailing list for the monthly magazine, and hundreds of small weekly jobs, were maintained by Merkle. After interviewing the competing companies, we elected to go with Kelly Press, primarily based on our relationship with the account representative, Rudy Yateman. Mike Kelly, the owner, met our every expectation and is a first-class guy.

In February, Ethelda returned to Washington to make it our permanent home. Of all the decisions I have made over my lengthy career, it was the wisest and most fulfilling. During the initial months, she was unemployed and missed her family in Cleveland terribly, returning for several weeks when I traveled to Peru. With her employment at the University of Maryland in late 1981, she acclimated to the area and adopted it as her home.

CHAPTER 12

Negotiations

Moe and Vinnie

Upon our arrival in Washington, the presidents of the two largest postal unions were under the leadership of old allies from New York who had played pivotal roles in the 1970 strike. Vince Sombrotto had been successful in becoming president of the National Association of Letter Carriers (NALC) New York Local in 1971, where he served with distinction until elected as national president in 1978. Vince had an apartment on Capitol Hill. A committed family man, he continued to maintain his home in New York and traveled there nearly every weekend. When Moe arrived in Washington, he secured an apartment in the same building where Sombrotto lived. The apartment was on my way to the APWU headquarters, so I picked Moe up in the mornings and Vinnie often joined us since the NALC headquarters was en route.

To assist Moe in the retention of his driving skills, I sometimes permitted Moe to drive the distance from his apartment to the office, but one day when he was close to having an accident, I observed that instead of turning the wheel or applying the brakes, he closed his eyes and inhaled strongly as though bracing for a collision. The other driver avoided the accident, but from that day forward, I did all the driving. Later, when Doug Holbrook purchased a home in Virginia where Moe had relocated after he married Collee, Doug assumed the driving duties to and from the office.

On one occasion, when Vince and I were waiting for Moe outside the apartment, we engaged in discussions about contract administration. Vince mentioned that I needed his approval as a part of the Joint Bargaining Committee (JBC) before I could proceed with grievances regarding interpretive issues. I told him that he was crazy and proceeded to address interpretive issues on my own. During the early years, I communicated with NALC through Vice President Larry Hutchins. We jointly addressed several subjects, most notably the excessive use of casuals and compliance with the 90 percent full-time employee ratio. We processed joint grievances and ultimately prevailed in securing employee compensation in the amount of $8.5 million for past violations and conformance with the limitations of part-time employees.

Of the dozens of major arbitrated decisions that we won over the years, I do not know of any that had more residual impact than the series of decisions won on the use of casuals. Following the national award, scores of locals, including the huge decision by the Pittsburgh Local under President Chuck Pugar, won tremendous back pay resolutions (over $60 million) for thousands of their members. The union's refusal to accept excessive casuals began with cooperative efforts between NALC and APWU through Larry and me.

The relationship between Moe and Vinnie cooled over time, caused in part by different approaches to representation. Each had a strong personality and believed that his decision on union matters was the right way. At one convention in Las Vegas, NALC and APWU held their conventions in adjoining ballrooms, separated only by a wall, but neither president was invited to appear at the other's convention.

Sellout

The 1980s will be remembered in the halls of labor as the era when union leadership became convinced that they could serve workers best by cooperating with employers. Workers' unity had been responsible for the significant gains of the working class that had been achieved through confrontation, strikes, and other militant actions. Now academicians had convinced labor leaders that gains could be achieved only through mutual interest. The movement permeated the halls of labor so much that even the AFL–CIO leadership, although refraining from an official endorsement, became a cooperative body and facilitated the spread of the disease. The theory defied the understanding that capitalism's driving force is greed and is further driven by self-aggrandizement, the very opposite of mutual advancement. Still many labor leaders were convinced that workers' interest could be advanced by cooperating with employers who had capitalistic objectives.

This movement blunted the edge of militancy necessary to demand the workers' share for their efforts. I suggest that the cooperative movement was planned in advance as a tool to blunt worker opposition to the one-sided international trade agreement NAFTA. The record shows that these systematic shifts in labor relations occurred simultaneously with the shift of production. While workers were engaged in discussions about incidental issues, their jobs were exported to distant lands. Unions could not have prevented the ultimate shrinking of the globe and the spread of capitalistic principles, but the approved treaties should have uplifted workers throughout the world rather than the resulting practice of chasing cheap labor and barbaric working conditions. Through NAFTA and its trade policies, the United States signed a pact with the devil in the name of profit. Absent the cooperative programs, American workers would have had the solidarity to fight compromise and achieve policies that promoted a level playing field.

Moe was a staunch opponent of cooperative programs no matter what postal management elected to call them—Employee Involvement or Quality of Work Life (QWL). While all of the other postal unions embraced cooperative programs with gusto, APWU was a committed holdout. In my meetings with Larry Hutchins, vice president of the Letter Carriers, we often debated the value of cooperative programs, to which he would end up giving his pat response, "Workers do not check their brains at the door," implying that through cooperative efforts we could improve the workplace. When the postal service had achieved its objective of modernization without worker resistance, it summarily jettisoned the programs. Today only the Mail Handlers continue the mirage of cooperation, and look what that has gotten them. I shared Moe's opposition to the misnamed Employee Involvement program, and the APWU message was clear: workers are best served when the lines of interest are clearly drawn and respected.

PATCO

The timing of our arrival in Washington coincided with the Professional Air Traffic Controllers Organization (PATCO) strike; a union that had supported the candidacy of Ronald Reagan overestimated its political influence and initiated a strike. The results were devastating for air traffic controllers and the labor movement. The APWU national officers joined with PATCO in a massive picket, and in private, Moe and I met with President Poli to discuss the coordination of our bargaining strategy.

History records that PATCO acted unilaterally with horrible consequences. There have been reams of analysis of the PATCO strike, dissecting the events leading to the strike and how events would have unfolded if the decisions had been different. President Poli was new to the position, and the membership had adopted a militant stance regarding their grievances. Drew Lewis, the newly appointed secretary of transportation, pulled the trigger, dismissing more than eleven thousand air traffic controllers without giving adequate time for passions to diminish, and the AFL–CIO sat idly by as a union was being broken for exercising the constitutional right of withholding their labor. There is sufficient blame to pass around, but the fact is the air traffic controllers were fired and banned from service in the federal government and that included employment in the postal service. The postal service broke ranks through Moe's insistence. Moe made their eligibility for postal employment a priority. He aggressively pursued their inclusion until the barrier was removed in 1993. During those years, no other federal union had equal impact on the labor movement.

Preparing For Negotiations

Shortly after we arrived on the Washington scene, it was time to begin preparation for the upcoming 1981 contract negotiations. We had campaigned on a platform of contract improvements and were determined to put our very best case forward. After researching records of prior negotiations, I was extremely disappointed in the style of the union's proposals in previous negotiations. Bernie Cushman, an attorney and lead APWU union staff member involved in negotiations, had a well-deserved reputation, but the past union's proposals reflected a total misunderstanding of the bargaining process.

The union had prepared proposals that consisted of the existing contractual language being crossed out and then the desired wording added in its place. In essence, the union rewrote the contract section by section, which was insane. The objective of negotiations is to engage the other party in discussions on issues of concern, convince them that change is mutually beneficial or deserving, and work toward a common goal. Negotiations involve dialogue about ideas that results in a mutually drafted contract. To start the process at the end eliminates the need to bargain. The opposing side is left with the choice to respond either yes or no, and more often than not they say no. I was appalled. That was not negotiations; it was "take it or leave it." I insisted that we change course and prepare the union's proposals in conceptual form, expressing the problems and any solutions in general terms.

Trip to Lima

As we began the early preparations for negotiations, the Postal Telegraph and Telephone International Union (PTTI) had scheduled a meeting in Lima, Peru, and the APWU was invited. Moe requested that I serve as the representative. I had been to Mexico and Canada, but going to Peru required securing a passport and checking with the embassy. This trip was my opportunity to see the rest of the world, and it would be my first international meeting.

The Communications Workers of America (CWA), National Association of Letter Carriers, and UFPC were among the founding members of PTTI and represented the largest block of financial support. As a novice on the world stage, I arrived at the Lima Conference with bags of APWU apparel—jackets, T-shirts, buttons—for distribution. That was considered taboo and fit the image of the "ugly American." I quickly learned the protocol of international relations. The meetings are conducted through interpreters. Each delegate is provided a headset connected to the interpreter of his or her native language. I met many of the attendees from other countries and went on to develop relationships with a number of them. It was on this trip that I was introduced to Keith Archer, president of the Telegraph Union of the Bahamas. Keith was a progressive unionist who was committed to expanding the rights of the workers and had even formed a credit union. We had much in common, and thirty years later, I still consider Keith a valued friend and communicate with him whenever possible.

Barbara Easterling, secretary treasurer of the CWA and a veteran of the Cleveland Labor movement, was an activist in international union affairs and attended the Lima Conference. Barbara and I had established a bond during the aborted takeover of the Cleveland central labor body, and as representatives of the local CWA and APWU unions, we communicated before my advancement to national office. When I arrived in Washington, we rekindled the relationship. It was good to see a familiar face at the conference.

At the time of my integration into global networking through PTTI, Glenn Watts was the president of CWA and the telegraph/postal sector of PTTI. He was succeeded as CWA president by Morty Bahr, who continued the tradition of American international leadership. Glenn and Morty knew Moe from the American labor movement in New York, and they were carbon copies of Stu Filbey, calm under all conditions and very smart.

At international PTTI meetings, traditionally the American unions—CWA, NALC, and APWU—would host a dinner for all of the representatives, and I gladly joined my sister unions in this endeavor. Lou Moore was the international representative for CWA, and he took me under his wing, explaining the customs of the host countries. He also explained that American unions were well respected throughout the world. Perhaps his best advice, though, was, "Don't drink the water."

As a tourist traveling beyond America for the first time, I endeavored to bring something back to the United States, a souvenir of my experience. Vendors lined the avenues with their wares, most of which had very little value. One item that caught my attention was a small cart filled with rocks that were imbedded with gold-colored flakes. They looked like gold nuggets in their raw state before being separated from the surrounding rock. Of course I knew they weren't real, but I thought they would make nice conversation pieces, so I purchased two for my personal collection. They weigh three pounds or more each, and they are displayed in my library today as a reminder of my educational trip to Lima, Peru.

Joint Bargaining

When I returned to Washington, we continued preparations for contract negotiations in coordination with NALC. Dave Noble, special assistant to Vince Sombrotto, was their contract specialist. He was paired with Richards and me to prioritize our bargaining demands. The APWU and Letter Carriers have different institutional interests regarding working conditions. APWU Clerk Craft employees work under constant supervision, and contractual rules governing workplace rights were a major factor in job satisfaction. In contrast, the Letter Carriers spend the vast majority of their workday without supervision, so the workplace rights do not have the same level of interest. The Letter Carriers could not understand our focus on changes to Article 19 to restrict the right of postal management to make midterm changes to negotiated provisions. The internal negotiations were tense and on occasion caused strains during the preparation; nevertheless, we prepared a package of joint proposals for presentation.

There were no internal disagreements over demands for wage increases, though. We both wanted more, and in preparation, the two unions retained the services of Joel Popkin, an economist who prepared an in-depth analysis of our wage demands. Joel was an accomplished professional and had previously worked on the government Consumer Price Index. We spent hours preparing our economic proposals with each word and figure backed by actuarial analysis. We presented the proposals to the postal service with much fanfare, justifying our demands with careful explanation. Despite our advanced preparation, the postal service negotiators were not impressed and responded with an overpriced and oversized postage stamp bearing the likeness of Moe and Vince.

Negotiations proceeded at a snail's pace. Few issues were resolved, and during the final days, Moe and Vince housed their executive boards in the hotel where the negotiations were taking place. As the deadline approached, the union officials were grouped in large ballrooms—one for NALC and one for APWU—where food was served and no one was permitted to exit. Moe and Vinnie wanted to keep a tight lid on information about the negotiations. They had planned elaborate communications networks to send messages to the locals about the status of the negotiations, and they did not want a loose cannon releasing information prematurely. Tempers were running high; as the deadline approached, there was tension about the possibility of a strike.

Few agreements were reached on issues of importance, but a memorandum was finalized recognizing that the Mail Handlers were, for the first time, not a part of the Joint Bargaining Committee. The prior contracts had included the Mail Handlers in the application of very sensitive contractual provisions, and at issue was their inclusion after severing bargaining ties. Moe, Vinnie, and I participated in a contentious meeting at USPS headquarters, where we discussed the issue and finalized the memorandum, which incorporated the Mail Handlers in the application of specific contract provisions but would be declared void if the Mail Handlers did not negotiate similar provisions.

During the negotiations, postal management informed the union that they intended to include cost of living adjustments for retirement obligations but would only contribute the postal share for retirement when employees were within three years of retirement. The economic benefit was that if the employee was not within the three-year window for retirement calculations, the postal service would save the 7 percent contribution to the retirement fund. This deferral without protection was unacceptable, so after intense negotiations, we finalized a memorandum to cover exceptional circumstances when the employee or heirs would be entitled to early qualification for retirement before the cost of living had been added to basic pay. The final agreement led to an annuity protection program memorandum that protected those employees who would have received credit for cost of living adjustments prior to the change. Almost immediately after the negotiations were concluded, it was necessary to arbitrate the 1981 memorandum as postal managers who were not a part of the negotiations sought to bend the intent to satisfy unachieved objectives.

I had been put in charge of negotiating a process to convert employees to full-time, and Tony Vegliante and I reached an agreement on a procedure requiring that part-time employees who worked thirty-nine hours or more per week for six months would require conversions to full-time flexible. The full-time flexibles would be guaranteed forty hours per week but would have flexible schedules. This agreement satisfied management's demand for flexibility and the union's demand for conversions to full-time status. All Clerk Craft employees are hired as part-time with the objective to convert to full-time and have predictability of income and work hours. Over time, the maximization agreement became the primary vehicle for conversions to full-time employment in the Clerk Craft, and hundreds of thousands of part-time employees benefitted from its application.

During the final hours of negotiations, Dave Noble of the Letter Carriers, Larry Gervais of APWU, and I were charged with paring down the dozens of pending union proposals to a handful of "must-haves." We worked for hours in a hotel suite with little success, and when Moe and Vinnie returned, there were still more proposals than we could reasonably be expected to achieve. Moe and Vince accepted our unfinished project and returned to bargaining, which was concluded several hours after midnight with an agreement by Vinnie and Moe on wages. They requested my presence in a room where they awaited management's return with a printed copy of the verbal agreement. The USPS representatives arrived and distributed a paper that Moe and Vince studied astutely. The blood drained from their faces with each line they read. Finally Moe or Vince threw the paper at a management official, proclaiming, "This is not what we agreed to."

Management had written a three-year proposal with yearly bonuses instead of pay increases. Moe and Vince protested that the bonuses were supposed to be on top of basic pay increases; disagreement ensued. The management officials left the room, and Moe and Vinnie went to their caucuses in the ballrooms to tell the officers of the disagreement. The atmosphere was tense and a strike was imminent. Moe and Vince held it together, and the following morning, twelve hours after the deadline, they succeeded in a negotiating a pay package that was a mixture of bonuses and pay increases, which settled the contract.

Pilot Grievance Procedure

The backlog of grievances had reached an unmanageable number, so to address the growing problem, I negotiated the Discipline Task Force, consisting of union and management officials designated to explore means of reducing the tremendous backlog. Following the negotiations, we explored new procedures to expedite the finalization of grievances and negotiated modifications to the contractual grievance procedure, putting the local parties in charge of the process. Through an agreement with postal management, we piloted a number of modified programs permitting the local parties to schedule their cases, select arbitrators, and facilitate the grievance process. I visited a number of sites with management officials, and we explained the new process that was designed to reduce the time in grievance processing and remove management's incentive to delay. Later this expedited process was expanded to include disciplinary action, permitting the local parties to agree to reduce minor discipline to no loss of pay while the grievance was being adjudicated. Many of these programs continue today.

Round Robin

Following completion of the negotiations, I returned to the office to organize the contract papers for distribution. I was creating stacks of paper when I noticed a document that I had not previously seen. It was a productivity standard that was anathema to Clerk Craft employees. In the early 1960s, postal management had experimented with productivity standards, and after the union challenged them, they discontinued the effort. It had become a joke as employees would surreptitiously secure the paper slips that indicated they had worked a full tray of mail, and at the end of a work day, they would add the pilfered slips to their legitimate slips and present them for count. Here was a union agreement to reinstitute a productivity standard, and I was not aware of its existence. The document was appropriately initialed, so I requested an explanation of its source. Moe explained that it was of little importance and insisted that I refrain from including it in the package for distribution. I threw the papers from my hands and left the building. I left the union office, and as I got in my car, Darryl Anderson, lead counsel, came running behind me, asking me to return. I refused and drove home, where I had not been in a week. I needed rest and home cooking.

Moe and I resolved our differences over the hidden document and proceeded to travel to each of the five APWU regions to share the new contract with local leaders and national officers. We began with a meeting in New York for the east and northeast regions and then traveled from there to Chicago for the central region. Following those locations, it was on to the southern region in Atlanta and finally the western region in Los Angeles. At the conclusion of what would later be named Round Robin, we returned home for rest and the normal grind. The contract was ratified, and we had passed our first test. The productivity standard was never implemented, and it never appeared in a contract.

CHAPTER 13

New Challenges

Union Finances

The finances of the union were in disarray. The revenues were insufficient to match the uncontrollable expenses. The dues assessment approved by the executive board was sufficient to get us to the national convention, but no attention had been applied to past and future expenses. The general understanding at union headquarters was for each officer to spend what he/she believed was necessary, track expenses, and request reimbursement. From a budgetary standpoint, this process was a financial dilemma that would follow Moe throughout his career. He did not incorporate budgeting in his management style, and the union's finances were consistently in the red, dependent upon the next dues increase for additional revenue.

When the five unions merged to create APWU, each of the more than ninety total officers made individual decisions regarding expenditures to do what they deemed was necessary to perform their duties, and they charged the expenses to the national union. No individual budgets existed, and this independence became so grotesque that some field officers would independently determine

Christmas bonuses for secretaries, funneling the cost to the national union in their monthly expenses. They justified their expenses by claiming that they were representing the best interests of the members. In their view, the role of the accounting department was only to record expenses and reimburse accordingly. The finances of the union consistently showed surpluses in the non-convention years and huge deficits in the convention years due to the high cost of holding the convention. It was no wonder that financial deficits were a constant for many years.

First Convention under New Leadership

In August 1982, the APWU delegates met in Miami to convene the sixth biennial national convention. It was the first convention under the leadership of Moe Biller, and it proved to be exciting and productive. The national officers arrived in the host city one week prior to the convention, and I was provided a suite in the Fontainebleau Hotel, which would later be used in the film *Bodyguard*, starring Kevin Costner and Whitney Houston. The principle guest speakers were former Vice President Walter Mondale and Coretta Scott King, wife of the slain civil rights hero. In a flourish of showmanship, Moe unveiled an eighteen-minute multimedia show produced by J. Walter Thompson Advertising Agency promoting the theme "letter perfect." When the show ended, Moe presented the resolution to increase the per capita tax in the amount of the assessment, and it was approved overwhelmingly. The delegates also approved changes to the officers' structure.

During the first day of the proceedings, New Jersey Local President Gerry Manzullo challenged the ruling of President Biller on a procedural question, and Moe turned the chair over to me while the question was being decided. As I approached the podium for the first time at a national convention, my nervousness was apparent as my voice elevated several octaves, but within minutes I engaged in the flow of the debate and felt quite comfortable in the role of chairman. The decision of the chair was sustained, and I proceeded to chair the constitutional changes that were decided. I had received my baptism in presiding over the democratic process of conventions.

Before the convention, Moe had charged me with the task of rewriting the APWU constitution to rework the officers' structure. Because of the merger, we had too many presidents, and we needed to establish a uniform title for field officers. In the merger, Filbey had agreed that each of the presidents of the merging unions would continue the title of president, with the top officers identified as general executives. In the drafting of the new constitution, I consulted the Craft presidents and regional coordinators and achieved a consensus approving the changes that removed the term "general" from the title of national president, executive president, and secretary treasurer.

Over the history of the unions that formed APWU, the majority of the field officers worked from their homes. This arrangement created all sorts of accountability problems. To reach the office of one field officer, it was necessary to go through his daughter's bedroom. So after restructuring the officers' structure, I realigned the field structure. I renamed the field officers as business agents and converted them to full-time employees assigned to specific offices. The change met with serious resistance as it eliminated abuse and required every officer to report to an APWU designated office. This issue was not finally resolved until we included several grandfather clauses that protected existing officers, most notably Steve Zamanakos and Leo Persails. Nevertheless, the changes were approved by the convention delegates, and we were successful in creating a permanent APWU footprint.

In drafting the constitutional changes for a new field structure, the Special Delivery Craft was particularly challenging as the Craft had fewer than two thousand total members and fourteen officers. I demanded that they reduce to one resident officer and two field business agents, one east of the Mississippi and one west. In an unruly meeting outside the convention hall, the Special Delivery officers rejected my proposal even though I informed them that the unlimited reimbursement for material, office furniture, and expenses for the continuing part-time officers would be seriously curtailed. The new field structure that included one full-time officer for the Special Delivery Craft was approved by the national executive board and the convention. These were hotly contested issues, and roll calls were required to confirm that the required two-thirds majorities had been obtained.

During the course of the convention, the Miami Local hosted a luau as entertainment for the delegates, which turned into a disaster when the catering company exhausted the supply of food and drink for hundreds of delegates who had purchased tickets. The issue was not resolved satisfactorily until months after the convention had been concluded. Despite the distractions, the convention was considered a success, having adopted the primary issues of constitutional changes.

Mail Handler Challenge

The delegates approved a resolution to collect petitions to decertify the Mail Handlers Union. There was natural friction between clerks and mail handlers as they had overlapping duties in the mail processing environment. Clerks were routinely assigned the manual tasks that generally fell within the mail handler's jurisdiction, and we considered them job related. In addition, with the introduction of automation, when scheme study became less of a factor, the lines between clerks and mail handlers became even more blurred, so there were constant grievances over duties. My companion, Smitty, whom I partnered with, was a mail handler working beside me performing the same duties. The duty of "hanging sacks" was a mail handler function even though I had performed the task as a substitute clerk. Mail handlers, on the other hand, were not assigned schemes, so they were not qualified to perform the work of the clerks. From management's perspective, they increased flexibility in the maximum use of clerks because they could work at more jobs. This was changing, however, as the scheme requirement was being phased out with the implementation of mechanization and automation, and fights over jobs ensued. As a means of resolving the issue, the decision was made to decertify the Mail Handlers Union and convert the disputes to internal issues for resolution.

This conflict led to institutional animosity between the two unions that boiled over, resulting in the Mail Handlers exiting the Joint Bargaining Committee. At the time that Stu Filbey engaged in merger discussions, it was reported that the Mail Handlers were receptive and that for a specific sum they would be willing to become a part of the merged union. This report has never been confirmed, but the animosity between the two unions grew continuously as the prime objective of the Mail Handlers Union was to extract jobs from the Clerk Craft.

The Laborers International Union (LIUNA) had wrestled control of the independent Mail Handlers Union through a vote of the Mail Handlers membership that, to this day, is suspect. The president of the independent Mail Handlers Union died under mysterious circumstances shortly after the questionable merger, and many of the mail handlers, particularly those in New York, became members of APWU. My mentors and friends John Smith in Dayton and Joe Anthony in Pittsburgh were among the Mail Handler leaders who elected to apply their many talents to APWU.

Lonnie Johnson emerged as president of the Mail Handlers Division of LIUNA. He was aggressive in seeking to expand mail handler jobs, and the conflicts forced a convention resolution requiring APWU convention delegates to initiate a nationwide program to decertify the mail handlers division of LIUNA as the representative union. Two-thirds of all postal mail handlers who were members of APWU were members of the New York Local, and when combined with the other mail handlers necessary to require a certification election, APWU would have to convince tens of thousands of mail handlers throughout the country to vote to decertify their union. Moe knew that the odds were extremely long and did not want to be diverted at the beginning of his presidency on an effort that could not succeed. He offered a motion at the executive board meeting to refrain from undertaking the decertification effort.

Kenny Leiner was a revolutionary who had been successful in defeating John R. Smith as director of the APWU Mail Handlers. As a member of the national executive board charged with implementing the convention resolution, Kenny was a leader in the adoption of the convention resolution and spoke at length of the obligation to go forward consistent with the convention decision. The debate was heated with no compromise from either side. Those supporting compliance with the convention resolution prevailed, and the union proceeded with the effort to decertify the Mail Handlers.

Over time, Ben Zemsky, Kenny Leiner, Mike Zullo, Jim Connors, and John Richards formed a coalition of resident officers with the Trine Council that was in opposition to everything Moe did. Moe took John's defection personally, and their relationship went downhill from there. John and I continued to communicate regularly, but his relationship with the newly formed Trine Council widened the Biller–Richards gulf and it never recovered. When historians look back, they may record the Biller decisions that the coalition opposed as failures, but it will be more difficult to find what the coalition did to improve postal employment. The human race is made up of those who do and those who critique. Moe was a doer, and the Mail Handlers decertification effort failed miserably.

Contract Enforcement

During this period, I authored a booklet on the Family and Medical Leave Act (FMLA) that was distributed to each employee for information and protection. The FMLA revolutionized the use of sick leave in the workplace. Postal rules had provided that all absences be classified as "failure to maintain"; extended sick leave for a serious health condition was no exception. Upon passage of the law, I met with postal officials to come to an understanding on the application of the law. We succeeded in reaching a series of agreements, many of which continue in effect today, but when the Republicans gained control of the Labor Department, many of the original protections were watered down. One of the agreements was unprecedented, requiring the acceptance of union-designed forms, which required less information. Steve Albanese, a business agent and friend who would later be a candidate for executive vice president on my team, became an expert on FMLA issues. He was a knowledgeable instructor and traveled throughout the country teaching the law and its application. We were successful in transforming the postal leave policy.

Later I went on to write a number of information books on various subjects, including MSPB, excessing, carpal tunnel syndrome, the history of APWU bargaining, and others.

Health Plan Fiasco

After settling in at APWU headquarters, Moe and I wanted to take a look at the hospital plan operations. The building was located in Silver Springs, Maryland, twenty-five miles from union headquarters, so we had to navigate through the maze of downtown DC and the immediate suburbs. When we arrived, we were escorted into the building by Ben Evans, the newly elected director. We were in for a shock. What looked like millions of files were stacked everywhere. There was no orderly system of paying medical claims, and as we later learned, there was not enough money to pay them. We knew a major overhaul was necessary, but we did not know where to start. We hired the professional consulting firm Booze Allen to advise us on how to dig out of the morass. Tony Pino was retained as the manager of operations, and he estimated that $75 million dollars in payments were included in row after row of pending claims.

Over the coming months, we began to dig out of the hole. We were entering the open season and had submitted our proposed premiums and benefits to the US Office of Personnel Management (OPM) for approval. We thought it would be perfunctory, but we were in for a surprise.

Moe and Vince had traveled to Japan for a meeting with PTTI and immediately prior to their departure, OPM had informed APWU that we had to modify our benefits to include significant coinsurance and deductibles. The APWU plan had a proud history of excellent benefits, and its selling point was its first dollar coverage. Director Devine, head of the OPM, demanded that we accept a plan with a thirty-dollar premium. We thought that he was bluffing, so Moe declined the OPM offer and departed for Japan.

Despite the time difference, Moe and I had several long-distance conversations about the OPM ultimatum. We both agreed that we would hold out to lessen the impact of the proposed changes, and until his return, I would resist efforts to seek an agreement to change the health benefits.

One evening after I had returned home from the office, I received a telephone call from Director Devine. After introducing himself, he informed me that if APWU did not agree to the modifications demanded, the APWU plan would be dropped from the Federal Employees Health Benefits (FEHB) program. Having discussed the issue with Moe, I informed him that we would not accept the ultimatum. The following day, APWU was officially notified that its hospital plan would not be continued as a plan in the FEHB program. Upon his return, Moe began a flurry of calls. He contacted congressmen, senators, the AFL–CIO, and anyone that could be of assistance. Finally he received assistance, and APWU was permitted to remain in FEHB, albeit with a significantly modified plan. We had created the emergency by refusing to modify the plan, but Moe performed a miracle in salvaging it.

CHAPTER 14

The Retirement Plan

1983 Election

The 1983 election of officers was a contest between the administration and the newly formed Trine Council. It was led by the anti-Biller forces, and they saw an opportunity to defeat Moe. Dave Daniel, president of West Virginia State, was selected as Moe's opponent, and he waged a vigorous campaign. I have since come to know and appreciate Dave as an articulate, dedicated unionist, but in 1983, he was the enemy, and he made a good run. He was supported by Kenny Leiner, director of the Mail Handlers, and the other anti-Biller national officers. Leiner was an effective campaigner. He was smart and organized, and it had been reported that he had been trained in Cuba as an activist to socialize the American Labor movement. He and his cohorts qualified for postal employment for the purpose of radicalizing the postal labor movement, and becoming president was an opportunity to be on the inside of a large union. Leiner spent hours organizing support for Daniel, who teamed with Janet Olsen of the Milwaukee Local. Olsen opposed Doug Holbrook, and she and Daniel came uncomfortably close to winning the election. I was unopposed but Moe and Doug were in a dog fight. Until the final day of ballot counting, it was not clear who would win. In the final count, we prevailed and were afforded another term of leadership. The Labor Board required a rerun of the election, but Biller and Holbrook were again victorious.

The Assault on the Civil Service Retirement System

In 1983, Congress began deliberations to consider changing the Civil Service Retirement System (CSRS), a type of defined-benefit plan, and as president of the largest union of government employees, Moe was thrust into the spotlight of opposition. APWU engaged in picketing, running television commercials, and a host of other activities intended to influence the outcome of the deliberations. Moe appeared on several television programs where he debated Patrick Buchanan, William Buckley Jr., James C. Miller, and John McLaughlin on the issues. The government retirement system was changed to a defined-contributions plan, but Moe was in the battle against the private investors who expanded their portfolios to include the retirement funds of millions of postal and federal workers. Just imagine the profits from the fees for the administration of all federal and postal employee investments. This change was a twofer for the Republican Party. They succeeded in reducing the liability of the taxpayer in funding retirement, and their supporters made huge profits in the exchange.

Political Connections

Because of Moe's political connections, he and I had the privilege of watching the 1982 congressional election returns from the office of Speaker of the House Tip O'Neill. The Democrats took a terrible beating, but we were impressed at having been invited, among a few other labor officials, to be in the presence of the second most powerful man in America. The image is captured in a photograph that I cherish.

In October 1983, I attended a briefing in the press room at the White House, and to the surprise of all in attendance, President Regan entered the room from behind the stage curtain less than twenty feet from the twenty or so union officials assembled. The purpose of the briefing was to justify the ongoing Grenada invasion, where the US military had been dispatched to quell an alleged insurgent uprising. Resistance was nonexistent, and within hours, the US military was in control. The president did not tell us anything that had not been reported in the press, so we left not knowing why the strongest military in the world had found it necessary to invade a defenseless island. The most memorable part of the briefing was the exit by the president, who needed painted footprints on the floor to direct his path as he left the room.

Mail Processors

The 1980s ushered in major modifications to the Clerk Craft, the largest group within APWU. As the postal service transitioned from manual and mechanization letter sorting machines (LSMs) to automation (OCR/BCS), it created a new job description: mail processors, with a lower rate of pay (grade 3). The optical character readers (OCRs) and bar code sorters (BCRs) were computer operated scanners that read the address and made appropriate sortation. The former LSM assignments required a greater degree of skill and were salaried at level 6. The postal service was proposing to replace them with level 3 duty assignments. We arbitrated the new position and succeeded in elevating its pay to grade 4, but it took many years before the employees were fully integrated into a universal pay grade for clerical employees.

The lower pay grade created many problems, most notably in the application of seniority. After assimilation into the workforce, the principle objective of postal employees is wages, followed by the use of seniority to achieve preferred assignments and hours. The mail processing operation is a twenty-four-hour-a-day, seven-day-a-week operation, and the senior employees assume the regular nine-to-five working hours. Employees who were classified as level 5 or level 6, which included 80 percent of the Clerk Craft, could not apply for the new level 4 assignments because they could not apply their seniority. Indignation was rampant when a mail processor who had been working for three years could obtain a preferred assignment that was denied an employee with fifteen years seniority. I was successful in negotiating the merger of the seniority lists, and we chipped away at the differences until we finally succeeded in incorporating mail processors into full contractual protections.

As the postal service made the transition from LSMs to OCR/BCS automation for the processing of mail, they faced conflicting contractual and legal obligations, as mentioned above. The operators who were classified as level 6 LSM employees were reassigned to level 4 OCR/BCS assignments. Employees who had served in the military were covered by the Veterans' Preference Act that included specific protections for veterans. It required the veterans to be provided a higher ranking than nonveterans if they were reduced in pay grade. The postal service was caught between the contractual provisions that required seniority as the determining factor and the Veterans' Preference Act.

Postal management searched for a solution, and initially I was the lead officer addressing the issue. I refused to solve their problem and succeeded in negotiating wage protections for thousands of LSM operators, which protected their contractual seniority. The APWU Clerk Craft officers opened discussions with management, and since the assignments in question were within the Clerk Craft, Moe insisted that I pass the issue to their jurisdiction. In a meeting filled with tension, Moe reassigned responsibility, whereupon the officers proceeded to negotiate a memorandum waiving the contractual seniority rights and permitted management to cherry-pick the employees subjected to excessing. This had been management's objective from the outset, and I never learned how it was in the interest of the employees.

The Officers' Retirement Plan

Another issue of major concern requiring attention was modification of the Officers' Retirement Plan. The liabilities, including previous postal employment that had not been funded, exerted constant financial pressure on the plan. An officer having been employed by the postal service for twenty years prior to election to union office was credited with the postal time when he or she retired from the APWU even though neither the union nor the officer had funded the postal time in the officer retirement system. The constitution dictated that the officers' retirement system be no less than that provided by civil service, and at the time of the merger, officers of the merging unions became immediately qualified for maximum retirement benefits. After consulting a professional actuary, I succeeded in rewriting the retirement provisions, sun setting the officers elected prior to 1983. In later years, I found a way to combine the pre- and post-1983 groups. Following the acceptance of the provisions by the executive board, Leo Persails, who was a member of the executive board and an opponent of the administration, approached me in private and expressed his appreciation for the adjustment that would increase his annuity. This change would not benefit Moe or me, but it was actuarially achievable, and it was the right thing to do.

1984 National Convention

The 1984 National Convention convened in Las Vegas, and we were honored to receive Bill Ford, chairman of the Post Office Committee, Congressman Mickey Leland of Texas (who later died in an airplane crash while on humanitarian trip), and Geraldine Ferraro, the first female candidate for vice president. The hot button issue for debate was the relocation of field officers to the twenty-two established offices. The delegate count was 3,213 certified delegates, and Sonja Leggett, delegate of the New York Local, was the first female to chair an APWU convention.

177

The Taj Mahal

Doug Holbrook began the search for a new headquarters building. The building at Fourteenth Street NW was beyond repair and undeserving of a proud labor union, and the neighborhood was less than desirable. One day, Moe and I were returning from lunch at a local restaurant and stopped in the bookstore next door to the union office. Moe asked the clerk if he could purchase a *New York Times*, which caused the clerk to laugh uncontrollably because the books and papers he sold were pornographic. Doug began exploring a number of locations and arrangements, and we came close to partnering with the Teachers Union in a new development on Capitol Hill. The existing building on Fourteenth Street was paid for, so we had some bargaining power and entered into discussions with realtors.

Once it became known that we were considering relocating, the union political opposition seized the opportunity to put a face on their constant dissent. If it had not been the building, it would have been something else. They just did not like Moe. Charges that the administration purchased a building without a convention vote were brought against the union, and a court case ensued. Much convention time was devoted to opposition, but when the dust settled, we had a new building—a brand-spanking-new building financed through the sale of the old building and a partnership with Sam Lehrman, cofounder of Giant Foods. It was a much-needed and beautiful building. The opposition gave it the nickname "Taj Mahal" because they thought it was excessive. Moe received all of the heat, but Doug and I convinced him that we needed to upgrade. At one point, Moe threatened not to sign the papers, but he took all of the blame for the Taj Mahal. We completed the move into the new office building and were able to group officers by functioning responsibility. The president and vice president were now on the same floor, all craft officers were on a floor, and one entire floor was dedicated to the secretary treasurer and his staff.

1984 Negotiations

In 1984, we spent ninety days sparring with a management that was determined to reduce wages. When the parties reached an impasse on economic provisions, postal management announced that it was their intent to impose a two-tier wage schedule that the unions had previously rejected. The unions filed an injunction in federal court, and Representative Silvio Conte of Massachusetts introduced legislation in Congress to prohibit the application of the two-tier wage schedule during the impasse. After mediation and fact finding, the unresolved issue of wages was referred to renowned economist and arbitrator Clark Kerr. After protracted presentation of contrasting evidence in arbitration, he issued the first decision interpreting the intent of the term "comparability," which is a legal requirement that kept wages comparable to the private sector. This decision concluded that "wages in the postal service had gone up substantially faster than wages in the private sector" and the means of correction should be "moderate restraint" of future wage growth. The arbitration decision was positive, and we achieved the highest negotiated/arbitrated wage increase (three 2.7 percent increases) in the history of postal bargaining. The agreement also included lower starting wages, expanding the number of years from entry level to top step from eight years to thirteen years.

We also succeeded in negotiating union control of the APWU membership list. Before the 1984 negotiations, management maintained the membership list, and Forms 1187 and 1188 (union membership and revocation forms) were submitted to management to add or remove employees from the union rolls. The contract set forth a specific time frame for membership revocation, but the union was unable to verify if those conditions had been met. We were aware that management oftentimes had held an untimely submitted revocation until the anniversary date was reached. In the agreement to transfer administrative control, we extended dues payments from one per month to biweekly, which increased dues receipts by two bi-weekly deductions per year. Those were major accomplishments. We also agreed to add Martin Luther King Day as a contractual holiday.

Penalty Pay

The 1984 negotiations resolved a continuing problem of excessive overtime. The unions had initiated many efforts to curb the obligation to work in excess of eight hours per day and scheduled off days. We were successful in 1984 in reaching agreement on the payment of double time for hours beyond the established limits (ten hours per day and work on more than one nonscheduled day).

This payment, called penalty pay, grew out of the strangest of circumstances. Overtime for employees had become excessive, and the national union office had taken all available steps to moderate abuses. Changing contractual provisions had become essential. Moe was engaged in direct discussions with Postmaster General Bill Bolger, who shared Moe's concern for the unusually high percentage of overtime and offered to pay double time for violations of the contractual limits. The Letter Carriers had previously won a celebrated arbitration case in which the arbitrator ordered double time for violations, and PMG Bolger was volunteering to make it a standard. Not knowing the myriad of contractual provisions that would have to be modified, Moe, Vinnie, and Bolger agreed to the basic proposition. During the discussions that were taking place on a Saturday, I was driving to attend to a personal matter, and Moe called me on the car phone. I attempted to advise him on the details that would have to be addressed, but a conversation while traveling in the car was not conducive to dealing with the myriad issues involved. Moe, Vinnie, and Bolger finalized a document reflecting their intent, but the following day when Postal Operations had the opportunity to review the Bolger commitment, they went ballistic and Labor

Relations began to include roadblocks in the application of the basic agreement.

Moe summoned Larry Gervais to come to Washington to spearhead the union's efforts to clarify and maximize the new provision. Moe often turned to Larry to address major issues. He was called upon to negotiate solutions to Section 6 of Article 1: jurisdiction with the Mail Handlers, light and limited duty, and penalty pay. Larry's efforts led to a series of national arbitrations, a memorandum ended up being ineffective, and penalty pay became clouded in local disagreements, principally on the provision requiring employees to work in excess of ten hours a day. Moe was extremely proud that he had achieved penalty pay and often said that he wanted it on his headstone.

The Assault on Wages

Arbitrator Clark Kerr had concluded that postal salary exceeded the comparability standard and ordered moderate restraint, so to buttress their proposals for radical reductions in wages, the postal service contracted for a special academic study of postal wages, employing Professor Wachter of the University of Pennsylvania. Professor Wachter's analysis of postal employees' wages and benefits was intended to convince arbitrators that wages exceeded the comparability standard. The study prepared by Professor Wachter was Exhibit #1 in each interest arbitration from Kerry (1984) to Goldberg (2000), with graphs and charts supporting their position, which was invariably to reduce wages. Secretly I took great pride in the part of his presentation showing that the postal service had a voluntary attrition rate that was among the lowest in the country.

The APWU and NALC countered the Wachter study and argued that the legal comparability referenced in the statute was intended to apply to union workers in the private sector, which supported our position that comparability had not been exceeded, but the national arbitrators to date have not accepted this position. The secondary position of the unions has been that postal wages determined by postal contracts do not include the discriminatory practices applied in the private sector, and after accounting for such discrimination of women and minorities, the USPS-supported wage premium does not exist. After five interest arbitrations, the novel arguments of the postal service and those of the unions have not prevailed.

Contract negotiations throughout the 1980s were extremely difficult and contentious. Each negotiation was merely a prelude to arbitration, but in each instance, we were successful in staving off the drastic reductions proposed by the postal service.

Five out of the eight labor contracts spanning twenty-three years, from 1978 to 2001—a major portion of the Biller presidency (1980–2001)—were decided in arbitration. (I was the chief negotiator in the 2000 negotiations, which were decided in arbitration) The postal service's Board of Governors was determined to reduce wages at all costs.

The legal standard established by Congress in the 1971 Postal Reform Act is and has been "comparability" with employees in the private sector performing similar activities. The unions successfully defended against radical change, and Arbitrators Healy, Kerr, Mittenthal, Clarke, and Goldberg decided that any downward adjustment in wages must be achieved through moderate restraint.

Smoking Policy

As the health community began the campaign to warn people about the dangers of tobacco smoke, the postal service's health department reached out to the unions to develop a new policy. As a former athlete, I refrained from smoking throughout my formative years, including my years of military service, only to succumb to the habit while searching for an identity in Steubenville, Ohio, after my military service in the 1950s. I smoked about ten cigarettes a day until the late 1980s when I quit cold turkey. I was able to refrain from the addiction for approximately eighteen months. During that time, I gained twenty pounds and decided that the trade-off was not worth the results, and since I don't inhale, I am at peace with the addiction.

In the mid-1980s, the post office policy of facilitating smokers was well established. Smoking was permitted with few exceptions, and a change would be resisted. Violations would lead to individual disciplinary action, and it was my intent to set a good example. I had chaired national conventions with a cigarette in hand, so the members knew me as a smoker; I had some credibility in the development of policy that permitted smoking only in certain areas. As a result of these efforts, postal service employees did not suffer the contradictions that existed in many workplaces when smoking was prohibited.

During my service as executive vice president, my office became the smoking area, and when officers or members visited headquarters, they came to my office to engage in their habit. When my friends Josie and Liz were in Washington during the workday, they could be found in my office. After the surgeon general issued his warning about the dangers of smoking and when I assumed the presidency, I realized that I was setting a bad example and refrained from smoking in the union office building. I requested that Ron Collins, director of logistics, construct an area on the loading dock that was protected against the weather for smokers. I wanted the officers and the employees to understand that I took the issue seriously and if I could go to the dock, they should follow suit. Several officers continued to smoke in their offices despite my example. Pat Nilan was notorious for smoking cigars at his desk, and when he refused to stop, I had the building mechanic remove his office door, exposing him. My smoking partners were Sharon Ingram, who has since taken the cure, Rodney Radcliff, Stacey Burch, Delores Sutton, and on occasion, Steve Raymer and Myke Reid. We solved many world problems on our smoking breaks.

CHAPTER 15

Getting Comfortable

Our First Home

After residing in apartments since our arrival, Ethelda and I began exploring the idea of purchasing a home and looked at several properties. I had restricted our search to Maryland because Washington was too congested and too expensive and Virginia had too conservative of a political record, including the state-sponsored closing of all public schools in response to the 1954 Brown decision. A realtor suggested that we consider building a new home. The only person I knew who built his own home was the eccentric Cleveland Local APWU business agent Richard Butler. My immediate response was, *You must be kidding me*, but the idea was intriguing. The realtor walked us through the process and told us about a neighborhood with ready-to-build lots for sale. We fell in love with a half-acre wooded lot that backed up to ten acres of state-owned land that could never be developed. We purchased the lot and began the search for a builder. Our luck held, and we found Steve Myers, a small builder who had just completed a project and was looking for another job. Together we designed a three-thousand-square-foot brick split level that was absolutely gorgeous.

The day we signed the papers for our dream home, we were married in the county courthouse. In celebration, Doug Holbrook and Moe Biller treated us to dinner at Duke Zeibert's restaurant. Duke's closed shortly after our wedding day, so Ethelda and I have celebrated every anniversary at the Willard Hotel, where I present her a rose for each year of our marriage. Today it is getting a little expensive, but I have the best wife in the world—well worth the price of all the roses in the world.

Interlaken, Switzerland

As we were moving into our dream home, the opportunity arose for us to travel to Interlaken, Switzerland, to represent APWU in the international postal and telecommunication community. Doug and I paid for our wives to join us, so Moe, Doug and Jackie (his wife), and Ethelda and I traveled to Interlaken. The three of us traveling together was unusual, but this trip was special. Nestled in the Swiss Alps and overlooking Lake Luzerne, Interlaken is one of the most beautiful cities in the world. Our trip was truly relaxing.

Switzerland has no official native language, and most of the citizens in the north speak German. On a peaceful carriage ride we took with our wives, Moe wanted to display his knowledge of the local language. He spoke at length to the carriage driver, who listened politely and with extreme professionalism remained silent as Moe displayed his limited knowledge of the language. When Moe paused to breathe, the driver politely asked, "Would you please speak English?"

Another memorable event was our visit to a restaurant high in the Swiss Alps with a spectacular view. We dined on American cuisine and shared several bottles of wine. After the meal, when the check came, I presented my American Express card. The waiter huddled with his superior and then returned to inform me that they did not accept credit cards. Knowing this in advance would have been nice. I presented several hundred dollar bills as payment. The waiter proceeded to raise each bill to the light for inspection. I was incensed. *How dare you question the legitimacy of American money?* I abruptly snatched my C-notes from his hand and announced that he would have to accompany me back to the hotel for payment after I exchanged my bills for local currency. Doug and Jackie were able to present sufficient local currency to pay the tab. Two Letter Carrier officers who had joined us for dinner watched the tense exchange and never offered to assist even though their meals were included in the tab.

We planned our trip so that we would spend several days in London on the way to Interlaken and several days in Paris on the way home. We were able to eat dinner at Wimbledon and ride to the top of the Eiffel Tower in Paris. These were special experiences. In London, Billy Hayes, president of the British Postal Union, and John Baldwin were gracious hosts, but they introduced me to a local dish called "mar mar," which is like caviar but in my opinion the foulest tasting food in the history of human beings. To get to Paris, we had to take a taxi to the airport in Bern, Switzerland, so early in the morning that the airport had not yet opened. When we finally boarded the plane, the stewardess served us a breakfast of hard rolls from a basket. When we arrived in Paris, our room was not ready, so we elected to go on a tour of the city. We fell asleep on the bus and missed our stop. When we woke up, we had no idea of where we were. Some kind passersby assisted us in finding our hotel. Overall it was a wonderful trip.

The End of the Biller–Leiner Feud

The 1986 election of officers was a repeat of 1983 and 1984, with Dave Daniels opposing Moe and Moe winning with increasing margins with each election. In the 1986 election, the opposition had obviously determined that leaving me unopposed was not wise, so they challenged me with the candidacy of Dave Herb, president of the Schenectady, New York, Local. The results were not close; Biller, Burrus, and Holbrook continued to lead the APWU. Biller did not experience a serious challenger for the remainder of his career.

Although we were victorious, the Biller team lost good union officers and friends. Wallace Baldwin was defeated by Jim Connors of Springfield, Massachusetts, and Mike Benner was defeated by Sam Anderson of the Chicago Local. Mike was retained as Moe's assistant and continued to play a vital role in union affairs until 2000 when he left for the Teachers Union to work as the president's assistant.

Biller, Burrus, and Holbrook experienced comfortable margins of victory, but the real victory was the end of annoying opposition. Ben Zemsky, director of organization who had devoted his career to opposing Moe, was defeated in the 1986 election. More significant was the end of the longstanding feud between Moe Biller and Ken Leiner. Kenny had defeated our friend John Smith in 1978 for the position of president of the national Mail Handlers Division and had been a thorn in Moe's side ever since. He had been a leader of a group called the Outlaws, which disrupted New York Local meetings, resorting to chair throwing and threats of violence. Kenny and his group also led the 1978 wildcat strike at the New York BMC, and despite Moe's advocacy to restore Kenny as an officer on the executive board, their relationship was volatile. If Moe proposed it, Kenny opposed it.

Moe recruited Norman Steward, director of the Mail Handlers in the New York Local, to oppose Kenny. Because 80 percent of the APWU Mail Handlers were members of the New York Local, it was anticipated that if Norman could carry his home local, he would win. On the last evening of the ballot counting, there was a ruckus in the back of the counting room. Massey, a member of the New York Local and a giant of a man, was holding Kenny by the back of his shirt, lifting him off the ground. He had caught

Kenny destroying ballots. Kenny had observed that he was losing heavily in the New York Local, so he had secretly removed several handfuls of uncounted ballots and was attempting to flush them down the toilet when he was apprehended by Massey. The police were called, and Kenny was escorted to jail. Over the following months, he was expelled from the union and found guilty in criminal court. Thus ended the Biller–Leiner saga.

1986 Convention

At the 1986 National Convention, the administration was successful in passing a resolution increasing the officers' salaries. This increase was a significant achievement as APWU officers' salaries were less than half of their counterparts in other unions and previous attempts had failed. I chaired the convention throughout the debate, which tested my skills as there was strong opposition. Certain delegates are opposed to any proposal supported by the administration, so to achieve a victory in increasing salaries was a notable accomplishment. To this day, I do not know the source of the gulf that exists in APWU conventions between some delegates and the administration.

Special Assistants

During the 1980s, Moe appointed selected local and state leaders as special assistants to work full-time for the national union. Bob Stutts was state president for North Carolina and was well respected throughout the union for his knowledge and folksy personality. Bob was a welcomed addition and among other things assisted the business agents in grievances, arbitration, and training. The appointment of these special assistants caused tensions with the elected business agents because the assistants were seen as encroaching on the agents' territory. Steve Zamanakos, a well-respected business agent who became influential in national conventions, was a force at national conventions. Don Foley, David Yao, and Steve had the pulse of the convention delegates and often thwarted initiatives sponsored by the administration. The issues of expanding the convention cycle, compensating advocates, and many other changes proposed by the administration were opposed by these leaders, and they were often successful in convincing the delegates to follow their lead.

Robin Enters

In May of 1987, Robin Bailey became my administrative assistant, responsible for the affairs of my office. She had previously worked in industrial relations after a brief stint in the president's office. While working for Moe, I recall an occasion when we were out of town and Moe called Robin to dictate a piece for his article for the APWU monthly magazine. The exchange was confrontational because Moe could be extremely abusive to office staff, and on that occasion, I felt empathy for the employee engaged in that conversation. A few weeks later, I interviewed three candidates for the vacancy in my office and selected Robin.

The position that she filled was within the OPEIU bargaining unit because I had resisted efforts to remove the top employees from the secretarial pool and convert them to staff. I felt strongly that the top position in my office should be filled by a union employee. Michelle Cochran was the previous vice president's secretary and she served me well, but after seven years of seeking advancement, she left to obtain employment at the AFL. I was fortunate to turn the responsibilities over to Robin, who would administer the affairs of my office for the balance of my career. Her services were invaluable, and to this day, she remains a trusted friend.

Burlesque

On a visit to my home local in Cleveland, I invited my friend Congressman Louis Stokes to dinner. After I had completed my union business, Lou's driver dropped him off to meet me at the union hall. We selected my favorite Cleveland restaurant, the

Theatrical Grill, located on Short Vincent Street in downtown Cleveland. The Theatrical was very similar to The Prime Rib, one of my favorite restaurants in the Washington area. As a young man, I often went to the Theatrical alone to soak up the atmosphere established by the jazz music provided by the local quartet. Many of the Cleveland movers and shakers dined at the Theatrical, and as a young man, I went to observe and learn. When I was dating Ethelda, I tried to impress her by taking her to dinner at the Theatrical, and I hit a home run. It was raining the night Lou and I pulled in front of the restaurant. I let Congressman Stokes off at the door so that he could secure a table while I parked the car. Lou entered the revolving door and before I could shift into drive, he had made a full circle and made a beeline to the car, proclaiming, "Bill, they have naked girls twirling on poles." Evidently, since I had left Cleveland, the Theatrical began catering to a different crowd and had gone the burlesque route. As a congressman, the last thing Lou wanted was for people to think that he was frequenting naked bars. We ended up eating dinner at the Top of the Town.

CHAPTER 16

Making Strides

1987 Negotiations

The negotiations of 1987 were successfully concluded without arbitration, but the untold story of that event is the failure of the negotiators to anticipate the effects of the significant change to the contract termination date. Negotiating pay increases, which happened in the '87 negotiations, has hidden consequences. The negotiators successfully managed a pay increase but only by moving the contract expiration date from July to November. On the surface, this move appeared to be no more than watering down the effect of the pay increase in the final year. A pay increase for a period of sixteen months has less value than one for twelve months, so the negotiators agreed to limit the total cost of the 1987 agreement by adding four months at the end. This decision was a calculated move to achieve agreement. What we failed to consider was the effect that the November expiration would have on subsequent negotiations.

In contract negotiations, each party has a limit within which they are willing to negotiate. These determinations are made prior to bargaining, and the job of the union and management officials at the bargaining table is to achieve agreement within those parameters. As bargaining proceeds, prior to the finalization of verbal agreements, if there are deviations from the anticipated issues, before agreement can be reached concurrence must be received by higher level management officials. In the selection of November as the termination date of the 1987 contract, we failed to address the specific impact of the month selected. By changing the expiration date to November, the agreements were finalized during the holidays when everyone was busy with family obligations that interfered with bargaining issues receiving their full attention. We should have foreseen the problems this would interject in the subsequent rounds of bargaining.

The failure to anticipate the impact resulted in the 1990, 1994, and 2000 negotiations being deferred to arbitration because the negotiators were preoccupied. Even when we were close to an agreement on the wage package, decision-makers were unavailable within the scheduled time frame, and the negotiators took the easy way, deferring the contracts to arbitration. The higher level management officials who must give their blessing to any agreement prior to a commitment were, to varying degrees, indisposed during that time. We could have extended the termination date of the contracts, but that would have diluted the momentum built up over the bargaining period. The resulting impact on the negotiations and the Mittenthal, Clarke, and Goldberg awards that perhaps could have been avoided taught us to pay closer attention to these issues, which do not readily come to mind in the heat of the final days of negotiations that involve huge sums of money. Such issues can be the difference between a future negotiated contract and arbitration where past gains will be exposed.

The 1987 negotiations did result in an agreement on a memorandum on child care in union-operated facilities, which had become a prime objective of the union. As the number of female postal employees increased dramatically, the need for child care expanded, and the intent was to incorporate centers in the workplace. The San Francisco Local successfully opened a center that was a model for the service. Those negotiations will also be remembered for a memorandum negotiated by the Mail Handlers that summed up their bargaining strategy to achieve benefits equal to APWU. It read as follows:

> If any of the subjects enumerated below, as set forth in the successor agreement to the 1984 APWU/NALC National Agreement, are more favorable to employees covered by the APWU/NALC National Agreement, with respect to the subjects enumerated below, than those set forth in the 1987 Mail Handlers National Agreement, such more favorable provisions shall be extended to the employees covered by the 1987 Mail Handlers National Agreement, on the same date that such provisions become effective for employees covered by the successor Agreement to the APWU/ NALC National Agreement.

In later APWU national negotiations, after the NALC had elected to bargain separately, there were extensive discussions within APWU on whether or not to introduce a "me too" clause as a bargaining demand. In internal confidential discussions, I strongly resisted this proposal. If negotiators are not confident in their ability to achieve the very best possible deal in negotiations, it is time to go to arbitration. (Moe once said to me to never use the phrase "That's the best that I can do." It's an invitation to the members to get someone who can do better.) Relying on the success of another union is unprofessional and not worthy of the largest union in the postal service.

Tony Frank

In 1988, Anthony "Tony" Frank assumed the position of postmaster general. He initiated policies that APWU found detrimental to the interest of the American public and postal employees. After repeated confrontations, Moe issued a public demand: "Frank Must Go." Moe's New York public relations consultant, Danny Frank (no relation), was brought in to initiate public demonstrations against the postmaster general.

Postmaster Frank's most devastating decision was the subcontracting of the remote encoding operation. Previously the letters that could not be read on the letter sorting machines (LSMs) were processed manually, requiring skilled employees who were knowledgeable about the distribution schemes. With the introduction of encoding, this process was automated. The images of the misaddressed letters were transmitted electronically to remote postal facilities where employees with the aid of computer programs, including a nationwide address system, replaced the address and returned the correctly addressed mail piece into the processing system. The system was designed to replace the highly skilled employees with lower skilled and lower paid employees to perform the same functions.

This process was a major blow to APWU as tens of thousands of manual distribution and LSM jobs were involved. The unions arbitrated the pay grade and succeeded in elevating the pay grade to level 4. Changing the pay grade did not resolve the issue of mail processing being performed in remote locations, but over time, we succeeded in incorporating the assignment into the national agreement. In later years, the number of REC sites was reduced dramatically, and the Goldberg arbitration award in 2000 eliminated the pay disparity. However, at the time of the implementation, this was a major issue.

1988 National Convention

The 1988 National Convention was held in Chicago and was attended by the largest number of delegates (3,396) in APWU history. Kitty Dukakis, wife of the Democratic candidate for president; Senator Stevens; Congressmen Bill Ford and Bill

Clay; and Chicago Mayor Sawyer were the guest speakers, but no issues of major importance were approved by the delegates.

In his opening remarks, President Biller reported that the APWU had more national officers than any union in Washington, DC. American Federation of State, County, and Municipal Employees (AFSCME) had over one million members and two elected officers; United Food and Commercial Workers (UFCW) had nearly one million members and five elected officers; Communications Workers of America (CWA) had more than 500,000 members and five elected national officers. APWU had 278,000 members and twenty-one elected officers. Moe's report was intended to set the stage for APWU restructuring, but the resistance to eliminating positions prevailed, and the convention was unable to make any progress on reducing the number of officers.

Because of the size of the APWU national convention, the host city convention centers compete with each other by offering a variety of incentives to the union, including free room accommodations for the top officers. The accommodations for Moe and me at the Chicago Hilton were lavish, with the two of us occupying the entire top floor. We even had a helicopter pad outside our doors, and President Biller performed a marriage ceremony for APWU members Jack and Regina Aiello.

Apartheid

Throughout the 1980s, the developed counties joined with the struggle waged by the black natives of South Africa to gain their freedom from the oppressive policies of apartheid. The European Union and Japan passed economic sanctions, and apartheid became a hot political issue in the United States. After four hundred years of slavery in the United States, followed by repressive state laws denying human rights, American politicians had the opportunity to make amends and support freedom in the native land of the American slaves, but Congress did not pass legislation until 1986. President Reagan vetoed the legislation with the support of many Republicans, but there were a sufficient number of legislators who believed in freedom for all people. They overrode the veto, and America joined with the world community condemning apartheid.

In 1989, the continued imposition of apartheid in Africa dominated the press, and labor unions joined with other organizations that demanded increased sanctions on the South African government. The Republican Party repeatedly opposed American sanctions, and there were frequent public protests. Moe was constantly searching for social issues, and the free Africa movement was a natural cause for the APWU. We participated in an illegal picket of the South African Embassy. The proceedings were orderly and peaceful, but we were all handcuffed, arrested, and taken to jail in a paddy wagon. During the ride to the police station, Myke Reid, Roy Braunstein, and I were seated in the police vehicle with our hands cuffed behind us, whereupon Myke ingeniously freed his hands. I warned him that, if discovered, he would face the additional charge of "attempting to escape." We were booked and later released on our own recognizance, but we were fingerprinted and have an arrest record. It was for a good cause.

When apartheid was lifted in 1994 and the first truly fair elections were held, I authorized eight APWU officers, including Sidney Brooks and Teddy Days, to travel to South Africa to serve as official AFL–CIO observers of the election. They returned with amazing stories of the hardships endured by Africans who were voting for the first time, and they brought me a sample ballot used in the election. Because of the dearth of educational opportunities, many of the first-time voters could not read, so the ballot was organized by colors and party symbols so that candidates could be identified. I proudly display the ballot used in the election of Nelson Mandela in my library.

Sears

In their continuing efforts to privatize postal services, management initiated discussions with Sears to contract retail service centers in their network of stores. We did not automatically oppose the idea, provided that professional postal clerks would staff the centers. When we found out that Sears intended to use their own employees, we strongly objected. As the discussions continued over several months, it became clear that a mutually acceptable arrangement was not forthcoming. The union engaged in nationwide pickets and demonstrations, and I drafted a letter for Moe's signature to Sears CEO Edward A. Brennen that respectfully but clearly informed him that APWU would not accept the transfer of postal jobs to nonunion Sears employees. The letter further stated that if they proceeded to finalize a contractual agreement, the union would call for a boycott of Sears among its members. Within a month, Sears announced that it was severing the private postal retail initiative. Years later, Hallmark explored similar arrangements, but they too were convinced that postal employees would protect their jobs. APWU has long supported the expansion of the postal retail footprint, but we adamantly opposed the use of private workers to perform postal functions.

My Mother

On November 22, 1989, my mother, Gertrude Rushian Burrus Morris, succumbed to cancer. She died peacefully and left behind her son, daughter, and husband who loved her dearly and miss her to this day. She was our mother. Jane and I formed a bond with our mother that lasted into adulthood. We had lived with Mother in Cleveland, and after she relocated to Detroit, she often visited us in Cleveland. Jane moved to Hawaii, and Mother and I traveled to her home for family gatherings. Frank Morris, Mother's husband, was a kind and gentle man who fostered our relationship.

My mother was blessed with good looks, and being the youngest girl in a family of five, she was spoiled, too. Her brother lived around the corner from us in Wheeling, and as a child, I often waited for him to come home from his job at the mill. He would stop and share snacks from his lunchbox with me, and we would chat uncle to nephew. Uncle Jack was my connection to my mother after she left the family during the early years. Years later, during my army service, Uncle Jack was killed in an automobile accident one week before my discharge. I did not know and when I arrived at his house in Wheeling, I was given the terrible news that he had been buried the day before. He was a good guy.

Finding herself in Wheeling, West Virginia, with two children under the age of four was obviously not consistent with Mother's expectations for her life's journey, and she did what she did. As a child, I was told that my mother was pretty, so I scoured *Jet* and *Ebony* magazines in the family-owned newsstand looking for a picture of her because that was where pretty colored women could be found. Years later as president of the union, I was honored to have my picture in *Jet* and *Ebony* magazines on a number of occasion as one of the 100/200 most influential African Americans in the United States, but I never found my mother's picture there.

The earliest memory I have of my mother is of when she came to Wheeling to visit Uncle Jack. She asked that Jane and I come to see her. We walked the block to our uncle's house not knowing what to expect. When we entered the room, there were several women there, and I did not know which one was my mother. When a beautiful lady opened her arms, we embraced, forming an instant bond. Our father was sufficiently kind, gentle, and understanding and never spoke an unkind word about our mother at home, so as we matured, we accepted the past and were able to build a wonderful relationship.

Jane and I visited Cleveland that summer to spend our vacation with Mother. She bought me my first bike and a BB gun. My father was not too pleased with the gun, but he let me keep it. The following summer, Jane elected to stay in Cleveland to attend school, but I wanted to return to be with our mother.

In 1988, I had the occasion to bring Mother to the San Francisco convention, where she sat in the visitors section and derided delegates for blocking her view of the big screens showing the convention proceedings. She announced to all who were within earshot, "Get out of the way; that's my son."

When I returned to the office, I was catching up on neglected business after being out to attend my mother's funeral, Moe suddenly entered and demanded that I explain where I had been. I was taught at an early age to take my responsibilities seriously, so I reported to the office every day for thirty-seven years, missing a maximum of only thirty days over that entire period. I was blessed with good health, so I rarely took a sick day or even an "I don't feel good" day. With the exception of several seven-day vacations, my leave consisted of one day before a holiday and/or one day after. I was always at work, and it was expected that I would be there, so Moe's question was not unexpected. Even though I had not announced my mother's death, I did not anticipate Moe's tone, and I am sure that he regretted it when I told him I had just attended my mother's funeral.

Shattering the Glass Ceiling

The 1989 election was when the APWU shattered the glass ceiling with the election of Joyce Robinson, president of Richmond, Virginia, as the first female resident officer—the director of research and education—and Elizabeth "Liz" Powell, national business agent, as the first female member of the executive board. In my early days of postal employment, there were few female postal workers, and through the years, many were denied inclusion. Joyce and Liz were among the first and have served admirably to date. Through her role as director of research and education, Joyce has trained an entire generation of APWU representatives who are simply the best in protecting the rights of postal employees.

Joyce and Liz were among the founding leaders of POWER, in tandem with their friend Josie McMillan, and Joyce has served as a mother hen over the intervening years. Upon my retirement, Joyce organized a tribute from POWER that stretched my imagination, and I will be eternally grateful. The POWER sisters who honored me were Joyce Robinson, national coordinator; Carolyn J. Watson of the central region; Rachel Walthall of the eastern region; Ivona Palmer of the northeast region; Gayle J. Vincent of the southern region; and M. Joanne Holiday of the western region.

Moe's Appointment to the AFL–CIO

In 1989, President Biller was appointed vice president of the AFL–CIO executive council. His predecessor, Emmett Andrews, had held this position, but for eight years after his election, Moe was denied the privilege, prestige, and honor. Doug and I were aware that this denial was a constant irritant to Moe even though he did not often speak of the snub. As a native of New York, steeped in the tradition of organized labor, Moe coveted the position of vice presidency of the council. It is suspected that the reason for the delay of appointment was because years before Moe had been caught up in Senator McCarthy's web of accusations and was charged with consorting with the Communist Party, a charge for which he was never officially cleared. Doug and I were extremely happy when Moe became a coveted member at the table of organized labor. We knew that he was proud.

Legal Challenges

In the early 1980s, the postal service changed the rules, permitting mailers to reduce American postage by diverting mail to international remailers. In response, the APWU and NALC sued the postal service in federal court, alleging a blatant violation of Private Express Statutes, which restricted mail delivery to the postal service. The unions prevailed at the Washington DC

Circuit Court of Appeals, but the decision was appealed to the Supreme Court, and Moe and I had the privilege to be present when Keith Secular, the counsel for the NALC, presented his oral argument before the justices. The Supreme Court ruled in favor of the defendants, citing archaic exceptions to the postal monopoly that workers do not have standing to bring suit.

Later, in a similar scheme to avoid US postage, the postal service would devise a scheme in partnership with React Postal Service to prop up a private mail delivery company that seriously modified the Private Express Statute. APWU legal counsel filed a restraining order and prevailed before Judge Bruce Jenkins. This decision was subsequently overturned by the Tenth Circuit Court of Appeals. The delay exposed the intended unraveling of the postal monopoly, and in 1985, the Salt Lake City firm lost financial backing and discontinued the mail processing business.

In 1989, the unions and the postal service joined efforts to remove the postal service from the federal budget. Moe retained the services of the high-caliber K Street lobbyist Leticia Chambers to lobby Congress on the union's behalf. We described the acts of Congress as treating the postal service as the "cash cow" for federal deficits, and on December 2, 1989, we succeeded in having the USPS revenues and expenses removed from the federal budget. During the period that postal revenue and expenses were recorded in the federal budget, Congress often found it convenient to impact postal solvency in addressing federal budgetary issues. This successful effort was later negated by the Postal Accountability and Enhancement Act (PAEA) of 2006 that found a new approach to shifting USPS resources to the federal books by requiring that the postal service prefund future health care costs. While we were making strides, there were always setbacks.

CHAPTER 17

Advances and Setbacks

Postal Employees Relief Fund

In 1990, a series of weather-related disasters struck the South and West, and APWU locals throughout the country wanted to be of assistance. Many locals rented trucks, purchased supplies, and transported emergency items to the stricken communities. I evaluated the assistance that could be provided by the national union without duplicating the efforts of others.

During my postal employment in Cleveland, I had initiated a savings scheme where all employees in a work center could commit to saving a specific amount each pay day: $5, $10, $15, or $20. They would receive the year's worth of savings on a date determined by a blind draw—and before making all the contributions. For example, if an employee committed $10 per pay day for twenty-six pay dates, the employee would receive $260 on a date determined by drawing lots, even before having contributed their $260. It was an interest-free loan. The key was ensuring that they contributed the agreed-to amount after they collected. Being the originator of the idea, I was the banker and was responsible for the collection and distribution of the money.

As you can imagine, I often had to chase down participants who had collected their money but had not paid for the year.

This experience inspired the idea of the postal unions and postal management creating a fund to assist postal employees affected by natural disasters. Each of the unions made an initial contribution of $100,000, and the postal service contributed $200,000. With this seed money, Attorney Susan Catler of O'Donnell, Schwartz, and Anderson filed the necessary paperwork to create the Postal Employees Relief Fund, and we began providing grants to postal employees affected by natural disasters. The fund solicited contributions from postal employees, and it became a part of the Combined Federal Campaign. I served as the initial chairman of the fund until taking office as president of the APWU in November of 2001. Upon my resignation as chairman, I designated Sue Carney, director of human relations, to serve as the APWU representative. Sue is an excellent advocate, serving with distinction as of this writing.

Robin Bailey, my executive assistant, served as the administrative assistant to the Postal Employees Relief Fund from its inception until I resigned the chairmanship in 2001. Over the years, the fund has provided tens of millions of dollars in financial assistance to postal employees who suffered major losses from natural disasters.

Moe's Compassion

Moe always had compassion for the underrepresented. When the students at Gallaudet University in Washington, DC, protested in anger when the board announced its decision not to fill the presidency with a deaf candidate, Moe eagerly lent support to the grieving students, and the officers and staff of APWU joined them in picketing the administration. APWU was the first labor union to show its solidarity with the deaf students, and they credited Moe in part for their ultimate success. Years later, while I was browsing in an airport store while waiting for my departure, a gentleman noticed my APWU briefcase and asked about the health of Moe Biller. He introduced himself as Mr. I. King Jordan, the first deaf president of Gallaudet, the one that we had supported.

The solidarity at Gallaudet, the apartheid struggle, and the battle to remove the federal employment ban for air traffic controllers were among the many social issues that Moe championed over his career. He was a defender of the underdog and could be counted on to support issues of conscience. During those years, no other federal union had equal impact on the labor movement.

Consistent with Moe's affinity for the underrepresented, he supported the efforts of the deaf and hard of hearing APWU members to achieve representation within the union. When the postal service transitioned from manual sortation to LSMs, they had aggressively hired deaf applicants under the misconception that they would be more productive due to their communication limitations. The expectations that lost productivity would be curtailed did not come to fruition; even though the employees were limited in verbal communications, hand signals were used. Integrating deaf employees into the mail processing environment created new and unexpected challenges such as issues of TTYs and interpreting services.

Moe understood the importance of empowering individuals to represent themselves and providing them equal opportunities, and we worked for inter-union identification and representation for the deaf and hard of hearing. At the 1988 National Convention, the delegates approved the next step and created the Deaf and Hard of Hearing Task Force, charged with coordinating APWU efforts of representing deaf employees. Now, by constitution, a deaf representative is included in contract negotiations, and the deaf and hard of hearing have become integrated in the full range of APWU activities. Through the years, with their counsel, we have removed many barriers to equal employment.

Mittenthal

The negotiations of 1990 concluded in arbitration that was referred to Arbitrator Mittenthal. His selection was a major mistake. In the past, Mittenthal had arbitrated a number of important national cases, including the relationship between light and limited duty and promotion pay. In each case, the final decision was constructed without rationale, indicating that Mittenthal hadn't evaluated all of the evidence before coming to a conclusion.

Moe, the APWU's legal counsel, and I were responsible for the selection of Mittenthal. Unfortunately we did not vet him properly even though all of the signals were there that his decision would not be based on the evidence presented before him but on his preconceived views of what the resolution should be. In a prior decision on a promotion issue, for which Mittenthal was the arbitrator, he ruled in favor of a promotional system based on terms that did not appear in any postal documents and on a management argument that was not supported by any evidence. Larry Gervais, national business agent and union representative, had presented a thorough analysis of the pay system based on historical practice and contractual language, but in the end, since it did not meet the objective, Arbitrator Mittenthal created a new promotional system based on a hypothetical standard ("most prevalent step").

The issue of promotion pay created such consternation among the membership that the president of the Denver Local and a personal friend, Paul Mendrick, organized a group of dissidents to protest the national officers. They called themselves the POP, which stood for "Pissed-Off Presidents." Their grievance was that they were not being informed of efforts to confront management initiatives. In response, I began writing a regularly issued information sheet titled "Update" that I continued through the balance of my career. It included a continuous recap of national activity. Moe also convened a group of local and state presidents to come to Washington to map out a strategy to confront the dispute over promotions. John Richards, who had returned to

Pittsburgh as local president, titled the group the "Share the Blame Committee." John had a way with words.

The selection of Richard Mittenthal as the 1990 interest arbitrator was unusual to say the least. The attorneys for NALC, APWU, and the postal service were meeting in the APWU boardroom, attempting to agree to the selection of an interest arbitrator. Having failed to agree on several names, each attendee was asked to write a name on a piece of paper and turn it face down. When the choices were uncovered, all had written the name Mittenthal. After making the selection, the attorneys met with Moe and me and revealed their recommendation. With some reservations, Moe and I concurred. The attorneys then called Mittenthal to determine if he would be receptive. Mittenthal had served the parties for many years as a national level arbitrator.

Mittenthal expressed his concern that, historically, if unions were dissatisfied with interest decisions they often discontinued the service of the arbitrator to interpret the agreements. We assured him that we would continue his service as an arbitrator, and he accepted the assignment. Following receipt of his irrational decision, Moe refused to renew his contract as an arbitrator, but Tom Neil, the director of industrial relations, continued to assign him cases until he was replaced by Arbitrator Daas.

We should have known better in our selection, but having made it, we should not have been surprised when he granted the postal service transitional employees (TEs). This decision was handed down even though there were no records that USPS negotiators had proposed the category during negotiations, and there was no record of a disagreement between the parties. Nevertheless, he imposed the new category with scant knowledge of how these employees would be incorporated into the bargaining unit. He compounded the problems with the decision by referring the many issues involved in their integration to the unions—NALC and APWU separately—and reserved final authority if the parties did not agree. In addition to the new category of employees—

the TEs—the 1990 award included modest salary increases; continuation of COLA; and a change to the staffing requirements from 90–10 to 80–20, which mitigated the success achieved in 1981 to increase the number of full time employees. He also added new entry steps and included the union request for a leave sharing program permitting employees to donate annual leave to coworkers.

Health Plan

During the 1984 negotiations, we agreed to establish a task force to explore a USPS health plan covering all represented bargaining unit employees. The negotiators did not make a serious effort to reach agreement on the structure of USPS health care administration. The JBC presented a proposal that allowed the health plan benefit to be converted to APWU/USPS and NALC/ USPS Plans, resulting in all APWU-represented employees being covered by this single plan. The proposal was that these plans be jointly administered and all decisions be made by the equally represented administrators. The new plan would save the USPS money and would release the parties from the jurisdiction of Federal Employees Health Benefits (FEHB).

One of the misunderstood features of USPS health coverage, though, is that FEHB does not actually provide health coverage. It only administers independent health plans like APWU and NALC to federal and postal employees. The question of concern was this: If the postal service or an independent federal agency filed for bankruptcy, would the retirees and active employees continue health coverage? The issue is complicated, but in general if the postal service filed for bankruptcy and the courts did not require the continued payment of the employer's share of health premiums, FEHB would not provide health coverage for employees of a defunct agency. The health care provider—Blue Cross, APWU, or NALC—would not continue coverage without payment. FEHB is not a shield against the loss of coverage in extreme situations.

The discussions were extensive, but the USPS negotiators insisted that the Financial Accounting Standards Board (FASB) would require the postal service to include health care costs in their annual financial reporting. The unions maintained that the FASB rules did not apply, but in the event that it was found otherwise, they would use their political clout to obtain an exemption. The discussions ended in a stalemate, and the APWU/NALC-represented employees continued in the FEHB program. Later the PAEA of 2006 proved that the 1990 negotiations were a missed opportunity that would have avoided the onerous payments of five billion dollars plus per year. As I write this memoir, the interest for a postal health plan has shifted from the unions to postal management that now appreciates the tremendous costs savings that could be generated from a postal only plan.

Upon the receipt of the Mittenthal decision, I was assigned as the APWU negotiator on the work rules for the newly imposed transition employees, and I reasoned that if Mittenthal had intended to integrate them into the regular pay scale, he would have done so in his initial award. This reasoning was my rationale in the subsequent negotiations that resulted in the placing of TEs in the pay scale but excluding them from cost of living adjustments and requiring an impact statement before hiring. I calculated that this arrangement would be better than resubmitting the entire subject of wages back to Mittenthal, who would have the latitude of creating a whole new wage scale applicable exclusively to transitional employees. I obviously calculated wrong because after APWU reached agreement, Mittenthal ruled on the USPS/ Letter Carrier impasse that letter carrier TEs would receive full inclusion in the pay scale with COLA. To this day, I do not understand why, if that was his intent, he did not decide the salary at the time he included them in the bargaining unit.

Mittenthal also deferred the issue of the division of health plan premiums between employees and the employer to a separate arbitration panel for resolution. The division of health plan premiums had become a hotly contested issue as postal management and conservative politicians argued that the health benefit contribution ratio of the postal service employees should match those of federal employees. The argument was bogus because the law does not compare postal employees to federal employees but to those in the private sector. Nevertheless, the issue gained traction, and it was clear that it would be addressed. The deferral by Mittenthal required an entirely different arbitration on the sole subject of the division of the premium. The unions were aware that adverse change was very possible.

After several weeks of hearing, the new arbitrator, Voltin, instructed the parties to prepare a "last best final offer" (LBFO), and he would select as his decision the one that more closely fit his desired solution. In the unions' preparation to write an LBFO, APWU and NALC differed sharply on its construction. NALC believed that the appropriate strategy was to take a strong position on the shifting of cost, leaving the arbitrator the option of maintaining the status quo. I argued forcefully that the unions should show flexibility and offer concessions. It was my opinion that in the LBFO we should gravitate toward the middle since the arbitrator will likely accept the more flexible offer—the lesser of two evils. I was successful in whittling the unions' proposal around the edges, but as the arbitrator defined it in his ruling, the unions' proposal "promises little relief, now or ever." We had gambled, and Voltin accepted the USPS's LBFO, which changed the division of health care premiums to the detriment of employees.

Retirees

The 1992 National Convention established the APWU Retirees Department, which was modeled in part after the Letter Carriers and incorporated retirees into the APWU. John R. Smith was appointed as the initial director and relocated to Washington. The objective was to create a forum for retiring union members to continue their involvement and affiliation with their former coworkers. It was recognized that retirees would be a major source for COPA contributions and other political activities as they were beyond the restrictions applied to active employees. Later in our administration, Doug Holbrook served as the director of the Retirees Department and skillfully made the department an integral part of the union. Retirees' COPA contributions were disproportional to their percentage of the union, and they played a major role in my achieving the one million dollar goal I had set. Doug was determined that they receive appropriate representation in the political arena. On one occasion, he took me to task for being ineffective in achieving legislation benefiting retirees.

Marvin Travis Runyon

Throughout the period of the Biller and Burrus administrations, we had difficult relationships with the various postmasters general, none more celebrated than that with Marvin Runyon. He had been preceded by Tony Frank, who came from the private financial sector. After serving as the chief executive of the Tennessee Valley Authority, Marvin Runyon assumed the reins of PMG with the intent of completely remaking the postal service. He began by replacing the USPS logo that had identified the postal service for over two hundred years.

Early in our contact with Runyon, in a private meeting with Moe and me, he promised to eliminate the handbooks and manuals that had been a source of disagreement between the union and management because they were not subject to the negotiation process and were routinely modified without full bargaining. This initiative was thwarted by postal officials, but Runyon followed through with his plan to reduce the size of the workforce by removing assignments that "did not touch the mail." Postmaster General Runyon did so much to remake the postal service that he assumed the moniker "Carvin' Marvin." We were happy to celebrate his retirement, but our celebration was short-lived because our experience with his successor, William

Henderson, was even more negative. With my experience of interacting with eighteen postmasters general, I conclude that my negative opinions are influenced more by our competing roles than any personal deficiencies. On a positive note, Postmaster General Runyon joined with me in the founding of the Postal Employees Relief Fund; on behalf of the postal service, he made an initial contribution of $200,000.

Discord

Fissures began to appear in the relationship between Moe and I. We were two strong personalities struggling to operate in unison. More often than not, we succeeded; but the relationship between us digressed to the point that Biller would grill anyone visiting my office as to the subject of our discussions. My policy had always been that my office doors were never closed. Members, officers, or staff could come in anytime they wanted, so anyone entering my office to engage in gossip or negative conversation would worry that someone might come in behind them and overhear the negative remarks. You would be surprised how some people in my office spent more time looking over their shoulder at the open doors than addressing me with their issue. Moe was the opposite. He instructed anyone entering or leaving his office to close the door behind them. I would continuously hear Moe's command, "Close that door," followed by his door banging shut. Even the secretaries were instructed to close the door.

Doug Holbrook served as peacemaker, smoothing out those rough periods, and we continued to administer the union. Moe is long deceased, so he can't share his side of the story, but even during our disagreements, my respect for his contributions to postal employees and his union was unwavering. We had disputes that can be attributed to each of us, but they did not detract from our efforts for employee representation. Individually and collectively, our focus was on the membership that we were privileged to represent.

CHAPTER 18

Realizing a Dream

The Election and Health Care Reform

In the 1992 election of officers, for the first time in his union career, Biller ran for president unopposed. Holbrook and I won handily, so we were poised for another term as the administrative officers.

In 1993, Moe became entwined in the debate over the structure of health care reform undertaken by Hillary Clinton on behalf of the president. The AFL–CIO was invited to engage in the discussions at the White House, and Moe was designated as a spokesman. He spent many days strategizing and planning the political strong points of a universal health care initiative. Lobbyists for the insurance industry brought out the big guns and finally succeeded in forcing President Clinton to withdraw his health care proposal.

During the Clinton presidency, I had the occasion to be invited to a signing ceremony on the White House lawn. I do not recall the specific legislation, but among the invited guests was Michael Douglas, who stood directly beside me for two hours. We engaged in small talk, and it never occurred to me to mark the occasion with a signed autograph.

Another Home

Early in 1993, Ethelda and I began musing about what kind of a house we would build "if" we were to do it again. Our neighbor whose home was built by the same contractor that we had used constructed a new home in an exclusive neighborhood. It was the same three split-level design of his former home, only larger. Ethelda and I wondered why he would build the exact same home. We began musing about how we would find a different style if we decided to build another home. We were perfectly satisfied with the home we had designed and built in 1985. The landscaping had matured and it was our dream home, but we liked the process of building and the closeness that came from creating something together.

We purchased a few books on home designs and began exploring possibilities. One particular house design caught our imagination, and over several months we discussed its unusual features. Finally I purchased the blueprints, and we began discussing how we might personalize the plans. We had to find a new contractor because we wanted to more than double the size of our home and our first contractor's operation was too small. We began searching for a lot suitable for such a grand structure, but nothing worked out.

After months of searching and disappointments, I was reading the Sunday paper between Christmas and New Year's and noticed an ad promoting land sales. The ad read "All lots 5 acres or more at a set price in Croom, Maryland." That December morning, Ethelda and I drove to Croom and walked the lots. At the time of our viewing, there were eight lots still unsold, all the same price. One was eleven acres; it was tempting, but the trees overshadowed the location where the house would be constructed. We inspected each lot in about three inches of snow and settled on lot 5, which was 6.2 acres on a hill with a three-thousand-square-foot tobacco barn and a small livestock barn. The barns were built before nails, so the planks were connected by wooden pegs. There were many tobacco barns in the Croom community as that was the area farmer's main cash crop. After the health community exposed the dangers of smoking, many of the farms were sold, and our area, West End Farms, was subdivided into thirty-five lots of five or more acres. The large barn on the property was for tobacco curing and storage, and there was an auction house several miles away in Upper Marlboro where the farmers would transport their crop for sale.

Upon selecting lot 5, I proceeded to inform the developer that we wanted to put a "hold" on the property. He responded that if we wanted it, we would have to buy it on the spot. We had come to look at property, not to buy it, but it was decision time. We elected to purchase the lot, and throughout the following two years before construction, we took friends and family out to see the land, picturing where the house would be built. I would scoop a handful of dirt and proclaim to Ethelda, "This is our land."

The relationship between me and the property was conflicting. I had read of the abuses of fellow human beings held as slaves in Maryland. They had been used to produce cash crops; now I owned the very land where they had been held hostage. To further compound the odd situation, the house that we would build on the land had more than a dozen huge white columns, the very image of plantations during the period of slavery. I guess each of us is full of contradictions.

When we built the house, digging a well was necessary as there was no water. There was no gas, public sewage treatment, or cable television. After construction began, we would drive the twenty-six miles from our existing home to monitor the progress and watch our dream take shape.

The architect finalized the conversion of the prints into construction drawings, and I began circulating them to interested contractors. The plans were for a Mediterranean-style structure, more commonly built in the South and Southwest, with no basement, a huge portico and veranda, and eight interlocking roofs. I didn't even know what the hell a portico or veranda was, but I was game. We added a basement and reversed the layout so that the garage was on the left side of the circular driveway and the bedroom windows had an expansive view of the wooded property. It is an eight-thousand-square-foot home that comprises more space than all of my previous residences combined. Every wall is angled so there is not a single wall that goes straight from corner to corner. The living room has a soaring twenty-five-foot-high ceiling, and the master bedroom and bath occupy more than one thousand square feet. We finally found a builder who was interested in quoting a price, and the bargaining began. I had spent my career negotiating, and this was personal. We went back and forth with proposals that culminated in a signed construction contract that was closer to my expectations than the opening bid. My secretaries must have been bored to death as I talked obsessively about the new house. Pictures and diagrams—they got the whole shebang.

Several years after we purchased the property, the house began to take shape to the point that one could discern the rooms, but there were no walls or windows. We decided to host a "construction party." We invited perhaps sixty of our friends, children included, to visit, and in each room we had a copy of the blueprint showing how that room would look when completed. The event was a smashing success.

Breakup Of JBC

In 1994, the Letter Carriers informed us that it was their intent to negotiate a separate contract and dissolve the Joint Bargaining Committee (JBC). The announcement did not come as a major surprise, but it was disappointing to the APWU. Moe and his disciples truly believed in the concept of one union, and if joint bargaining was the closest we could get, it was better than nothing. The Letter Carriers could not achieve their highest priority, a universal upgrade, with three hundred thousand clerks, motor vehicle, maintenance, and special delivery employees who had to be included in any pay package.

So for the first time in the history of postal bargaining, APWU was negotiating alone. The negotiations once again were finalized in interest arbitration, and the APWU repeated the 1990 debacle in the selection of an arbitrator. We selected Jack Clarke, an arbitrator educated at Auburn University and steeped in the traditions of the Deep South.

Clarke's final decision was a reasonable one, but it reflected a bias against wages received by postal employees. In the selection of Clarke, we did not consider the cultural biases he inherited from being in a nonunion environment throughout his formative years. As a southerner, he was exposed to a wage structure influenced by the inability of workers to make collective demands, and the salary of postal workers exceeded that of many professionals in his community. As a lawyer, his firm's staff was compensated competitively for the area, but the postal workers in the same community received wages far exceeding the employees in his office. So when deciding our dispute, he brought to bear those biases, and we ended up with a decision that was convoluted.

We got a four-year contract and new pay steps that merged into the continuing pay scale, and we lost several COLAs. Included in the Clarke award was a modification of the calculation of pay for work between the hours of 6:00 p.m. and 6:00 a.m., referred to as night differential. It had been the practice long before postal collective bargaining to pay the night differential 10 percent more than regular hourly pay. When hourly wages were increased, the night differential would increase as well, but Clarke elected to apply a fixed reduced amount for the differential, which resulted in a significant pay reduction. During the hearing, no testimony had been offered to change the calculation of night differential, but Clarke decided to reduce labor costs in this novel way. I did not think that the decision was fair, based on the evidence presented.

The Clarke award eliminated the delayed COLA roll-in that was initiated in 1981 and allowed the postal service to avoid paying the retirement contribution. The postal service had been under continuing pressure from OPM over the delayed payments, and Arbitrator Clarke removed the separation between base and basic pay.

During the Clarke arbitration, APWU counsel Art Luby was presenting the union's case on maximizing the number of full-time employees, and I was exasperated over the line of questioning. Sitting beside Art Luby, I interjected comments as he presented the case, and in an act of frustration, Art instructed me to proceed with the presentation. Arbitrator Clarke observed the confusion at our table, and after a limited number of questions from me, he sent a clear signal that he would not permit me to function as counsel.

Since I served as a union official, concluding that my views of the Mittenthal and Clarke awards were biased was easy. However, over the many years of my career, I have learned to accept a reasoned decision as valid, provided that it is based on the evidence. One can say that evidence can be influenced by one's perspective, but black is black and white is white. I reject the conclusion that white is black.

Discounts and Contracting

In their continuing effort to reduce mailing costs beyond the use of rate discounts, the USPS began to partner with large mailers in the performance of sortation functions before entering mail into the mail stream. The policy of reducing postage equal to the postal cost avoided led to a billion-dollar industry, and when money in that amount is in play, the recipients will find novel ways of qualifying. Under the leadership of Biller and Burrus, the APWU aggressively opposed these blatant violations of universal rates. With the help of Senator Lieberman, we were successful in tying the discounts directly to the postal costs avoided, but that has not been adequate to stem the loss of billions in revenue. As the postal service has become more efficient in the processing of mail, the volume of mail processed by postal employees has been reduced. This reduction actually raised the cost per letter. The more productive that the postal service became, the greater discounts the large mailers demanded. This practice has piggy-backed on relationships formed by mailers through their proximity to postal officials who allocated office space to the mailers in USPS headquarters at L'Enfant Plaza. As single-piece first class declined because of the increase in electronic diversion, the Mailers Technical Advisory Committee developed unique strategies to maintain their subsidies, and Moe and I constantly waged battle with those parasites to first-class volume.

One way large mailers reduced their postage costs was by convincing postal management to outsource entire mail processing functions. They concluded that having the work performed by low-paid, nonunion private-sector workers would generate increased profits for their executives and also continue low cost delivery of their product. They were not merely satisfied to enjoy the cheapest postage in the world but were determined to keep it that way, so they convinced postal management to outsource the processing functions of priority mail. After a series of perfunctory meetings, a contract with Emery Worldwide was finalized, and the processing of priority mail was outsourced. Despite the APWU's protests, the outsourcing continued for several years until the cost to Emery exceeded the original expectations. When the contract was up for renewal, the postal service balked at paying the high increase, and at that point, I was able to negotiate the return of priority mail to the postal service. If the postal service returned priority mail to be processed by postal employees, the activity would be fully governed by the collective bargaining agreement. In difficult negotiations, I agreed to modify the percentage of non-career employees in the priority mail facilities and to waive the payment of penalty pay, but in return, I not only wanted the return of priority mail but also a resolution of the ongoing dispute regarding promotion pay.

Promotion Pay

In this ongoing promotional pay dispute, the postal service had interpreted the pay provisions to require that when an employee received a promotion, in many circumstances, the promotion would result in a loss of pay depending upon the step placement at the time of promotion. Mittenthal and Clarke added new steps to the pay schedule that contributed to this problem. The new steps created lower starting wages, but after a prescribed period the employee would merge into the former pay scale. The result was enormous increases when the employees were integrated into the old pay scale and created a pay anomaly when the employee could earn more if not promoted. The union had arbitrated this unique reading of the regulations, and Arbitrator Mittenthal had decided against the union, applying an invented term of "most prevalent step," determined by the dollar amount that was repeated most often in the step progression system. We had to find a way to overcome these arbitration decisions, and I decided to use the return of priority mail as the vehicle.

I had leverage because the postal service had rejected the conditions demanded by Emery for contract renewal and had decided to assume the processing of priority mail. I demanded resolution of the promotion pay issue, insisting that promoted employees would receive pay increases in all circumstances, and after tense negotiations, they agreed. After I had reached an agreement, I turned to my trusted technician, Phil Tabbita, who had designed the new pay scale and requested a remedy. Phil engaged in protracted discussions with his management counterpart, and after tense negotiations, we agreed to a remedy providing thousands of employees with lump sum payments to compensate for the losses. In addition, we had succeeded in eliminating the pay anomaly by restructuring the pay scale with equal increases between steps. This accomplishment, as well as the modification of the BMC keying stations, was truly revolutionary in that a labor union had such influence on employment decisions.

The mail handlers were livid about the delay in returning priority mail as they did not have a dog in the promotion pay dispute and were salivating over the new jobs in the PMCs. I was not particularly concerned as to how the mail handlers felt, and we proceeded and resolved that thorny issue.

Friends and Family

In 1995, there was a PTTI meeting in the Bahamas, and as usual, I secured transportation at our expense for Ethelda because I wanted her to accompany me on any trip out of the country. Ethelda had formed relationships with her coworkers at the University of Maryland, and when she learned that Jimmy Scafone, a maintenance worker, and his wife, Barbara, would be vacationing in the Bahamas during the same week that we would be there, she extended an invitation that we meet while there. This invitation was the beginning of a relationship to the extent that Jimmy and Barbara were our constant companions to many places, far and near. Barbara is different but Jimmy is cool. It rained every day in the Bahamas, and I accused Barbara of having her own personal rain cloud.

Ethelda often visited her family, who is from Kentucky just like my father's family. They lived a short distance from Cincinnati, Ohio. Her mother, LouElla, was a member of the Bond family, and much of the clan continues to reside in the area, including sisters-in-law Earnestine and Hattie Mae as well as cousins Thelma, Penny, Tiny, Pam, Dicky, Philip, Isaac, and Marty. Her father, William Harkins, was also a Kentucky native from Louisville as was her uncle Richard Hawkins, who was among the first group of black marines during World War II at Montford Point. The family is extremely proud of his receipt of the Congressional Gold Medal. For reunions, the family members—including Uncles Richard and Buddy and Aunts Eloyis, Jean, Janie, Alma, and Virginia—would assemble. The distance between our families in Kentucky was too great to expect a historic relationship, but our ancestors shared the common geographical area after slavery and eventually migrated to other sections of the country.

Ethelda's family is extremely close. She has a brother, Doctor Derrick Harkins, the minister, and a sister, Sylvia. Each relocated with their spouses and children to the Washington metropolitan area after Ethelda and I settled in DC. Her parents fostered their children's relationships, so they are extremely close. Upon the death of Mr. Harkins, LouElla relocated to our home, and the entire family was within a twenty-five-mile radius of one another. Sylvia has since moved to Tallahassee, Florida, to spend time with her grandchildren as they grow up, but she and Ethelda talk on the phone every day. The relationship brings back memories of my sisters and me.

Ethelda's sister, Sylvia Glover, accompanied us to many APWU functions, beginning with the 1976 National Convention in Las Vegas. She has been Ethelda's constant companion at many union events while I was engrossed in union affairs, and Sylvia became known to many of the APWU union members. Sylvia has also been especially helpful with gatherings at our home when we entertain large number of guests. I do not know what Ethelda would do without her.

Light Duty Bidding

Over the course of my career, I addressed hundreds of workplace issues sufficiently voluminous that a book, the *Burrus Book*, has been compiled devoted exclusively to those accomplishments. My memory of the specific issues fades over time, but one issue that seemed to be of little consequence at the time stands out for the hundreds of phone calls and letters it generated. The postal service had created major repercussions when it switched to the letter sorting machines as the primary means of mail sortation. Because of a faulty design, employees suffered work place injuries, and to contain their liability, postal management initiated a number of disincentives for employees seeking compensation for their injuries. The intent was to reduce the number of fake injury reports. One such disincentive was to deny injured employees the opportunity to bid or change work assignments by virtue of their seniority. This denial became a constant source of irritation. I was made aware of a decision in which the mail handlers were successful in processing a grievance on light duty bidding, and as I embarked on a search for a solution, I extracted from their resolve wording that would permit employees on light duty to bid for other assignments. An agreement was reached, and injured APWU-represented employees were afforded bidding opportunities.

Another issue that stands out is automatic retreat rights for excessed employees. When an employee was excessed from his or her assignment or facility, he or she was entitled by contract to return to the first vacancy in the former section or facility. Often the excessed employees would not know that vacancies existed, and they would fail to bid and would lose their retreat rights. My objective was to find a way that excessed employees could automatically submit a bid to their former work center from which they had been excessed. Under the postal policy at the time, excessed employees no longer had notice of available vacancies, and failure to bid negates the opportunity for excessed employees to return. Postal management would void multiple numbers of employees with retreat rights in the posting of a single vacancy. I negotiated a provision that permitted excessed employees to inform management at the time excessed of their desire to return and to have their seniority automatically applied when awarding an assignment. The newly negotiated provision leveled the playing field. There are dozens of other mutual contract interpretations that have proven to be equal in importance to newly negotiated provisions.

Two additional issues stand out in my recollection of successful representation: the right of employees to use leave without pay (LWOP) for approved absences and management's obligation to fill posted vacancies. The discussions of these issues took place over a period of years, but I finally succeeded in achieving management's concurrence that when an absence is approved, the employee may elect to use a combination of leave and leave without pay (LWOP) and may use leave in increments of 1/100 of an hour. This is important when an employee will be absent for a period that will exhaust his or her leave balance and the employee has not satisfied the requirement of six years of continuous service to achieve lay-off protection. A leave balance as little as one hour can be spread over several years, enabling the employee to receive continuous credit for being in a pay status.

An equally satisfying agreement was a provision requiring the filling of posted duty assignments. Local management had developed a practice of posting vacancies, and if there were no bidders, management would revert the assignment far beyond the limits of the contract (twenty eight days). The agreement required that the vacancies must be filled through the assignment of unencumbered employees or through the conversion of PTFs to full-time. This resolution created thousands of new full-time employees to fill the vacant assignments.

Strategy for Contract Enforcement and Unfinished Business

Traditionally grievances are contractually initiated at the local level and, after being denied at steps 1, 2, and 3, are then pursued at the national level. I found this process to be defective in that all of the facts of the original grievance clouded the interpretive question. Instead, during the early years of my service as executive vice president, I developed a strategy of writing a narrative in a letter to postal management that included specific contractual or handbook language and posed an interpretive question that had been addressed in a different form so the management response was dictated by previously resolved dictum. If management disagreed, I would initiate a grievance, but if they agreed, I had a mutual interpretation of a contractual provision. Over time, this practice became less effective as managers were instructed to ignore my inquiries.

One important issue that I failed to resolve was the seniority standing of women who were employed as temporary workers during the 1960s. The antidiscrimination laws enacted in the intervening years called into question whether these employees should be provided seniority for the years that they were denied career status. I had initiated a grievance while president of the Cleveland Local, and upon my election as vice president, I intended to raise it as a national issue and pursue it in court. In a similar case in the private sector (steel industry) in Pennsylvania, a case was taken to the US Supreme Court that decided that a seniority system that was not discriminatory could not be challenged based on past discriminations. I was denied the opportunity to make whole the thousands of female postal workers who were clearly the victims of discrimination.

Another issue of unfinished business was the botched drug sting arranged by the Cleveland postal inspectors. The inspectors had teamed with a postal employee who agreed to serve as a confidential informant. After a number of unsuspecting employees were arrested, it was discovered that the informant was not buying drugs from coworkers but was pocketing the bait money and arbitrarily identifying coworkers. In fact, it was the postal inspectors who were being shammed. Upon learning that the sting operation had gone astray, the postal service returned some of the fired employees to work, but a young man, Dukosta Smith, was not returned. Dukosta was the son of Dorothy Smith, who had housed me in Steubenville, Ohio, following my army service, and I demanded to know the criteria applied to return some employees. I initiated a grievance, and at the time of my retirement, it was still pending at the national level.

Candidates for Leadership Team

The 1995 national APWU election of officers exposed the periodic differences between Moe and me. Following the process initiated in our first election in 1981 and continued in subsequent elections, we assembled a team of officers consisting of the incumbents and new candidates who shared our philosophy of union representation. Tom Neil, who had succeeded John Richards as director of industrial relations, announced his retirement, and we wished to offer a candidate in the position. Moe favored Cliff Guffey, who was serving as the assistant director of the Clerk Craft. I was committed to Greg Bell, president of the Philadelphia Local and chairman of the Presidents' Conference. I had observed Greg in his roles and was convinced that he would serve in the director's position with distinction. I believed that Greg would bring a different perspective that would not be provided if the position were filled by an incumbent national officer. On the evening that the team met to select our candidate for the director's position, the protracted debate was filled with passion, but I was able to secure more votes for Greg than Moe did for Cliff, so Greg became a member of the 1995 leadership team, won his election, and has served continuously to date.

Modified Workweek

After the 1994 negotiations, I began exploring a modified workweek for postal employees. The forty-hour workweek of five eight-hour days was under attack. The federal government and growing numbers of private companies were exploring other options. I was a convert to the idea and engaged postal management in extended discussions, leading to a modified postal workweek. The most common alternative was four ten-hour days without overtime, but I did not want to be restricted to a single alternative. Forty hours can be divided into various components over a seven-day week, and I did not want to be restricted to only one option. After agreement was reached on the parameters of contract application, we agreed to pilot the concept in twenty-one offices where the local union and management volunteered.

At the end of the twelve-month testing period, I assigned Teddy Days, assistant director of motor vehicle services (MVS), the task of surveying management, employees, and local union leaders to determine the positives and negatives of the program. Teddy had served as president of the St. Louis Local and was among the representatives that I selected to observe the South African elections. He was a highly respected activist within the union, and I had every confidence in his judgment. Bill Downes, vice president of labor relations, was my partner in resolving many contractual interpretive issues and assisted me in this effort as well. Bill designated a headquarters' management official to join in the reviews, and the results were overwhelmingly positive. My intentions were to incorporate the workweek option into the national agreement, permitting the local union and management the opportunity to negotiate the application of this provision. However, somewhere in the bowels of postal management, there was opposition at the highest levels. A stumbling block in my discussions with Bill Downes was management's lack of authority to designate an entire section of employees for modified workweeks if one or more employees were opposed to the change.

I entered these discussions with a firm commitment to the five-day workweek as an employee option. I wanted to empower the employees to be able to choose which option worked best in their personal circumstances. I recognized that there were mothers who could not secure child care for ten hours a day, plus travel time, and employees who had supplemental employment and could not make the adjustment. There were also elderly employees who could not physically work ten-hour days. I wanted each participant to be a volunteer and rejected a forced modified workweek for those who did not want it. The system could work as I envisioned, but management pulled the plug.

AFL–CIO Election

Moe led an APWU delegation to the 1995 AFL–CIO convention that promised to be electric. President Lane Kirkland had announced his retirement, and for the first time in the history of the American labor movement, the office of president of the AFL would be contested. The APWU supported the candidacy of Tom Donohue, who had served with distinction as secretary treasurer for many years. The faction that supported Service Employees International Union (SEIU) President John Sweeney originally attempted to draft Tom Donohue to oppose Lane Kirkland, but out of loyalty to Lane, Tom refused. When it was determined that Lane intended to retire, opposing him was no longer an issue, so Tom was willing to run and announced his candidacy. By that time, the unions that wanted Tom to oppose Lane had shifted their support to John Sweeney.

The APWU, NALC, CWA, UFCW, and other unions with loyalty to Tom were unshaken in their commitment, so it came down to a test of support. Moe and I participated in a series of political meetings with supporters of Tom Donohue leading up to the convention, and consistent with Moe's intent to include activists in important events, Josie McMillian and Liz Powell were certified as delegates to be in attendance. The vote was close, but the overwhelming numbers of AFSCME, SEIU, and other large unions carried the day and John Sweeney was elected president. In the heat of the campaign, because of our support for Tom, threats were made that perhaps Moe would not be included in the Sweeney election slate, which would have meant that he would not be reelected as vice president since the slate of the victor for president carries the down ballot positions. They did not follow through with the threats, and Moe was reelected.

Following the election, in the middle of the convention, the chair was transferred from Lane Kirkland to John Sweeney. On the advice of the parliamentarian, John Sweeney announced that the dues increase was a part of a committee report, requiring only a majority vote for its adoption, and could not be amended. This move was clearly a violation of Robert's Rules, which specifically references the impropriety of attaching dues increases to committee reports. Despite my challenge to the propriety of this tactic, the chair proceeded, and dues were increased.

Merger

Moe began discussions with Morty Bahr, president of CWA, on the possibilities of a merger between APWU and CWA. I am not aware of how far they had proceeded, but Morty was invited to attend an APWU executive board meeting to share his concept of a merged union. I opposed the idea of a merger outside the postal arena while postal employees continued to be fractured among four unions (APWU, NALC, Mail Handlers, and NRLC). The APWU executive board was hostile to the idea, and I am not aware of any further discussions on an external merger.

Andy Stern, president of SEIU, was a strong advocate for the combining of all unions within an identified "sector." If enacted by the AFL, the governing union of postal employees would be either all government employees or in a communications union, depending on how narrow the divisions would be drawn. There are valid arguments for and against the concept. Andy became frustrated with the lack of interest on the part of many craft unions that have long and distinguished histories and removed his union from the AFL, forming a new federation called Change to Win. This academic argument supports the concept of unionism, but real life is not always consistent with logic. We are centuries away from the ideal union structure, and Andy was an impatient man.

Moving In to Our Dream Home

On December 31, 1996, after a year of construction and weather delays, our house was finally finished, and Ethelda and I moved into our dream home. We thought the first one was fabulous, but this one was a castle with fifty-two windows, a portico, and a huge veranda. We purchased a white, computer-operated piano for the sunken living room and suspended the seat from the twenty-five-foot ceiling with white chains. While dining with Josie and Liz at Jezebel's restaurant in New York, I noticed that the seating was suspended by chains and upon returning home discussed the concept with Ethelda. She thought I was crazy but warmed to the idea after Josie sent us a picture while construction was under way. We contracted with a three-hundred-pound carpenter who built the swing and assured us that it would carry his weight. I purchased the chain from the local hardware store and painted it in the garage. We now have this conversation piece as you enter through the front doors.

We also installed a shower in the master bathroom, a feature that I had not enjoyed in my previous homes. When I was in school, I showered following football and basketball practices and games, and showering was the only means of bathing during my three years in the army, but I had never used a shower in my private residence, not even in the house that we had built in 1985. The one we installed was not just a shower but one enclosed with glass blocks in a huge circle. We moved in on New Year's Eve; while the world was celebrating the dawn of a new year, we were supervising the movement of furniture and placement of boxes. For the next week, we devoted all of our time to relocating, and each day we marveled at our dream taking shape. Ethelda often tells associates that on the first morning in our new home she awoke and refused to open her eyes, praying, "Please, God, let this be for real."

In the summer of 1997, we held a formal open house. It was

a special black-tie and gown evening. Two drivers chauffeured the guests from the church parking lot two miles away to the entrance, where a long red carpet was laid across the portico. As each couple arrived, our friend Jimmy Scafone snapped their pictures that Ethelda included in a thank-you note the guests received weeks later. Barbara and our niece Christen conducted tours throughout the house. A young man with a violin circulated among the guests, and waiters served beverages throughout the house. It was a grand evening, and occasionally we view the tape and remember that magical evening. There were approximately two hundred guests in attendance, including APWU employees Conrad Carr, Angela Ross, Michelle Cochran, and Tad Kumlachew, who were all beautiful. All of the resident officers were invited, but Moe, Tunstall, and Guffey chose not to attend.

Toward the end of the evening, Ethelda and I ascended the steps to the balcony to toast our friends. To this day, Ethelda regrets that she didn't address the guests. Her mother and father were present as well as many other family members. My sisters, Jane and Effie, were present to represent my family, and Jane asked if she could say a few words. Who was I to dictate her right to speak? She shared with those assembled how proud our father would have been.

We have since added many features to our dream home, including a picture library overlooking the living and dining rooms where we display thousands of pictures and a walnut-paneled elevator that connects the master bedroom to the library below. The elevator is enclosed in glass walls, facilitating an unobstructed view of the property as it descends.

CHAPTER 19

Decision Time

Moe Experiences Health Problems

Moe began to experience health problems. Having turned eighty-three, he began to display medical conditions. On one occasion, he was dining with the board of governors at Duke Zeibert's restaurant when he collapsed. A member of the board who was a licensed physician resuscitated Moe, restoring his vital signs. I was not present, but the attendees consistently conveyed the seriousness of the situation to me.

Another situation that caused concern arose at the Philadelphia installation of officers. Because of my respect for the Philadelphia Local leadership, I had been at their installation of officers for many years, so Ethelda and I were in attendance for the installation of President Gwen Ivey, a lovely woman and strong supporter. The affair was proceeding wonderfully, and I was relaxed because it was a rare occasion that I did not have to give the keynote address because Moe was present.

The hidden secret about the positions of president and vice president is the expectation that they give an interesting speech on every public occasion. Your every word is followed with rapt attention. Another significant demand on the elected officers is the requirement to travel. The APWU represents members in every city. While serving as vice president, I traveled an average of two times a week, which meant waking early in the morning, traveling to the airport, and as often as possible returning home on the same day, even when visiting faraway places like Las Vegas and Seattle. On that night in Philadelphia, I didn't have to travel far and Moe was the speaker, so I could relax and enjoy the evening.

Moe began his presentation in his New York style, extolling recent events and the struggles ahead, when in mid-sentence, he fell strangely silent. For sixty agonizing seconds, he was frozen in place, making no motions and speaking no words. I caught the attention of the master of ceremonies and asked that he seat Moe and proceed with the program. After a brief period, Moe could communicate normally again and appeared to have recovered. I do not know the cause of the temporary loss of functions, but at that point, I realized that Moe's service as our leader was coming to an end.

Years later, I experienced a similar circumstance. Greg Bell and I had just landed after returning from a Presidents' Conference held in the East. As I rose to deplane, I experienced a violent dizzy spell for a brief period. Requiring Greg's assistance, I struggled to deplane and then had to wait ten minutes or more on the tarmac before I was able—with Greg's help—to walk to the terminal. The union's driver drove Greg home first, which was in the opposite direction of my home, so the drive lasted for a substantial period. By the time I arrived home, the dizziness had subsided. For the next several years, occasionally I would experience dizziness while flying, but my doctor could not identify the problem. Nevertheless, it brought my mortality to my attention. The problem subsided over time, but I drastically reduced my air travel. To this day, I am apprehensive when boarding an airplane.

Let Roy Speak

As we prepared for the 1998 election of officers, the political team met to form a slate of officers. During the discussions, Moe rejected Roy Braunstein as a member of the team for reasons that were never explained. I considered Roy to be an effective officer and good friend, so I insisted that he continue as a team member. An extremely confrontational meeting to resolve the issue ensued. The meeting lasted well into the night as Moe and I held fast to our positions. All of the team members in attendance knew that we had to include Moe as the leader, so a solution had to be found. The final agreement was that the team would not support any candidate for legislation director, but the team members were free to support a candidate of their choice. Moe supported Jim "Moose" Musumeci, president of the Brooklyn Local, and I supported Roy, who won handily despite a vigorous campaign by Moose.

I could never identify the animosity that Moe felt toward Roy. There was constant tension between the two of them that erupted from time to time into shouting matches and insults. Roy was a valuable contributor to postal issues on Capitol Hill, but Moe simply did not like him. Roy and his wife, Marilyn, became personal friends, and their sons, Rick and Daniel, helped Ethelda navigate her routes in the cities of the national conventions.

During the early years of our administration, Moe and I were engaged in restructuring. One of the positions we targeted was that of assistant legislative director. We believed that the position required knowledge of the political system that was not commonly found among postal employees. We proposed to eliminate the position, and as had been experienced in all other efforts to eliminate positions, there was stiff opposition. Myke Reid, who had served as staff in the legislative department, resisted the change despite assurances that his services would be retained.

Later at the 1998 convention, we attempted once again to remove the position of assistant director. As the convention delegates voiced their opinions, Roy refrained from speaking on the issue until the question had been called to close debate. When I asked the convention to vote, the delegates cried, "Let Roy speak." I was chairing the convention and had followed the mike rotation when the question was called for. Roy, having passed up the opportunity to speak in the rotation, had been silent on the issue affecting his department, so his supporters used his failure to speak as their battle cry. I permitted him to speak even though debate had been closed. He opposed its elimination. The resolution was defeated, and subsequently Roy became the director and Myke the assistant director.

Pig with Lipstick

The 1998 contract and its aftermath further exposed the separation between Moe and me. I do not blame Moe for the differences because I am sure that I played a part. During the final days of the 1998 negotiations, management made an anemic pay proposal (2 percent and 1.4 percent) that I considered inadequate. The fact that they made a proposal to increase wages indicated that there was flexibility, and I wanted to push to the limits. The postal service had experienced several years of surplus due to increased employee productivity, and it was my belief that the employees were entitled to a share.

Moe and I discussed the issue on the day prior to the deadline in the union office at the hotel where the negotiations took place. Moe agreed to push back and informed me when we retired for the night that he would contact me first thing in the morning to renew our discussions with management. I went to my hotel room and, upon waking early the next morning, went down to the union office to await Moe's arrival. When I arrived in the office, Randy Sutton, who was in charge of organizing the negotiations process, was nonresponsive when I asked if he had heard from

Moe. After several moments of small talk, he informed me that Moe had already reached an agreement with management.

I was livid. While there was no constitutional obligation for Moe to clear his decision with me, I had expected to be given an opportunity to have input into the final decision. We had worked as a team throughout the negotiations, and the night before we had agreed to reconvene before further discussions with management. The pay package was in the range of respectability, but we had been in agreement that there was more money on the table and that we would be remiss if we did not maximize the employees' wage increase.

Josie McMillan, president of New York, was the chairperson of the Rank-and-File Committee, and while she understood my views in opposition to the wage package, she was a strong supporter of Moe, and her endorsement made the difference. I was not swayed by the decision of the Rank-and-File Committee and proceeded to publically oppose the contract. During the ratification process, I called the tentative agreement "a pig with lipstick." The ratification was achieved with a comfortable margin, but I had decided to take a stand.

NALC Upgrades

The 1998 negotiations were a milestone for the letter carriers. In arbitration, they overcame a long-held objective of upgrading every letter carrier from level 5 to level 6. During the entire period of our joint bargaining, the letter carriers argued that their unique activities justified a higher rate of pay. Vince Sombrotto, an excellent advocate, had achieved their number one priority.

The success of the letter carriers obviously created great expectations among the APWU membership, and our conventions were dominated by resolutions on upgrades. Upgrades were something that I was only able to achieve incrementally, but in 2006, I successfully duplicated the NALC feat and negotiated the upgrade of every APWU-represented employee.

Harvard

Because of my standing as one of the few African American labor leaders in October 1998, I had the distinct honor and privilege to participate in an economic summit at *the* Harvard University, where I presented a paper, "Should There Be a Marshall Plan for the Inner City?" I shared with the attendees my views on the unlikely event that America would initiate a rescue plan similar to ones that had been provided to European countries following World War II. The capitalistic principles influencing our democracy resist the taxing of one segment of the population for the purposes of enriching another. Inner cities that had fallen victim to globalization were required to increase revenue streams to maintain public services. Failure to achieve the necessary balance of government revenue and expenses would lead to the ghettoization of the communities deserted by the middle class, and new communities would rise to become the town centers of America.

On a later occasion, when I was traveling first class on a flight from the West Coast, I engaged in conversation with the gentleman sitting next to me who was a fundraiser for the Republican Party and expressed negative opinions about the 2008 presidential election. During the conversation, he informed me that he was a graduate of Harvard and would work to defeat Obama in the next election. I told him of APWUs involvement in the Obama victory, and to counter his arrogance about graduating from Harvard, I informed him that "I had lectured there." His attitude of superiority was deflated just a bit.

The Letter

There were days following the 1998 negotiations when Moe and I barely spoke. He was suspicious of my every move, and I rebelled against his decisions. Looking back, notwithstanding the fact that Moe could be impossible at times, my actions were undisciplined and unacceptable. In anger, I wrote a factual letter itemizing Moe's imperfections and referencing the darker side of Biller. I forwarded it to Legislative Director Roy Braunstein, knowing full well that the contents of the letter would become public, but I was unprepared for Roy's decision to mail a copy to Gerry Monzillo, the New Jersey president, who distributed it nationwide. I immediately regretted writing the letter expressing my frustrations; to this day, I wish that I had handled the situation better. There was consternation throughout the union over a public dispute between the president and executive vice president. The dismay was short-lived as Moe and I quickly mended the riff and joined together on the team for reelection.

Another incident had occurred in my hotel suite at the national convention as we were convening key members of our political team to discuss strategy. Moe was late to the meeting, and just as I was informing the small group that no decisions could be made without Moe's input, he burst into the room accusing me of trying to "take over." I was incensed. At the very moment I was deferring to his authority, he was accusing me of usurping his leadership. In anger, I physically evicted him from the room, and if it weren't for the intervention of the participants, bad things might have happened. We were able to put the outburst in perspective and proceeded to administer the convention activities and campaigned as a united political team.

Through these isolated events, I grew to value solidarity in leadership and refused to paint the relationship between Moe and me with the colors of dissention. We administered the affairs of a major union through our combined efforts for twenty-one years. We both had our faults, but we worked toward improving the lives of postal employees because that was our primary objective.

Private Sector Organizing

After contentious debate, the 1998 convention delegates approved a resolution dedicating funds for private sector organizing. This resolution had been a hotly contested issue within the union, specifically among the motor vehicle craft members who had a concern that the private sector drivers would divide the efforts of the union. Moe had initiated programs to expand the union membership. He authorized Greg Proferl, Mark Dimonstein, Rich Shelly, and others to engage in organizing efforts on behalf of APWU. DHL was a promising target, but many factors, including interference by the Teamsters Union, prevented a major breakthrough. Even though APWU invested millions of dollars in the efforts, we were not successful in organizing private sector workers. The anti-union forces had erected major barriers to organizing, but the APWU team was committed. At the convention, the delegates established constitutional funding for organizing, and I vacated the chair to support the issue.

Steve Raymer, who went on to become the director of Maintenance Craft, was instrumental in assisting me in drafting the resolution dividing the funding between locals and the national union. As a member of the national executive board, Steve was always a force in the debates on important issues, and I welcomed his counsel. The union had grown from ad hoc organizing to a well-funded stream with mechanisms to achieve our objectives. Reality later dampened our enthusiasm, but in 1998, we were headed in the right direction.

Decision Time

In 1999, I received a telephone call with news that Josie McMillan had been defeated as president of the New York Local. Josie's defeat came as a tremendous shock. She was a dear friend and a hell of an advocate for working people. Moe had been instrumental in her ascension to the local presidency, and they shared an unbreakable bond. Through the years, Josie had been there for the Biller administration, and we assumed that she would be president for life. William Smith, an employee at the New York Bulk Mail Center, had seized on the general unrest among the New York members and defeated the most respected local labor leader in the union. As the reality settled in, I reflected on her defeat politically; the New York Local was by far the largest in the union, and Moe and his team could always depend on it for support.

I concluded that if the national leadership was to change in an orderly fashion, this was the time. Moe had passed his eightieth birthday, and the event in Philadelphia exposed unknown medical conditions. When I considered the previous incident in the restaurant, it was obvious that Moe had health problems, and if I aspired to take the next step, the time had arrived. A month later, I informed Moe that I would be a candidate for the office of president. He responded with a nod of comprehension.

My announcement for president created tension between me and Moe's closest associates, Executive Assistant Mike Benner and Communications Director Tom Fahey. They were his confidants, and many suspected that in the later years the two of them spoke on Moe's behalf, even making decisions for him. Moe's absences were more frequent, and Mike or Tom handled most of his day-to-day administration duties. His marriage had ended badly, and he was alone much of the time.

Greg Bell had become my closest ally, and in our daily meetings, we discussed my intended candidacy and plans for the future. As the 2000 national elections approached, I was prepared to be a candidate for president.

CHAPTER 20

A New Era

21st Century Postal Worker

In 2000, a dissident APWU member, Mark Campassi, created an Internet forum for postal communications titled "The New APWU." It was beyond the control of the national office and invited equal access to all APWU members. Protecting the interest and identity of the national union, the legal counsel intervened, insisting that the use of the APWU logo be discontinued.

Later the ownership and administration of the site was transferred to Randy Zelznick, an activist in the Philadelphia BMC Local. Randy changed the name of the site to "21st Century Postal Worker" and continued to moderate a forum for the exchange of opinions on a wide range of subjects. I have grown to respect the free exchange of thoughts sponsored by this forum, and I admire Randy for his work. During my presidency, I paid little attention to the Internet posts about the union. At the time, I was not computer literate. I used my office computer exclusively as a word processor. The only time I ventured to visit the Web, Sally Davidow, the director of communications, assisted me by performing the necessary key strokes. In my daily meetings with

Sally to review the news, she would not identify her sources, but I am sure that she included in her briefings information gleaned from various Web sites, including the 21st Century site. Since my retirement, I have frequented various Web sites, and Randy Zelznick's 21st Century site is among my favorites. I have even written on my own Web site about postal and union matters and how Randy's site contributes to the dialogue.

My First National Contract

On the collective bargaining front, Moe requested that I serve as chief spokesman in the 2000 negotiations. I had participated in each negotiation since 1981 and routinely led the union discussions on noneconomic issues; however, this would be the first occasion that I would serve as chief negotiator.

During the negotiations, I was determined to change the process that had developed over time. The accepted procedure had been to defer the discussion of wages and benefits until the final six hours of the ninety-day period of negotiations. The wages and livelihood of three hundred thousand employees were discussed and finalized in just six hours, after less important matters occupied the early months of the process when we would meet as infrequently as one day per week. I informed postal management that the APWU's team would be available every day, including weekends, throughout the ninety-day process. Management was committed to the abbreviated schedule and refused to appear more frequently, so on several occasions, I publicized pictures of APWU negotiators facing empty chairs where management should have been sitting. This practice created a level of animosity among management's officials, but it was not my objective to make them happy. The negotiations proceeded with little progress, and soon it was apparent that we were headed to interest arbitration once again.

In the arbitrator selection process, the attorneys for management and the union narrowed the list of arbitrators to a handful of names. The APWU had failed miserably in the selection of Mittenthal and Clarke, so I was extra meticulous in the 2000 selection. Included on the list was Arbitrator Stephen B. Goldberg, and after thoroughly vetting him, I approved. Postal management concurred, so the attorneys were instructed to contact Arbitrator Goldberg to determine his availability, but as fate would have it, he was vacationing in the south of France for several months.

The arbitrator selection process had dragged on, and the union members were becoming impatient for the process to begin. I offered Goldberg private air transportation to and from his resort on a frequency that he determined, but he demanded that his availability would be dictated by his schedule. I was determined not to repeat the mistakes made in selecting Mittenthal and Clarke, so postal management and I agreed to delay the arbitration while we waited for Goldberg's availability.

When his schedule finally permitted, the hearings proceeded as expected. The postal service and the union presented their contrasting evidence about employee pay, and the final decision reflected a fair analysis of the presentations. At issue was the legal standard of wage comparability. Were postal employees receiving similar pay compared to employees in the private sector performing similar activities? The lawyers had developed canned arguments for and against this basic question. The union presented evidence that the workers were underpaid, and management argued that they were overpaid. It was the responsibility of the arbitrator to decide the dispute.

As the deliberations commenced, my primary concern was that he would require employees to absorb a much greater share of their health expenses. Arbitrator Goldberg sent several signals that this option was under consideration, and I warned APWU attorney Darryl Anderson that it would be unacceptable to me. If the decision made drastic modification to the division of health premiums, I would consider an illegal strike. We were in the aftermath of the anthrax attack; two employees had been killed, and dozens were experiencing serious health conditions. I would not accept that they might have to pay a significantly higher percentage of premiums for their medical conditions. Darryl suggested that I meet with Senate Postal Committee Chairman Fred Thompson to give him a heads-up that job action was possible. We met and engaged in limited conversation that was intended to put him on notice that the negotiations were at a serious stage. Goldberg elected not to include drastic modification to health benefits, so I was not faced with a decision.

The 2000 contract ended up including a 4 percent increase in the contributions by APWU represented employees for health care, which was the employer's primary objective beyond wage adjustments although their proposal was much more severe. This contract had been the second occasion when health care costs had been shifted from the employer to employees, but in the prior arbitration, Arbitrator Voltin had sent a clear signal that postal division of health costs exceeded the comparability standard.

The 2000 negotiations also included the full contractual coverage for transitional employees (TEs), and effective December 31, 2005, all TEs, with the exception of the Remote Encoding Centers (RECs), were converted to career status, thus ending fourteen years of dual class postal employees represented by APWU. This had been a long struggle beginning with their inclusion in the bargaining unit by Arbitrator Mittenthal.

In a well-reasoned decision, Arbitrator Goldberg ruled that a wage premium had developed and the means of adjustment should be "moderate restraint." In response to the employer's argument that the USPS's finances should be the primary factor, Arbitrator Goldberg reasoned that

> The Postal Reorganization Act provides for compa-
> rable wages and benefits and does not condition that
> comparability on the long-term financial health of the

Postal Service, as opposed to longer economic trends that affect wage and benefit comparability. If the current legislative system for financing the Postal Service is no longer functioning well due to technological changes in the means by which Americans communicate, it is for the Congress to provide an alternative financing system, not for this Panel to require Postal Service employees to subsidize the long-term structural deficit of the Postal Service by working at wages and benefits less than those earned by employees doing comparable work in the private sector.

The decision mirrored the interpretation of the statute by the four previous arbitrators who denied the USPS proposals to dramatically reduce wages.

In each negotiation from 1981 through 2010, Moe and I set a course consistent with our beliefs. We believed and espoused that rate discounts were excessive, the burdens imposed by the Postal Accountability and Enhancement Act were unjust, and any corrections to comparability excesses should be made through moderate restraint. These positions were not merely rhetoric but our firm belief and commitment.

Also included in Arbitrator Goldberg's award were giant advances for APWU-represented employees. We received wage increases including COLA and basic wages that, when accumulated over a six-year period and including the contract extensions, equaled $19,420 for a grade 5 employee. We also converted tens of thousands of part-time flexible (PTF) employees to full-time. I received a warm letter of appreciation from an employee, Debra L. Harrison, expressing her joy of being converted to full-time after serving eight years as a part-time employee. It was letters like Ms. Harrison's that made the job rewarding and worthwhile.

One for the President

Moe and I were invited to dine with President Bill Clinton several weeks after he left office. We were among a group of eight to ten labor leaders selected as dinner guests with the former president at a downtown restaurant, the name of which escapes me, but the experience is etched in my memory.

We were served a broiled salmon dinner. I am not a big fish eater, having grown up far removed from a major body of water, but the salmon was served with a sauce that was delicious. The conversation was deferential to the former president, and since he truly is at ease in the presence of others, the afternoon was enjoyable. Moe and I left the restaurant and returned to the office before departing for home. When we arrived at the office, we had some unfinished business with Tommy Thompson, a Clerk Craft officer, and were engaged in discussing a union issue in Moe's office when suddenly I felt nauseated and excused myself to go to the restroom accessed from the office. Immediately I fell to the floor and regurgitated repeatedly into the toilet bowl. I lost consciousness for a brief period and awoke to find myself in a pool of body fluids.

Knowing Moe's sincere concern about the health of others, I wiped off my suit to conceal my condition, and when Moe called out to inquire about my extended absence, I lied and said that I was fine. If he had known my condition, he would have insisted that I be taken to the hospital, and I was determined not to go to the hospital. Upon recovering sufficiently to walk back in the office, I excused myself and went to my car to drive home. Three times on the way home, I was forced to stop the car and "relieve" myself out the window. As soon as I arrived home, I retrieved the garden hose and proceeded to rinse off the entire front of my suit, tie, and shirt. As chance would have it, Ethelda was in her mother's room where she was able to observe me engage in the strange activity of hosing myself down. When I was finished, I went straight to the master bath without even greeting Ethelda, removed my clothes, and took a shower. After that, I went straight to bed and slept until the next morning. When I awoke, I had recovered sufficiently to spread two tons of wood chips on a treed section behind the house.

While in President Clinton's company years later, I shared the general experience and told him that "I had taken a bullet for him," as the spoiled salmon was likely intended for him. He smiled and said, "I'm sorry."

Stack the Deck

The direct mail community took note of Arbitrator Goldberg's decision regarding its being Congress's responsibility to ensure financing and, understanding its future impact, initiated efforts to amend the law requiring the arbitrator to consider the USPS financial condition in his/her decision. Management advocates had routinely introduced the USPS financial position as a factor that should influence the arbitrator's decision. Each arbitrator had rejected this conclusion and decided that postal wages were governed by the law and the law required comparability. While both postal and union advocates had routinely presented arguments relative to the postal service's financial condition, management's intent was to stack the deck and have USPS finances as the sole determining factor for wages.

The concern of the union was ratified years later when Congress passed the Postal Accountability and Enhancement Act, which applied future health care costs to the financial debate, so essentially what the mailers favored was a strict relationship between employee pay and postal finances, which would have been influenced by the congressionally imposed future health care cost. A plausible case could be made that if Congress desired to fund health care costs they could have achieved that objective through a surtax on mailers, but their intent was to require employees to fund the USPS share through reduced wages. I consistently opposed the PAEA and did everything in my power to prevent it from becoming law. The APWU and the letter carriers had strong disagreements over the legislation that promised to release the postal service to compete with the private sector. The large mailers received the cover of several postal unions; their coalition even held meetings at the letter carrier building. I maintained that the legislation was a mirage and was not worth tying rates to the CPI. An additional change required by the PAEA was that injured employees would be required to use their leave while recovering from work-related injuries. The PAEA provisions did not include the mandate for arbitrator decisions, but the onerous requirement to fund future health care has put a strain on postal finances for years to come.

My Candidacy for President

As we approached the 2001 national elections, Moe had not announced his intention to retire or to be a candidate for reelection. I was aware of a survey that had been conducted by Communications Director Tom Fahey to determine the level of support if Moe decided to run. The results of the survey were not released, so I did not know the outcome, but it was my intent to be a candidate. I informed Moe in his office, and he acknowledged my intent without a response. As the election proceeded, Moe did not request petitions, so it was apparent that he chose not to be a candidate.

I did not make a formal request for his endorsement because we had functioned together for twenty-one years, and I did not want to put him in an awkward position. In the ensuing election, he did not publicly express a preference, but I was confident that my record of working on behalf of the members would prevail. I requested that Steve Albanese be a candidate for executive vice president. My respect for Steve and his talents was without limits based on his service as president of the Boston Local and as a national business agent. Steve was a leader at conventions and had been a confidant when I needed advice during negotiations.

He accepted the offer, and we became a team for the election. We formed the Burrus–Albanese–Tunstall team and were optimistic of our chances.

We were opposed by a team organized by Leo Persails for president and Clerk Craft Director Cliff Guffey for executive vice president. (I had asked Cliff Guffey to remain on my leadership team, but he declined, seeking a higher office.) Leo had previously been a candidate for president against Stu Filbey in 1976, and he opposed John Morgan for clerk craft director in 1978 and again in 1980. After these unsuccessful efforts, he finally succeeded in his candidacy for business agent in 1983 and later succeeded in achieving the position of regional coordinator. In 2001, he once again was a candidate for president.

As the Burrus–Albanese–Tunstall team prepared for the upcoming election, we needed to fill the position of assistant director of the Clerk Craft. Indianapolis President Sharon Stone and I had discussions about her joining our team. The problem was that a dear friend, national business agent Pat Williams, had expressed interest in the same position. I met with Pat and Sharon to determine if either was flexible in their plans. To my disappointment, both were committed friends but also committed to opposing one another.

Later I called Sharon and inquired if she would consider instead being a candidate for Central Region coordinator to fill the vacancy created by the retirement of Jim Williams. She told me that she would consider my request, and later that same day, she called to tell me she would be willing to run for the regional coordinator position. I was relieved. The final vote in that race was very close. Secretary Treasurer Bob Tunstall had notified Tom Maier, a business agent, that he had won, but after several recounts and a few false reports, Sharon ended up being victorious by the slimmest of margins. Tom graciously accepted defeat, and contrary to the normal practice of automatic appeal, he supported the seating of Sharon Stone in the position. So Pat Williams and

Sharon Stone were both victorious, and we had two strong voices at the national level. I commend Tony Turner, chairman of the Election Committee, for his equitable handling of the very close Stone–Maier election as well as numerous others over his long career. I always slept better during elections knowing that Tony was in charge.

Anthrax Attack

Acts of terrorism were always a national concern, but the country was not prepared for the disaster of 9/11 and the subsequent anthrax attack. The nation was reeling from the dramatic destruction of the Twin Towers and the assassination of thousands of American citizens when the news reported the mysterious death of an employee of a travel company in Boca Raton, Florida. The report did not suggest a national attack, and it wasn't until Senator Daschle's office was targeted that the authorities concluded that the US postal service was the common link.

The post office had been used as a vehicle of mass destruction. Postal employees were impacted, and three fatalities were identified as being directly related. A sense of panic engulfed the entire postal community. A biological agent that could not be readily identified by sight or smell was reported as the agent of death. The postmaster general hastily called meetings to discuss exposure and arrive at the various steps to be taken to avoid more fatalities. Following the incident in Florida, two deaths were reported of employees in the Washington, DC, office: Joseph Curseen and Thomas Morris Jr., with Leroy Richmond clinging to life. Scores of postal employees nationwide were affected by the exposure. The national union election was underway and the committee was exposed, requiring the members to engage in a regimen of Cipro, the antibiotic used to counter the effects of anthrax.

Deana Briscoe, an employee of the Washington, DC, Post Office emerged as a leader of concerned employees and created a forum for the multitude of issues that had to be addressed.

(She was later elevated to the position of local president, where she continues to serve. Dena is a lovely lady and effective representative.)

To keep abreast of the many issues involved in the attack, postal communications arranged a briefing of the PMG's staff by federal safety specialists, followed by a phone meeting with postal labor leaders. On the second day of the briefings, Greg Bell overheard my telephone safety briefing with Postmaster General Potter and suggested that the daily briefings by NIOSH and OSHA should be combined with the labor briefings so that we would all receive the same information from the original source. I conveyed this suggestion to Postmaster General Potter, and he consented that the entire group would meet daily.

The media went into a frenzy, and reports of exposure were constant. Assisted by APWU's Safety Specialist Corey Thompson, I initiated changes in the processes used in handling mail, some that were effective and some that were cosmetic, like wearing masks while working in the plants and retail units. My primary concern was the safety of all employees and alleviating the fear that could freeze the mail system. Reports of exposures were rampant, and individual employees made judgments about their employment: Had they been exposed and could they expose others beyond the workplace?

Within days Postmaster General Potter was conducting one of many news interviews and made the statement that "the mail was not safe," which was devastating news for the multimillion-dollar direct mail business. From that day forward, Deputy PMG Nolan became the official spokesman during the anthrax crisis. I attempted to project a sense of calm and reassure members that things were under control, realizing that this was the livelihood of hundreds of thousands of workers who depended on the postal service.

In the midst of this crisis, the APWU Presidents' Conference held a meeting in Miami; as anticipated, a main topic of discussion was anthrax. Everyone wanted to know what the union was doing. After my presentation, which was well received by the local leaders, Miami Local President Judy Johnson held a press conference announcing that postal management was at fault. Beyond blaming the perpetrator who introduced the poison into the mail stream, I had intentionally avoided blaming management. I saw no upside to this traditional approach. We needed calm and a dedicated workforce that would continue to report each day and process America's mail. If we had closed the post office as suggested, how could we justify its reopening? I interrupted Judy's press conference, informing the press that I was the president-elect of the national union, that our stand was that an evil individual had chosen to use mail as a vehicle to distribute poison, and that we were taking steps to protect the employees and the public. My message was broadcast on C-SPAN on two occasions, conveying to postal workers and citizens throughout the country that it was the act of an individual and not postal management.

Before the record is closed on the anthrax attack, I submit that it was necessary at the time of the attack for the postal community to "sing off" the same page, so I deferred placing blame. The fact of the matter is that postal management's decisions were the main contributors to the tragic events that followed the attack. APWU had long advocated eliminating the use of compressed air to clean postal processing equipment, but management continually refused. As the mail was processed, it was compressed in a pinch point through the equipment; at that point, the air in the letters expanded and was discharged into the environment. This process caused the anthrax in the letters to be expelled and deposited on the surfaces of the equipment and other areas of the building. It was then distributed widely through the practice of using compressed air for cleaning the machines. The two postal employees who died—brothers Curseen and Morris—were working near machines that had just been cleaned with compressed air. Following the attack, this practice was changed, but the residue of anthrax was discovered in other buildings, most notably in New Haven, Connecticut, where President John Dirjius enlisted the assistance of Senator Lieberman in the cleanup.

Following the 9/11 and anthrax attacks, a lunatic terrorized American citizens again by placing bombs in the mail. For several months, children refrained from retrieving mail, and every package was suspicious. The postal community again rallied to initiate procedures to identify suspect packages and protect employees as well as the public. There were many false sightings of suspected powder and bulging packages, but postal employees received no serious injuries from these malicious and insane attacks.

Continued occupation of contaminated buildings spread to a national dispute as postal management became less cooperative as time passed. In several postal facilities in New York, Connecticut, and other areas, we argued for the relocation of employees during cleanup efforts. With the intervention of NIOSH and OSHA, the union was successful in mitigating employee exposure, but our trust in joint safety was destroyed.

Election Results

The elections of 2001 were bittersweet. I won the election handily, and Sue Carney was successful in winning the race for director of human relations, defeating a dear friend, Sidney Brooks, and my teammate Steve Albanese lost the election for executive vice president. He lost by fewer than two thousand votes, and I was disappointed because I was looking ahead to my retirement and wanted him to replace me. I had every confidence that Steve was the right officer to succeed me as president. One can speculate that the turmoil in the airline schedules resulting from 9/11 contributed to his defeat. Thousands of air schedules were canceled, and mail—including election ballots from the New York area where Steve was especially popular—was directly affected. Even though the deadline for return ballots was extended, I believe that the turmoil affected the final outcome. Steve's defeat tempered my satisfaction, but I had won. I had succeeded as none before me. As an officer of African American descent, I had broken new ground in being elected by the membership as president of an international union. As I had served as executive vice president for twenty-one years and been involved in the executive decisions of leadership, the transition to president was more in title than day-to-day administration, but there is but one president and that was I. Moe honored me with the ceremonial transfer of the gavel, and even though he made no endorsement in the election, he was truly proud that his protégé had succeeded in the ride to the top.

PART FOUR:

Assuming the Reins

CHAPTER 21

President Burrus

President Burrus

The formal installation was an event that defined the journey I had taken from humble beginnings to becoming the first African American in the history of the nation to be elected by the membership to the position of president of an international union. A. Philip Randolph, John Sturtevant, and a few other accomplished African American labor leaders had previously been elected as president, but their elections were by convention delegates. Because of the unique "one member, one vote" feature of the APWU's constitution, APWU members from every community in the country invested in me the mantle of leadership. *I could feel the fog.*

I was sworn into office by John Sweeney, president of AFL–CIO, on November 16, 2001, and appointed to the position of vice president of the AFL–CIO on the same day. My election as president was a testament to thousands of individual postal employees who respected my contributions and trusted my ability to continue the proud tradition of APWU leadership. I will forever be grateful.

Organizing the Office

Having served with Moe in shared leadership, I was not overwhelmed by the transition from vice president to president. The anthrax emergency passed and the contract arbitration was completed, so I devoted my initial efforts to internal changes. It was necessary that I assemble a staff of capable assistants, and my first appointments were Robin Bailey as my confidential assistant and Steve Albanese as the executive assistant. Mike Benner, who had served as Moe's assistant, had resigned his APWU position and continued employment with the American Federation of Teachers (AFT), where he served for many years with distinction. Communications Director Tom Fahey had conducted a survey prior to the election to determine the level of support that Moe had for another term as president. I considered that unacceptable and determined that he would not be retained. To fill his position, I asked Sally Davidow, editor of the Philadelphia Local and wife of Greg Bell, who had become my closest confidant, if she would serve in my administration as editor. Sally, having been trained in journalism, was fully prepared for the task. With new staff, I was prepared to begin a whole new era within the union.

One of the first acts of my administration was to restructure the headquarters office. The operation had become bloated over time, and I had the opportunity to make changes. I identified unnecessary staff positions and provided generous severance packages to the incumbents, who were all dedicated and good employees. The supply room had grown to include hundreds of thousands of dollars of office supplies, and the union was locked into a contract with Pitney Bowes for more than $1 million a year for copy machines in twenty-one field offices and headquarters. The department was staffed sufficiently to run a first-class printing company. I closed the library and the supply room and, with the executive vice president's assistance, restructured the contract for copy machines throughout the union to reduce costs. Every secretary's station included a closet of supplies that could be obtained from any office supply store within twenty minutes. The union network, including field offices, hoarded office supplies. Cliff brought organization to the chain of supply and the restructuring of the offices at headquarters; Tunstall consolidated field office expenses. I was also determined to maximize income potential from the headquarters building, so I asked Cliff to reduce APWU's footprint to seven floors of our twelve-story building, freeing up five floors for private tenants. I was determined to drastically reduce administrative costs.

Historically the union had provided donuts and pastries to the employees for coffee and lunch breaks. There were gourmet coffee machines offering a number of choices. I ordered that all pastries be discontinued and replaced with seasonal fruits. It made no sense to continue contributing to the ill health of employees. The gourmet coffee machines were discontinued, and instead we provided a single brand of coffee.

For the final transition to a new administration, I ordered the remodeling of the seventh floor of APWU headquarters and put my new assistant, Robin Bailey, in charge. We completely updated the offices and the décor, replacing the doors to the president's office with glass to provide a sense of openness. As before, my doors were always open and all were invited at their pleasure. I had sufficient seating in my office, so even if I was busy, someone could be seated and wait. I hated the aura of secret discussions behind closed doors. The outcome of these changes reflected a positive backdrop for a democratic organization.

I continued my practice of personally responding to every letter forwarded to me by a postal employee. If employees took their time to compose a letter to me, it was my duty to respond. Over my thirty-seven years as an elected official, I never delegated such correspondence to a secretary or staff member. Likewise I personally took every telephone call either at the time received or at a follow-up time. I was never too busy to respond to the employees who entrusted me to attend to their business.

On occasion it was challenging to personally respond to the many of the 250,000 members who would have reason to contact my office, but from my perspective that was the job for which I volunteered.

Arbitration

With the intent of making the office of the presidency more available to local presidents, I often visited local offices to interact with the membership. On one occasion, I was requested to serve as a witness in a local arbitration case. Because of my respect for Joe Shevlin, president of Red Bank, New Jersey, I consented to his request. My assistant, Robin Bailey, made the necessary travel arrangements, and I departed armed with a familiarization of the issue. When I arrived at the airport, there was no one to meet me at the gate or in the baggage area, so I went outside to meet the driver dispatched to pick me up. After I inspected cars for several moments, President Joe Shevlin and Vice President Mike Levine arrived with apologies and transported me to the hearing. The management advocate objected to my serving as a witness, but the arbitrator overruled the objection, commenting that she would not deny the president-elect the opportunity to testify in the hearing. I provided brief testimony regarding the intent of the negotiated provision, and the management representative passed on the opportunity to cross-examine. The entire period spent in arbitration consumed less than four hours. This event did not involve important conditions of employment for thousands of employment, but it was consistent with my commitment to the members at all levels of the union.

JCIM and Byers

In the 1998 negotiated contract, we had reached an agreement to develop a Joint Contract Interpretation Manual (JCIM) to clarify competing interpretations of contract language; three years later, we had not lived up to our commitment. Throughout my life I have been devoted to being true to my word. I believe that if you say you are going to do something, you have a personal obligation to follow through. You owe it to yourself. This belief applied equally to contractual terms, and it was unacceptable to me that I had agreed to finalize a JCIM and over the course of many years, APWU had not lived up to its commitment. I removed the project from the Industrial Relations Department and requested that Regional Coordinator Elizabeth Powell undertake the task. Over the course of a year of continuous effort, I proudly affixed my signature to the first Joint Contract Interpretations Manual. Subsequently the manual has been updated each year to reflect successive contracts and newly identified joint interpretations. Coordinator Powell performed yeoman's work in its completion.

The interest of the members was also served by the selection of an additional arbitrator to the national panel. With the removal of Arbitrator Mittenthal, the national panel had been reduced to one, Arbitrator Daas, left to handle the numerous cases pending national arbitration. Under normal circumstances, twenty to thirty cases are appealed to national arbitration each year, and the arbitrator(s) will render decisions on no more than six cases per year. The backlog of important issues awaiting arbitration can become overwhelming. While having multiple arbitrators on the national panel raises the possibility of multiple interpretations of the agreement, having but one arbitrator to decide so many cases is ridiculous. I felt that this was a disservice to the membership and, after thorough review, approved the utilization of Linda Byers as a national arbitrator.

Communications and Convention Changes

The newly staffed Communications Department converted the APWU monthly tabloid back to a magazine. I had not been a fan of the tabloid style favored by Moe and thought that a newsmagazine style projected a better image of a first-class union.

Throughout my presidency, each day I received a briefing from Communications Director Sally, reviewing postal issues. Based on the issue of the day, I drafted outlines that she and her staff edited and refined into a final article that went into the magazine's "Updates and News" bulletin. For the monthly magazine, Sally's team selected a theme and artwork that reflected the main story advanced by my article. I was consistently satisfied with the work of Sally and her staff.

To organize and facilitate the national conventions, we relied on convention committees made up of local members. In the past, these members were selected directly by the national president. This policy created circumstances where a convention appointee might have been a political opponent of the local president or the local president wanted to reward a particular officer or member with the exposure and the reimbursement payment associated with serving. I changed the process by asking local and state presidents to recommend convention appointees, and then I selected candidates from those recommendations.

In addition, I changed the reimbursement policy for members servicing the convention. The long-standing policy was that the national union would reimburse for travel expenses and lost time. Since the local or state union already assumed their members' transportation costs, this expense was excessive and duplicative. I changed the policy so that the national union would no longer reimburse transportation expenses, and I changed the LWOP reimbursement to a flat dollar amount. I also restricted appointments to the Constitution Committee to local or state presidents. These and other modifications reduced the cost of national conventions from more than five million dollars to three million dollars.

The convention budgeting process had always been problematic with surpluses in non-convention years and deficits in convention years. I changed the budgeting system so that convention expenses would be allocated to each month between conventions. I also set a limit on how much each of the eighty-five officers and staff could spend in the performance of their duties. These changes made the budgeting process more consistent and reduced expenditures for mailings, copying, training, travel, and all other expenses that were controlled by individual officers. The previous policy allowed each of the officers and staff to make individual financial decisions without a budget. That could not be sustained, and despite some opposition, we were able to contain expenses with some predictability. Bob Tunstall was a strong supporter of these changes, and despite his lukewarm support to my candidacy for president, we were an effective team.

Arbitration Advocates

The processing of grievances is always a challenge. There are postal employees in every city and township in this vast nation, and that means there are a great many cases pending arbitration, placing a huge burden on the elected field officers, so Moe initiated a policy of appointing local and state members and officers to provide assistance to the national business agents through an "arbitration advocate program." By the time I assumed office in 2001, the program had ballooned. It was extremely difficult to administer and was growing extremely expensive. Some advocates were earning in excess of $50,000 per year in lost time and expenses, and factoring in the elected field representatives reimbursements on top of that, the costs were prohibitive. The appointments had become political, no longer based on qualification.

Upon becoming president, I limited appointments to once per year, requiring the nomination to be made by the local president, and furthermore I required each appointee to have prior official APWU arbitration training. I also capped the amount of expenditures per advocate, per year. The changes were not enthusiastically accepted, but they were necessary to exert central control and to rein in costs.

Postal Reform

In 2002, the postal service had experienced three consecutive years of financial deficits, and Congress renewed its interest in postal reform. The sky was falling and what better way to achieve political objectives? Hearings were held, and President Bush appointed a presidential commission. It was readily apparent that it was a stacked deck. I immediately exposed the commission, holding press conferences and providing congressional testimony. I predicted the anticipated conclusion of the Commission with the purpose of blunting the impact of a negative report when it was released. As expected, the commission permitted the "mailing interest" to dominate the presentations, and their final report was as expected. My repeated warnings countered the negative proposals, and the report was generally accepted as not credible.

Efforts of postal reform continued, and the APWU was isolated in its opposition. Through the presence of the APWU Legislative Department, I developed a relationship with Congressman Henry Waxman of California, who was chairman of the House Energy and Commerce Committee, and we were able to keep a lid on reform.

Private Sector Organizing

The promise of organizing private sector workers was not living up to the enthusiasm of the organizers, and even though they were committed to the task, the expenses were not justified by the results. After a thorough review, I determined to demand a comprehensive plan for future organizing activities. I had been committed to the principle of always measuring your commitments to determine their effectiveness. As I was leaving office, I had the occasion to counsel the newly elected Director of Organization Martha Shunn-King, and my advice was "always measure."

2002 National Convention

Prior to the opening of the national convention, we presented the delegates the opportunity to express their dissatisfaction with the George Bush administration and marched the 2,500 delegates to a picket of Vice President Chaney. We had big fun.

I had the privilege of inviting all of the former APWU national officers to the 2002 National Convention, and it was a pleasure to welcome the former officers to join in fellowship with the many friends made over their careers. Those in attendance were introduced to the delegates and were permitted access to the convention floor, where they were able to renew relationships. The most memorable event was a video conference with Moe Biller, who could not be in attendance due to failing health, but his voice was strong. He shared good wishes to delegates of the sixteenth biannual convention.

The political speeches that had historically dominated the opening day of the convention were continuously subjects of debate, so at the 2002 convention, I determined to shift the focus of the principal guest speakers, which had historically been reserved for politicians, and invited Jerry McEntee, president of the American Federation of State, County, and Municipal Employees (AFSCME), and Andy Stern, president of the Service Employees International Union (SEIU). Both made excellent presentations, and APWU delegates were exposed to giant labor leaders on the world stage.

Contract Extension

In 2003, I engaged Tony Vegliante, the vice president of labor relations and my primary contact with postal management, in discussion to explore the possibility of reaching mutual agreements on the contractual provisions in regard to planned consolidations of many processing plants. During the discussion, he raised the possibility of a contract extension. His request caught me off guard, and I was not prepared to provide a response.

In the history of postal bargaining, the contract had never been extended, so the suggestion required serious consideration and review. Upon returning to my office, I discussed the possibilities with Greg Bell. Further meetings with postal officials identified the parameters of the issues that would be included. After intense discussions over several weeks, the issues to be included were identified, and I presented a package to the national executive board that voted its approval.

The extension of a contract is no trivial matter as it defers the opportunity to address pressing unsatisfactory conditions. While marginal issues can be included—and they were—the postal service was experiencing serious financial difficulties, and it was recognized that wage increases would be seriously contested. Consolidations that had generated the initial discussions were of major concern, and the extension presented an opportunity to benefit union members nearing retirement eligibility who desired "early out" opportunities. These issues were covered in the extension, so the choice was either to roll the dice in arbitration or to maintain the stability of an extension. I chose the latter, and the membership overwhelmingly endorsed the decision. We achieved wage increases for all employees, upgrades, and a moratorium on excessing. However, in the months after the contract had been extended, major disagreement surfaced on retirement eligibility, requiring arbitration. It was worth it, though, for employees such as Marilyn Braunstein to be able to spend the rest of their lives engaged in activities of their choosing.

In 2003 and 2005, I successfully extended the APWU contract to avoid the battles of negotiation and to preserve past gains during a period of postal financial uncertainty. The postal service was emerging from a period of declining volume and depressed revenues, and I believed that if we could weather the storm we could continue on our road of improving conditions for our members. As a part of the extensions, I succeeded in upgrading five groups of employees and achieved significant wage increases. This was the second consecutive extension, and one APWU activist gave me the name "The Great Extender," which was humorous at the time because I took the obligation of contract negotiations seriously.

Volume Decline

Postal reform continued as a major concern of Congress, using decreasing mail volume and repeated deficits as justification for drastic political change. APWU was in the forefront of opposition to reform efforts and countered the misleading propaganda that the Internet and the postal service could not coexist long-term. We suggested that the reduction of mail volume and the growing use of the Internet were not related, presenting statistics confirming that in each instance when new means of communications were introduced, mail volume actually increased from expansion of the economy. I disputed the commonly-held belief that the reduction of individual use of the mail as a means of communications would adversely affect postal volume.

Personal mail had not exceeded 8 percent of total mail volume for many years, and the driver of increased volume was the economy. When the telegraph was introduced in 1844, mail volume increased 531 percent; when the telephone as invented in 1876, mail volume increased 1,075 percent; when the computer was developed in 1944, mail volume increased 134 percent; and when the FAX/Telex came into use in 1972, mail volume increased 125 percent. So the connection between these analog and digital means of communications and letters was false. In 2006, just four years after this debate, mail volume soared to a record-high two hundred and twelve billion pieces, confirming my position in 2002. APWU prevailed and postal reform was shelved for the time being.

CHAPTER 22

Closing a Chapter

APWU Takes a Stand on the War

Having achieved ascension to the presidency, I intended to continue Moe's efforts to engage the union in civic debate. President Bush had accused the Iraq government of storing weapons of mass destruction and not adhering to an arbitrary timetable for their destruction. In violation of all international treaties, he commanded the invasion of a sovereign nation, which would lead to the longest war in US history. On January 14, 2003, I presented the following resolution to the national executive board:

> The APWU National Executive Board opposes the pending war with Iraq. This declaration is based on the information made available to the American public at this time. We abhor terrorism, and we endorse all action—diplomatic and military—to appropriately respond to acts of aggression. However, preemptive attacks against sovereign states are not consistent with the principles of freedom and respect for all people.

On March 11, 2003, I requested that the board approve the following resolution in support of the American troops: "The National Executive Board extends full support of the American troops placed in harm's way and expresses hope for their safe return home."

Both resolutions were approved, and history has recorded that the APWU resolutions were confirmed by subsequent events.

Ethelda Calls It A Day

On February 1, 2003, Ethelda retired from employment as a supervisor at the University of Maryland in College Park. Shortly after her arrival in Washington in 1981, she had gained employment at the university. I often reference her looks as what attracted me to her, but for those twenty-two years, she demonstrated that there was so much more to her than I could have imagined. Not only did she go to work every day; she also maintained our home and took care of her son, Antwon, and me. She cooked a full meal for supper each day. We never, ever ate a dinner prepared by someone else unless we went out to eat. Over my career, I have invited union members and coworkers to our home unannounced, and I was never concerned that some areas would be untidy. Her retirement enabled her to spend quality time with her mother for years before she died. If anyone was deserving of retirement, it was Ethelda, and I will do everything in my power to ensure that she continues to enjoy it.

Jane

May 17, 2003, is etched in my memory as the day that I received a second dreaded phone call. In our household, because I'm used to having staff, out of habit I let Ethelda answer the phone. That day, after determining that the call was for me, Ethelda handed me the phone, announcing that Hal wanted to talk to me.

Halford Elston was my sister's husband, whom she had married after the dissolution of her marriage to Frank Johnson, her college sweetheart and the father of her only child, Kevin. Hal and I had a good relationship, and during the period when we all lived in Cleveland, he and Jane routinely entertained Ethelda and me after work with lemonade or mild drinks and small talk. They moved to Hawaii in 1976, and I often visited their beautiful home. After ten years, they returned to the Cleveland area, relocating in Chesterland, Ohio, and I often visited when I was in Cleveland for union affairs. The Hawaii and Chesterland residences were lovely and well kept. They were well furnished with imaginative decorations, and in Hawaii Hal and Jane had a swimming pool with a sliding board from the upper deck.

A very unusual feature of their Hawaii residence was that the windows and doors did not have molding. I liked the clean look of framing the openings with drywall, so when contracting our home, I told the builder that we did not want woodwork. He did not fully understand the finish that I was attempting to achieve, but the subcontractor was able to perform what was requested, and the look is smooth and attractive.

Jane and I often spoke about our father and his continuing efforts to prepare us for the world. For two years, Jane went to a high school in Bridgeport, Ohio, using the address of a former foster home where we had lived. Bridgeport was separated from Wheeling by two bridges. The schools were integrated, and the high school, Bridgeport High School, is best known as the beginning of a sports career for John Havelcheck, who would go on to Hall of Fame recognition with the Boston Celtics basketball team. I refused to get up two hours early and make the two-mile walk just to go to school with white kids.

My sister and I were inseparable. During our early teen age years, our father volunteered our services to clean the vacation home of the bank president prior to his family's relocating for the summer months. We were transported to the remote location and went about cleaning everything that had accumulated dust and dirt over the winter. While cleaning the kitchen, I noticed several

275

cases of unmarked clear soda bottles that were either club soda or ginger ale. I liked ginger ale, but it was necessary to taste the contents before knowing if the right bottle had been selected. I must have emptied out at least three bottles of club soda in order to drink six bottles of ginger ale over the course of the cleaning project. With each bottle I emptied, Jane admonished me.

There were so many treasured memories that my sister and I shared, and there is not a day that I do not think of her. The last memory that I have is her standing in the doorway of her home in Chesterland, waving good-bye and voicing the words, "I am proud of you."

During her stay in Hawaii, Jane continued postal employment for several years but then returned to school—having completed two years of college at West Virginia State—to qualify as a foster parent. After certification, she accepted foster children into her home as a means of employment. While in Hawaii, she had three lovely female Asian exchange students live with her; they thought of her as their mother. When she relocated back to Ohio, she continued taking foster children, but by then, having received advanced training, she moved it up a notch, accepting only those with a troubled past who were given a last chance in the foster home system because of bad behavior. Jane brought the foster boys to my home in Maryland to expose them to further evidence of the reward for living a clean life and doing the right thing.

My sister's foster home in Chesterland, Ohio, became front-page news when one of her former wards returned to the home and convinced one of the boys under her care to accompany him to rob a gas station. During the robbery, a young woman was repeatedly shot and killed as she begged for her life. Another girl was wounded. The foster kid, Marcus Moorer, sneaked back into my sister's home and pretended to be asleep in his bed. In short order, the police came, and he was booked and ended up confessing to the crime. He is serving a lifetime prison sentence. The entire little city was outraged that a black family was operating a foster home in their community. The issue was all over the news for months with even state and national politicians getting involved, but by May 17 the situation had subsided and things were normal.

Hal's phone call informed me that Jane had died. They had converted their three-car garage into an indoor basketball court, complete with floor markings and a coin-operated soda machine, to facilitate the basketball prowess of the foster children. While she was cleaning the area, she had leaned forward and died. Similar to our father's death thirty-one years before, Jane had not demonstrated any life-threatening conditions, so we were not mentally prepared. I was left with no member of my immediate family (excluding Effie) in the time it took to hear those words: "Jane died."

Two weeks prior to the phone call, I had visited Cleveland on union business and had made my special visit to her home. We spent hours in her kitchen reminiscing over what we had done with our lives and our plans for the future. The conversation was all over the place, from music—and one of our favorite female jazz vocalists, Lorez Alexandria—to our childhood and our father. These conversations were not unusual because we shared personal bonds of experiences; when we had the opportunity, we would just talk. We never had an in-depth discussion about her reasons for housing foster children, but our early childhood must have played a role.

She will be greatly missed.

Moses "Moe" Aaron Biller, 1915–2003

On September 5, 2003, Moe Biller passed away in a hospice care center in New York. After dedicating his life to improving conditions for postal employees and giving them dignity and respect, he left this world alone and with little notice. What I will remember about Moe are the good days—the days when he succeeded in advancing the cause of postal workers, raising us to new heights. History will never record the homes purchased, the children educated, the lifesaving medical expenses covered, the financial ability of postal workers to lend a hand to others, and the pride instilled in employees to be affiliated with their union—all because of the efforts of Moe Biller.

His style of leadership was unusual in that he was confident enough to share responsibility. During our administration, he willingly permitted me to lead the union's efforts in contract administration. The result was that local leaders look to national officers to handle their workplace disputes, giving credit for the achievements to the officer involved. This structure obviously played a role in the conflict between Moe and me as I handled most of the contract issues identified by local leaders, operating almost independent from Moe's supervision. There is no room for two presidents, and on occasion, my independent actions were the focus of our disagreements.

Recognizing that this relationship was not in the best interest of the union, during my presidency I initiated a policy that any document committing the union to a financial or legal matter must bear the signature of the president. Although that was not Moe's style, all of the advances that we achieved can be associated with the leadership of Moe Biller, and he is appreciated and missed. Appropriate services were held by the union with acknowledgement of his contributions. At the ceremony honoring his life, I offered the following on behalf of the APWU membership:

> I come representing the APWU family and personally to pay tribute to our leader and my friend, Moe Biller, President Emeritus and a good man. Moe's contributions to the House of Labor and the cause of justice were enormous. To name just a few, he helped lead the fight to establish Martin Luther King Day as a federal holiday; was a pivotal figure in the

establishment of the Federal Employees Retirement System; when APWU was expelled from the Federal Health Program, Moe worked tirelessly for restoration; and perhaps his proudest achievement, Moe established penalty pay for postal employees, unprecedented for federal employees. He often joked that penalty pay would be etched on his headstone. Moe prized democracy within our union and in society and was the prime force in establishing one man, one vote within APWU. He was recognized in the halls of Congress and often met with presidents to advance the goals of working people. But most importantly, Moe was a kind and gentle man. He was a true New Yorker, and his twenty-one year stay in Washington did not diminish his love for home. Moe was also a strong man who loved the challenge of adversity, and perhaps some of his greater moments were when he faced down those who would deny dignity and respect to working people. To Michael, Steve, and the lovely granddaughters who formed his immediate family and his surviving brother and sisters, thank you for sharing Moe's life with postal employees. And on behalf of the 300,000 APWU members, thank you Moe and God Speed!

Secretary Treasurer Changes Hands

On February 4, 2004, Bob Tunstall, the union's secretary treasurer, after many years of dedicated service, retired due to health conditions. We lost a good officer and a friend. He was the secretary treasurer when I assumed the presidency, and we had worked as a team in initiating the necessary changes to stabilize the union finances. Bob has since passed on, and I have been unable to maintain constant contact with his wife, Rae, who exerted a positive influence in our personal relations.

Bob's retirement made it necessary for me to nominate his replacement to the national executive board. I had a short list of candidates that included John Dirzius, president, Greater Connecticut Area Local; Elizabeth Liz Powell, regional coordinator, north east region; and Terry Stapleton, regional coordinator, southern region. I considered a number of factors and selected Terry Stapleton, who was approved by the board. To fill Terry's vacancy, I selected National Business Agent Frankie Sanders.

Terry recommended Allen Mohl, president of Broward County, Florida, to be his executive assistant, and we embarked on a period of positive change throughout the union. Terry was full of ideas, and Allen was a master of implementation. There was not a single area within the union that Terry and Allen did not examine and make suggestions to or initiate change in. I drew a line at the administrative control of the field operation, though. I reserved that for myself as president. Terry disagreed, and on one occasion, he argued about the jurisdiction of the field so vehemently that I had to expel him from my office. Throughout the years to follow, Terry Stapleton was a positive force in APWU, and with him, the secretary treasurer's office was in good hands.

Golf and Flowers

In our continuing efforts to develop the property of our new home, Ethelda and I decided to install a one-hundred-foot artificial putting green on the spot where the tobacco barn had been located. In anticipation of my retirement, I wanted a pleasant diversion close at hand. I succeeded in finding a location on our property within a short walk from the veranda. Not to be outdone, Ethelda requested a greenhouse where she could pursue her love of plants, so we had one constructed adjacent to the master bedroom.

We thought that these additions would complete our house, but as my retirement approached, we began to discuss where we would display the many lovely gifts I had received from postal union presidents throughout the world over a long career. We talked to the architect who helped design the house about adding a room to the basement, but because of the angles in the house, it would have had to be a long, narrow room. After several drawings, we determined that adding a room to the exterior would not work. We looked at the area above the dining room, which has twelve feet of space above the ceiling in the attic but concluded that since footings had not been constructed beneath the dining room it would require major renovation. We even looked at the space beneath the veranda outside the house, but it would have required major excavation and integration with the existing basement. The final decision was to convert the basement into a library and connect it to the master bedroom above with an elevator. This idea was exciting to us after we included glass walls from the basement to the bedroom so the elevator had a view of the wooded area behind the house.

After many changes, Ethelda and I had completed our dream home, and we were enjoying another chapter in our lives.

CHAPTER 23

Historic Gains and Losses

COPA Milestone

In 2004, with the yeoman's assistance of Roy Braunstein, Myke Reid, and many committed activists, the APWU succeeded in surpassing one million dollars in COPA contributions from members. When I assumed office, the highest amount contributed was $387,000 for a year. I set one million dollars per year as a goal, and as an incentive to local and state unions, I changed the convention seating to reward those locals that met their assigned goals for COPA.

Because of the size of the APWU convention, delegate seating by locals and states is spread over a very large ballroom. Though we incorporate large video monitors throughout the hall, preferred seating is closest to the dais, and the delegates consider it a coup to be seated in the front. This change created some consternation, but it soon became the accepted norm and resulted in incentivizing locals to become involved in the political process. The one million dollar political war chest gave APWU a presence on Capitol Hill as a major player in the political process and gave prominence to Myke Reid as director of legislation.

Money is the grease that lubricates the American political system, and to play with the big boys, you have to be a player. There are ingenuous fund-raisers that generate lists of donors, and these lists are reviewed when legislation is under consideration. The system is not so corrupt that one can buy specific legislation, but most legislators spend more time fund-raising than legislating, and if one wants to be influential, it takes political donations to get in the room where decisions are made. We succeeded in raising the profile of COPA contributions, and APWU finally had a real political presence.

I later attempted to duplicate the successful NALC structured political operation and appointed five APWU grassroots coordinators charged with mobilizing political activity at the field level. My target for COPA contributions became two million dollars per year. We were also successful in having legislation introduced by Congressman Lynch to require bargaining when subcontracting is contemplated. This was the first piece of legislation sponsored exclusively by APWU, and it was successfully introduced in Congress. As a testament to the raised APWU political profile, during his campaign for president, John Kerry visited the delegates to the Boston APWU Presidents' Conference. On that occasion, I had the opportunity to express the support of APWU and that of our membership in the election.

Holiday Leave an Added Benefit

Upon the death of President Ronald Reagan, I achieved a notable contractual improvement in negotiating a new application of holiday leave, and represented employees were granted an official holiday emanating from the actions taken by APWU. In 1994, upon the death of Richard Nixon, I had challenged the USPS's decision to afford holiday leave to selected employees. The grievance proceeded to arbitration, where I was victorious in a decision that confirmed that the contractual holiday pay rules applied for a national day of mourning to all postal employees.

After receipt of the arbitration decision confirming that the arbitrary assignment of holiday leave violated the contract, I entered into discussions with postal management and reached agreement on the application of the leave policy on a national day of mourning. The other postal unions adopted the APWU settlement, and now all postal employees enjoy an additional holiday that is not included in the collective bargaining agreement.

2004 National Convention

The 2004 National Convention considered dues increases and changing the election cycles—but the main resolution was the issue of dues. In preparation for the expected loss of union membership, I opposed all efforts to address the expected revenue shortfall through dues increases. The delegates rejected these resolutions, and the issue of revenue shortfall was left to the constitutional authority of the president. As I had informed the delegates, there was sufficient authority in the constitution to reduce expenses commensurate with the membership loss. Terry Stapleton and I began the arduous process. Allen Mohl and Danielle Shillam, executive assistants to the secretary treasurer, were assigned to reducing employee and administrative costs and were key lieutenants in effecting change. We began a program of purchasing APWU field offices and renegotiating leases and took other steps to reduce expenses.

Throughout the nine years of my presidency, we experienced budget surpluses in each year. Elizabeth Connolly and Twee Nguyen of the comptroller office are commended for their efforts in support of these goals. Paul Delaney, an officer of the Montgomery County Local, served as chairman of the convention's Finance Committee and provided assistance in training locals in the performance of financial duties. Without the stellar assistance of these professionals, Terry and I would not have been successful in stabilizing APWU finances.

2004 Election

The 2004 APWU election was historic. Once again, I was opposed by Leo Persails. Having the experience of being a candidate for president on two prior occasions and a candidate for a resident officer position in four previous elections, he mounted a vigorous campaign. However, I prevailed with the highest margin in the history of APWU presidential elections, receiving the endorsement of 73 percent of those voting. This election was also historic in that no member of the incumbent leadership team was defeated.

Because Leo Persails and I had been opposing candidates a number of times, people wondered whether or not there was animosity between us. We had our differences on a number of issues, but there was nothing personal. We merely viewed some issues through different lenses. I have continually expressed my admiration for his tenacity as an arbitration advocate, and from my perspective, our relationship was positive throughout my service as executive vice president and president. We both shared a love of vintage cars and often discussed the many restored cars that he had owned and my 1980 Corvette and 1985 Jaguar.

Andrea

The year also marked the addition to my staff of a knowledgeable, efficient, and lovely young lady, Mrs. Andrea Chapman from Kansas City. I had been invited to perform the installation of officers in Kansas City earlier that year and was so impressed with Andrea that I made a mental note to hire her if the opportunity arose. When Roy Braunstein retired and Myke Reid won his seat as legislation director, Steve Albanese, who had been my assistant, ran for the position of assistant director of legislation and won. This created a vacancy in my office. I called Andrea and offered her the job of executive assistant. I was extremely pleased when she accepted, and APWU became the beneficiary of a "two for one" as her husband, John, volunteered his services to assist her on many projects. Subsequently I had the opportunity to appoint Andrea to director of the per capita department, ensuring that locals and states get all of their money on time.

Hurricane Katrina

The devastation of Hurricane Katrina shocked the world, including the postal community. The media broadcasted the horror of New Orleans and the surrounding communities being destroyed. The nation and postal service had experienced the 9/11 attacks, then the anthrax attacks, and in their wake, we had built on the union's communications systems that had been developed. We quickly determined that the relief agencies would respond with emergency assistance, so we focused on assisting employees in rebuilding their lives.

I met with postal officials to determine how best to assist APWU-represented employees. The Postal Employees Relief Fund expedited the process of approving claims while I focused on continuing employment. We reached unprecedented agreements, including the temporary placement of all APWU-represented employees who were displaced by the disaster into neighboring or faraway post offices. Affected postal employees were transferred in large numbers to Houston, Galveston, and other southwestern offices. Some were reassigned as far away as Pennsylvania.

There were some abuses, but no APWU-represented employee was denied the opportunity to continue employment. We negotiated special contractual provisions for placement, including seniority rights. As the emergency subsided, management's commitment weakened and disputes arose over the application of retreat rights, but during the emergency, postal employees received protection way beyond other members of the community.

During that period, employees were in various stages of recovery, and local management used the disaster to favor some employees and disadvantage others. Grievances filed over violations of the Katrina Memorandums are still pending arbitration eight years later; nevertheless, I am proud of the response to this disaster. Throughout the devastated communities, postal employees continued to receive payment for jobs that did not exist.

Postal Reform

The cry for postal reform reached a feverish pitch in 2004 as lobbyists sought to achieve political agendas. A continued decline in the use of mail served as their justification to overhaul the entire system. Politicians were calling for consolidation of processing centers in an effort to save money. The cry for reform became so absurd that the postmaster general voiced opposition for the first time.

To entice the labor unions to join the phony reform efforts, the large mailers and other unions proposed to include a labor seat on the board of governors. I was not swayed and continued firmly to oppose political interference into postal matters. With four labor unions and one seat, the selection process would pit one union against the other, and a single seat on the board would not tip the balance on important decisions, yet as a member, we would be bound by the rulings. APWU did not fall for the ruse, and it was soon dropped from the legislation.

Despite our efforts, the APWU was not successful in fighting off reform, and in 2006, President Bush signed into law the Postal Accountability and Enhancement Act (PAEA), imposing a financial albatross that would seriously affect the postal service. It was the mistake of the century.

The pending consolidations of processing centers continued to demand the union's attention, and we waged opposition on a number of fronts. We were able to slow the consolidations to a trickle, but it was known at that time that such efforts would continue requiring continued vigilance.

Among the many challenges that I faced was the search for a solution to postal solvency. APWU successfully introduced HR

22, which was the equivalent to HR 1351 in the early 2000s. These bills expanded the USPS's authority to use its network of retail centers to generate revenue by offering non-postal products and services without the onerous baggage of the PAEA. The PAEA included a CPI cap on rate increases and the obligation to prefund sixty billion dollars in future health care costs. We made a good run at getting it passed but, in the end, were unable to garner enough support to bring it to law. These issues will haunt future union administrations as hard-copy communications continues to find its place in the ever-changing universe of technology.

CHAPTER 24

Further Negotiations

Breakaway

As a vice president on the AFL–CIO executive council, I was directly involved in the internal discussions prior to the breakaway of seven major unions to form Change to Win. The seeds of a breakaway were first planted in 2005 when Andy Stern and Jimmy Hoffa began taking strong exception to the AFL's allocation of resources. They continually advocated more resources for organizing with less attention to politics, but they could not achieve a majority on the council. A secondary issue was the increasing number of international unions representing workers that overlapped jurisdiction. For the postal community, Stern and Hoffa were proposing a single union with the possibility that all federal workers—including postal workers—would be restricted to one union. After failing to receive support, they planned their departure. I expressed on numerous occasions during the debate that the formation of Change to Win was a repudiation of basic democratic principles. If elected president of the AFL–CIO, Andy Stern or Jimmy Hoffa would have had the constitutional authority to impose many of their changes, but lacking the numbers to prevail in the democratic process, they "took their ball and went home."

The disaffiliation of seven of the largest unions, including SEIU, Teamsters, Laborers, and Unite Here, struck a major blow to the labor movement. As president of the tenth largest union in the federation, I was appointed to the executive committee charged with restructuring the AFL to meet the declining revenue. The discussions were intense as each member had an agenda, but we succeeded in securing a committed labor movement that won smashing political victories in the national elections of 2006. Despite fractured support, labor-supported candidates won overwhelmingly, putting to rest the debate over the division of resources between organizing and politics.

One issue that stands out in my memory of our activities was the committee's discussion on the future relationship with the constituency groups—Coalition of Black Trade Unionist, CLUW, A. Philip Randolph, Pride at Work, Asian Pacific, American Labor Alliance, and the Labor Corps for Latin American Advancement. Historically the president of the AFL–CIO made appointments to the executive council, including members of the constituency groups. Not every affiliated international union president is included on the council, so some international unions aren't represented. I thought that this was unfair and proposed to rectify the perceived injustice as we amended the constitution. I was the only African American officer on the committee, so while my suggestions were not dispositive, they carried weight on this subject.

A group of African American labor leaders led by Bill Lucy requested a private meeting with me where they expressed their unhappiness with my position. They didn't want to include automatic membership on the council for constituency groups in the constitution because to identify some would exclude others. This concern could have been worked out by drafting language that gave the president discretion, but they were opposed to the concept. I relented and withdrew my proposal, but later events confirmed the fairness of the concept that I had advanced. Several years later, the political differences between AFSCME President Gerry McEntee and Bill Lucy, former secretary treasurer of ASFME, became so tense that Gerry challenged Bill's right to serve as an elected officer of the AFL–CIO. Gerry relied upon an AFL constitutional provision requiring all officers to be members of an affiliated union. Since Bill had retired from his position as secretary treasurer, technically he was not a member of AFSCME and could not serve.

There is no international labor leader whom I respect more than Bill Lucy. Bill had a long and distinguished career of fighting for workplace justice, having been in the trenches with Martin Luther King Jr. As the founder and president of the Coalition of Black Trade Unionist (CBTU), he had been one of the most respected voices on the AFL Executive Council. His proposed expulsion was reprehensible, so to satisfy the union membership requirement, I bestowed upon him membership in the APWU Cleveland Local. He currently pays the required dues and through his membership qualifies to retain his seat on the AFL Executive Council, representing postal workers. Adoption of my proposal to include some of the presidents of the constituency groups on the council by virtue of their office would have addressed the problem because the president of CBTU would have automatically been a member of the executive council.

Following the breakaway of the dissident unions, I received a call from Laborers International Union (LIUNA) President Terry O'Sullivan, whom I respected very much. He wanted to discuss with me the possibility of a non-raiding pact between APWU and the Mail Handlers' Division of LIUNA. When LIUNA disaffiliated from the AFL, they no longer enjoyed the protection provided by Article 21 of the AFL constitution, and Terry was seeking a separate pact because, although the Mail Handlers membership is but a small percentage of LIUNA, the

Mail Handlers Hospital Plan is a revenue generator that they wanted to protect. I declined to reach such an agreement because the APWU constitution included the objective of one postal union and such a pledge would be in conflict.

Terry was a professional and accepted my position without recrimination. However, a rift surfaced between the APWU and the NALC on the issue of the Mail Handler re-affiliation with the AFL. NALC President Bill Young and I openly disagreed at the AFL Executive Council meeting that voted on the partial re-affiliation.

When AFL–CIO President John Sweeney left a message giving an ultimatum on my position regarding the Mail Handlers re-affiliation, I was engaged with the final stages of contract negotiations and did not have the time to engage in lengthy discussions about the Mail Handlers. The council voted to re-affiliate the Mail Handlers, but later I informed John of my displeasure at his timing. He put the relationship with President O'Sullivan ahead of a continuing-dues-paying affiliate. The Mail Handlers were readmitted, but it still does not make sense to me that an international union can affiliate a division.

Violence

Following the 1986 massacre in Edmond, Oklahoma, when a postal employee killed fourteen employees and customers, followed by similar tragedies in Ridgewood, New Jersey, and Royal Oak, Michigan, the media adopted the phrase "going postal" to describe workplace violence. Over many years of struggle, I worked to change the narrative, insisting that acts of violence by postal employees were symptoms of our society and as such unrelated to their place of employment. These were deranged individuals who would have engaged in antisocial behavior no matter their place of employment.

In early 2006, Charlotte Cotton, an employee of the Santa Barbara post office, was brutally attacked while working her assignment. On February 2, 2006, I joined with Postmaster General John Potter in attendance at a memorial honoring her service. After years of struggle, I had succeeded in separating the isolated acts of violence by postal employees from a public perception that the post office was a place of terror. Over the years, we were able to overcome the misconceptions and live down the journalistic expression "going postal" so that Ms. Cotton's service was given the dignity it deserved.

Later, following the All-Craft Conference and the announcement of my retirement, on December 23, 2009, the media reported that postal employees in Wytheville, Virginia, were being held hostage by a deranged gunman, bringing back so many memories of previous tragedies. I contacted postal officials, and we monitored the event, which ended without bloodshed. This was a victory for the hostages and for the post office.

MTAC and Reform

In 2006, with the assistance of Phil Tabbita, I initiated a lawsuit seeking entrée into the private meetings held by Mailers Technical Advisory Committee (MTAC), alleging a violation of the sunshine laws, which require public meeting. I believed it important that APWU find a way to disturb the unhealthy relationship between mailers and the post office. It had evolved to the point that mailers were being provided office space inside postal headquarters; proximity spreads poison. The battle was for admission to MTAC meetings where postal management provided briefings of intended actions and responded to mailers' proposals. We engaged in protracted judicial proceedings that did not provide the admittance that I preferred.

In the ongoing campaign to sway public opinion, disagreements with the large mailers reached the boiling point. Gene Del Polito, a smart and effective spokesperson for the mailers, and I exchanged terse editorials in our respective union magazines. Del Polito challenged me to identify specific issues that the union favored that included change. My position had been that the volume of mail and thus the postal service revenue was not negatively affected by the Internet and therefore there was no need for large mailer discounts to enhance postal efficiencies. This led me to post online and in the union magazine a vision of how the postal service could best serve the American public, including the large mailers. My vision was verified at the end of the postal fiscal year, when the postal service released their 2006 annual report, confirming the APWU's position that the sky was not falling. Postal volume had reached an all-time high of 212 billion pieces. As I had predicted, mail continued to be a major means of communications.

Discounts

I continued to expose illegal mailer discounts at every opportunity, often finding myself on the opposite side of the Letter Carriers, who believed that if discounts generated increased volume they were good policy. The conflict erupted into a public disagreement at a congressional hearing where the Letter Carriers were seeking legislation banning the subcontracting of delivery. I testified that Congress had no business in the collective bargaining arena, and I opposed the initiative. I found it hypocritical to oppose congressional interference when it was contrary to one's objective and solicit it when it was to one's advantage.

I deeply respected President Bill Young, who had succeeded Vince Sombrotto in 2002. He was a strong advocate for Letter Carriers, very smart and a bulldog advocate in representing their interests. In this instance, we disagreed, and I felt no solidarity to support their cause since they had been AWOL on ours.

After the postal service suffered consecutive years of reduced volume and revenue caused in part by the illegal mailer discounts, I made a public offer to convert APWU-represented employees' salaries to one cent below the discount rate of 10.5 cents per piece. The Postmaster General never responded to my offer, and in the

2006 contract negotiations, the proposal was met with awkward silence by postal officials. The offer must have struck a nerve because a spokesperson for the large mailers found it necessary to characterize the offer as trivial. However, in the world of economics, an offer to perform a task at the rate of one cent less than the current rate performed by the mailers cannot be ignored.

Throughout my service as a national officer, I fought rate discounts and postal reform. I lost more often than I won, but I kept the issue in play, and there was no misunderstanding where APWU stood.

2006 Negotiations

Reflecting the union's determination to continue moving forward, contract negotiations repeatedly ended in arbitration, so the 2006 contract was an exception when we finalized a negotiated agreement. I had negotiated the 2000 contract that was referred to arbitration and the extensions in 2003 and 2005. The 2006 results exceeded my expectations. We were able to achieve unprecedented advancements. The agreement included an upgrade for every APWU-represented employee, severe restrictions on the use of casuals, conversion of thousands of PTFs, decent pay increases, and more. With the upgrades, I had achieved an accomplishment equal to that of the Letter Carriers in 1998. In the entire forty years of bargaining, a general upgrade had never been achieved in negotiations. Prior to the 1971 Postal Reform Act, all employees received an upgrade by Congress, but this was before bargaining. The Letter Carrier success in 1998 had been achieved in arbitration, so this was a new milestone for APWU. In the extensions, I had previously succeeded in upgrading selected Maintenance, Motor Vehicle, and CFS clerks, so in the span of four years, some employees received two or three upgrades in addition to increases associated with step placement.

To achieve advances for the workers, union officials must have counterparts who are willing to bite the bullet and find ways to make mutually beneficial changes. Throughout my service as executive vice president and president, I was able to communicate with labor relations executives Bill Downes, Tony Vegliante, and Doug Tulino, who were true to their word and were willing to try new approaches.

Included among the many new initiatives, I reached an agreement on reemploying retired postal employees. This subject had been under discussion for several years. The stumbling block had always been the legal right to continue receiving an annuity while employed at the postal service, but legislation was passed solving that dilemma. I truly believed that the hiring of retirees in lieu of casual employees was a win–win situation. The former employees could supplement their annuity, and the postal service would get skilled employees on day one. Despite the agreement, there was still some postal management opposition.

The 2006 negotiations involved a shift of payment for health premiums. Although the employee contribution increased, I was able to balance the hike with an agreement that the postal service would pay 95 percent of employees' premiums if they enrolled in the APWU Consumer Driven (CD) Plan. I had pointed out to manager Tony Vigilante that if the USPS paid 100 percent in the APWU's CD Plan, the costs to the postal service would be less than 80 percent of the regular plan. We verbally agreed to 100 percent, but when Tony presented it to higher authorities, they objected. Because of my respect for Tony, I did not insist on the earlier commitment. Our ability to continue communications was of greater value than the small amount that would have been generated.

During the 2006 negotiations, I wanted to include the membership in the process. I requested that each resident national officer designate one APWU rank-and-file member who did not serve as a local union representative to come to Washington to be present during negotiations so they could personally experience the activities. A group of rank-and-file employees was able to witness the exchanges between the union and management on issues that would shape their careers.

My philosophy of bargaining did not include sacrificing the wages and benefits for future generations to achieve present gains. Throughout my thirty-seven years of bargaining, not a single negotiated contract included different standards for employees hired before the effective date and those hired after. Mittenthal and Clarke did impose new entry levels for new employees in arbitration, but in each instance, affected employees were integrated into the continuing pay scale to the maximum salary.

CHAPTER 25

Hope and Change

Early Retirement and Tour 2

In their efforts to downsize the workforce, the postal service initiated a policy of assigning surplus employees to "stand by," to record excesses to the complement. The solution to the excess of employees was to convince eligible employees to retire. The postal service offered a series of Voluntary Early Retirement (VERA) opportunities without incentives, and I cautioned employees to refrain from the opportunity absent of monetary incentives. After repeated discussions with Postmaster General Potter, I convinced him to offer an incentive to encourage eligible employees to retire. I informed him that the cost would be recovered through the savings generated. After negative results from the VERAs, the postal service agreed to offer a $15,000 incentive spread over two years, which softened the immediate impact on its cost. When retirement had been offered earlier without an incentive, I advised APWU members to stay because the union's demand for incentives had not been approved. My warning was ignored by some employees who later blamed the union when incentives were negotiated and they were excluded.

Another way management intended to reduce the size of the workforce was abolishing Tour 2 in mail processing centers, incentivizing senior employees to retire voluntarily. They did so without consultation, which contractually was required. Thousands of senior employees were reassigned to other tours. We were unsuccessful in the arbitration of this event. Concurrent with the reassignments, management expressed a new interest in modified workweeks to accommodate the new employee schedules, but I rejected such overtures intended to facilitate the elimination of Tour 2.

Another Loss

Ethelda adopted a female kitten that we named Misty. She has become a treasured addition to our family from a shelter. She is an adorable tabby and does not like to be in the presence of strangers, but she is lovable and receives our constant attention. When permitted to go outside, she is tethered to a thirty-foot cat leash because we cannot imagine her roaming the expansive countryside in our community with predators behind every bush.

In 2008, Ethelda's mother, LouElla Harkins, passed. She had moved in with us after the death of her husband, William Harkins, in 1998, and she was a pleasant addition to our home. When Ethelda retired from the University of Maryland in 2005, Mrs. Harkins served as her daily companion. She had not been ill, so her death was unexpected, and to this day, we miss her presence. Misty was a welcome distraction in the wake of our loss.

Leadership

Toward the end of my union career, I was invited to speak at the Letter Carriers 2008 National Convention by President Bill Young, who, in a courageous move, broke a long-standing precedent. Over the long careers of Vince Sombrotto and Moe Biller, neither president was afforded the privilege of speaking at the other's convention. Bill Young broke this historic snub and extended an invitation that I proudly accepted. My speech was received with enthusiasm by the Letter Carrier delegates, and I was proud to represent the APWU members before the largest assembly of union delegates (seven thousand) in the United States. I reciprocated with an invitation to the following APWU convention, and the delegates gave Bill a well-deserved ovation for being bold and true to the cry for labor solidarity. Bill Young has since retired and was replaced by Fred Rolando, whom I have grown to respect for his firm commitment to the betterment of postal employees.

Obama's Endorsement

In 2008, the highlight of the year was the APWU endorsement of Senator Barack Obama for the Democratic Party nomination for president of the United States. The battle was waged in hard-fought primary contests with Senator Hillary Clinton. She waged an aggressive campaign for the nomination, and labor unions were divided in their allegiances. I was in attendance at the Chicago convention of the AFL, and all of the Democratic candidates were invited. Senator Obama's message was not inspiring, so I left the convention as a lukewarm supporter of Hillary Clinton. We had witnessed the campaigns of Jesse Jackson and Reverend Sharpton for president, so this was not about black pride. We wanted to support a winner.

I invited Senator Clinton to the 2007 APWU Craft Conference. She was unable to attend, but the campaign sent former president Bill Clinton, who delivered a fine speech to the delegates. In private discussion at the convention, I shared with him the story about getting sick in the aftermath of the earlier dinner engagement. The former president posed for many photos and left a feeling of goodwill, but despite my respect, the results of Super Tuesday convinced me that Obama had a real chance.

I wanted APWU to be in on the ground floor. Because the Democratic nominee was selected before the Democratic National

Convention, if we wanted to be influential in the process, it was necessary for the APWU executive board to act. The Obama endorsement by the APWU executive board was later confirmed by the delegates to the national convention who expressed their support in a unanimous vote

APWU was among the early endorsers of Senator Obama, and the future president personally expressed his appreciation in a phone call to my home. It was around 8:00 p.m. when the phone rang, and as usual Ethelda answered. The caller informed her that Senator Obama requested to speak to William Burrus. Her first reaction was "sure," but she handed me the phone, and I spoke to the future president of the United States. As a reminder, our caller id still has the phone number.

The AFL executive board was divided in its selection for the Democratic nominee, so the APWU endorsement after several failed attempts led to repeated confrontations between me and Clinton supporters on the Counsel. For the historic Democratic convention, I authorized the purchase of an APWU ad in the convention program that proudly displayed the support of APWU members for Obama. During the presidential campaign, I received a call from Gerry McEntee, president of AFSCME, who was meeting with Reverend Al Sharpton. McEntee asked if I would be receptive to discussing a bus caravan that was planned by Reverend Sharpton to travel through the South to encourage voters to engage in the election. Gerry informed me that AFSCME had committed $25,000 to the project and was requesting that APWU make a contribution. The Sharpton entourage arrived at my office, and we engaged in small talk about the campaign and other occasions when we had met. The reverend then asked if APWU could make a contribution, and to his astonishment, I committed $100,000. At the time, AFSCME had 1.5 million members as compared to the APWU's 200,000 members, and the mention of the $25,000 was intended as a hint of what would be expected. But I thought so highly of the project that I wanted it to be successful. It was a good investment because Obama was elected, and I am sure that Reverend Sharpton's caravan played a role.

Obama Wins

The election was historical and extremely satisfying on a personal level. I was amazed that the United States, with centuries of racial baggage, could rise to the level of equality necessary to elect a black man as president; I was proud of APWU's role in his success. On my watch, we had progressed from civil rights legislation that made all men equal under the law to the office of president of the United States. What a journey!

The union joined in the festive celebrations honoring his victory. We rented a hotel ballroom to allow any APWU members visiting the city for the inauguration a comfortable venue to watch the event, and we certainly needed it because it was a bitterly cold day. When Obama took the oath of office, I beamed with pride. In the span of 238 years, we had progressed from slavery to president, a journey as far as from here to the moon.

After the historic election and prior to the installation, President-elect Barack Obama, his wife, Michelle, and their children attended services at the Nineteenth Street Baptist Church in Washington, DC. The pastor was my brother-in-law, Reverend Derrick Harkins, who is the eleventh pastor in the 173rd year of the history of one of the most prestigious Baptist churches in Washington. The day was bitterly cold, but the parishioners were lined up for blocks to worship with the new first family. The Harkins family, with Ethelda and me in tow, was escorted into the church, where we sat directly behind the presidential family. Reverend Harkins wrote a sermon particularly for the challenges facing the Obama family, and in private quarters before departing, they expressed their appreciation and posed for a photo with Reverend Harkins's family. It was rumored that the Obama family would select the Nineteenth Street Baptist Church as their permanent place of worship, but later after the experience with Reverend Wright in Chicago, they decided not to join any particular church. It's too bad; I had been looking forward to having the president's ear every Sunday so that I could apprise him of postal issues.

Notice of My Retirement

At the All-Craft Conference in 2009, I announced my intended retirement in the coming election of 2010. After fifty-two years of spending every waking moment consumed with postal issues, I had decided to move on with the rest of my life. Ethelda stood at my side for the entire period in Washington, condoning my many absences and family interruptions. I wanted to be able devote all my time to our joint pursuits before "my ticket was punched."

On the night prior to my announcement, I held a meeting in my hotel suite with my closest supporters to inform them of the news that I intended to break at the conference. They expressed their reservations but respected my decision.

My announcement to the assembled delegates was an emotional moment as almost my entire working life had been dedicated to their well-being. Many delegates shared their disappointment about my retirement, and I was touched, but as I expressed, it was my desire to live another life and my time had arrived. Over the final months, I was afforded many tributes and honors, for which both Ethelda and I are very appreciative.

CHAPTER 26

From There to Here

Trumka Takes Over

On September 15, 2009, Rich Trumka assumed the presidency of the AFL–CIO following the retirement of John Sweeney. I supported Rich, who had a sterling reputation after serving for fifteen years as secretary treasurer, but I withheld APWU's support for his selection of secretary treasurer. Elizabeth Schuler was a staff member of IBEW, and she had never served as a president of an international union on the executive council. Moreover, I did not know Ms. Schuler and did not feel comfortable committing the APWU membership to her support solely on the recommendation of others. Liz Schuler won as expected; our relationship was not affected by the withholding of support, and she has performed admirably.

After the election, President Trumka requested my presence, along with four other international union presidents, at a meeting with President Obama to discuss the challenges facing labor unions. I was the third president to address him. The union presidents who spoke before me requested his support for their union issues, but realizing that the president's staff and cabinet attend to policy issues, I did not follow their lead. Instead I shared with the president how proud we were of his accomplishment. I told him that although he was of a different generation and therefore did not have to experience on a personal level the kinds of struggles my generation and previous generations did, as a nation we had overcome so much and applauded his achievement.

Over the ensuing years, I continued to have major disagreements with many AFL–CIO vice presidents who repeatedly found fault with the Obama administration for every unachieved demand. I pointed out that organized labor has no option except to support candidates of the Democratic Party even when they cannot or do not deliver expected relief. The alternative would be devastating to working people. Republican legislators are staunch opponents of the basic rights of workers to organize for mutual benefit. Republican-controlled administrations shift the debate from positive change to a struggle to survive. I constantly reminded outspoken council members that the choice was not between the Obama administration and the delivery of expectations but between Democrats or Republicans, who have included on their agenda the elimination of the right to bargain.

My service as a vice president on the AFL Executive Council and Executive Committee is full of cherished memories of my activities on behalf of working people. While we often engage in spirited disagreement, the women and men who serve are committed to the working people. The assembled presidents represent all of the positive features of outstanding representation. I formed special relationships with Presidents Rich Trumka (AFL–CIO), Cecil Roberts (UMW), Harold Schaitberger (IAFF), Gerry McEntee (AFSCME), Larry Cohen (CWU), James Andrews (North Carolina State Fed), Bill Lucy (APWU), John Wilhelm (UFCW), Greg Junnman (IFPTE), Leo Gerard (USW), John Gage (AFGE), Lee Saunders (USW), and the other distinguished officers who serve working people. My respect for them is unlimited.

Budget Decisions

In 2009, Allen Mohl and Elizabeth Connelly, APWU senior staff on financial matters, entered my office with grave looks on their faces. They informed me that we were experiencing a cash flow problem and unless changes were made it would be necessary to tap the union reserves. Upon assuming the presidency, I had informed the secretary treasurer office that it was my intent to operate the union with annual surpluses, and they were informing me that this would not be possible without the curtailment of expenses or increased revenue.

We discussed the options, but within weeks, there was a stroke of good fortune when it was discovered that the USPS had violated the contractual casual limits. It had been agreed to in the 1975 negotiations and continued through subsequent contracts that only 5 percent of employees would be casuals, or temporary. This restriction continued through the 2006 negotiations that resulted in a process that would track the casual usage for appropriate remedy. I assigned Phil Tabbita to monitor the compliance as compared to the restrictions, and the record showed that they had exceeded the contractual limitations. Phil negotiated remedies in two major cases, and more than fifteen million dollars was paid to the national and local unions in February 2009 and March 2010. The timing could not have been better.

To address the uncontrolled union expenses, I had initiated a travel budget for each elected officer and significantly modified travel authority for resident officers. Moe had required that all officers' travel be approved in advance by the president, but I wanted to remove the office of the president from individual travel decisions and permit officers to travel at their discretion within budgetary limitations. I also reevaluated our focus on private sector organizing and compared the organizing results to monies spent. After the review, I curtailed those initiatives that had not generated new members or concrete projections for new members. I also limited the right of officers, secretaries, and staff

309

to generate unlimited printing costs. The practice had been that each regional office and staff member could place orders with Kelly Press and at the end of the month the secretary treasurer of the national office would be presented a bill. Now printing had to be on budget and approved by the president in advance.

A New Secretary Treasurer

In 2009, Terry Stapleton resigned from his position of secretary treasurer to obtain a position at AFL–CIO headquarters. I was disappointed to lose a dedicated officer of his caliber. Terry's capable assistant, Allen Mohl, had already left to work at postal headquarters. As a team, they had initiated major changes in the Secretary Treasurer's office. Terry's counsel was appreciated and respected, and together we had improved the union throughout the period that we worked in tandem as executive officers.

Having already considered Elizabeth "Liz" Powell for the position of secretary treasury at the time of Terry's original appointment, the selection was easy. I contacted Liz and inquired about her interest in the position. Upon her acceptance, she was appointed, and the executive board approved.

Throughout my tenure as president, Ms. Powell performed admirably in the positions of northeast regional coordinator and secretary treasurer, and upon my retirement, she organized the outstanding tributes to my service at the national convention.

Responsibilities

The responsibilities of president bring undesirable tasks, and I was obliged to issue an ultimatum to Frankie Sanders to resign his position of regional coordinator or face serious charges of falsifying expenses. Frankie had been appointed to fill the vacancy created when Terry assumed the position of secretary treasurer. The charges were confirmed by documentation. Frankie elected to resign, and I selected Bill Sullivan, a national business agent, as his replacement. The executive board approved my appointments, and Frankie was indicted by the Labor Board and convicted and incarcerated.

Potter Retires

In 2010, Postmaster General Potter announced his retirement. I was as surprised as the APWU membership. Despite our disagreements, I recognized that postal employees were in a better place when he departed than upon his arrival. Mr. Potter and I developed a working relationship throughout his period of service as PMG, and I expressed my "surprise and disappointment" at his announcement. He had initiated a regular schedule of meetings with the union presidents. The meetings often turned into forums where the presidents would advance the problem of the day specific to their crafts. As a career postal employee, Potter had an understanding of the employee issues, and we were able to address issues of importance.

Conventions

The national convention is the highest governing body in the union, and no one is more aware of that authority than the APWU delegates. Over the course of the fifteen national conventions that I had the privilege to chair, I was always conscious of the supreme authority of the APWU members in attendance. As could be expected, we differed at times on issues of importance, but it was always the delegates who decided.

During the course of the conventions, we had moments of triumph, humor, and disappointment. Perhaps our biggest failure in terms of achieving specific objectives was that we were unable to reach the required majority to reduce the officers' structure. The unavoidable conclusion is that the structure that was achieved to accommodate all the officers in the merger resulted in the union having more officers than can be supported by the dues base. Reducing the number of officers has been a primary objective and issue of dispute at each convention, but a required two-thirds majority always eluded our grasp. Another issue of dispute was whether or not to increase dues to compensate for the decline of members. I consistently opposed dues increases, believing that the financial burdens of the union should not be shouldered on the backs of the declining membership.

I am among a dwindling few of current members who have been in attendance at every APWU convention (1972–2010), and each convention has had its own character. Some were more confrontational than others; perhaps most notably were the debates on the timing of the national conventions and the reimbursement for arbitration advocates. Perhaps the most raucous conventions where the ones that involved debate on the subject of field office locations, Private Sector Organizing (POWER), representation for support services, and, of course, the officers' salaries. Steve Zamanakos and Don Foley, both national business agents, and David Yao, a union activist in Seattle, emerged as prominent voices for the delegates, playing active rolls in the convention proceedings. Of the many mistakes that I made over the course of my career, one was my failure to include Steve, Don, and David in the internal discussions prior to developing convention resolutions. I had met with Steve and Don before a convention once, but we didn't have the same perspective on the issues. They had the ability to influence the debate over important issues and could easily influence enough delegates to block the two-thirds majority required for constitutional change. The ego of the president tends to be a hindrance to admitting that others have sufficient influence to prevent change. If they had been made a part of the process, I expect that they would have joined with me in the adoption of positive change.

Each convention brings memories, mostly humorous ones. The "What lights?" by the chair after the intricate administration communications system was discovered was classic. A member of the administration would blink the stage lights to send a message to the delegates signaling support or opposition. When challenged, my response was, "What lights?" The exchange about whether campaign material on my clothing was covered by the rule banning campaigning from the podium was entertaining. The debate on resolution 6 will go down in history, including the spirited remarks by Joyce Robinson defending the president's right to make appointments. Moe's abandonment of his lifelong commitment to the industrial union concept of presidential appointments was disappointing. We brought laughs from the delegates when in the 2000 convention, in response to the repeated desire of individual delegates to insert in the record a specific birthday, the chair invited every delegate who would have a birthday that year to rise and be recognized.

Throughout the numerous conventions that I had the privilege to chair, the continuous challenge was to keep the delegates on track and arrive at decisions. This inevitably involved limiting the remarks to the subject at hand and preventing delegates from gaining recognition out of order by using the privileged status to achieve non-privileged objectives. We were able to complete all of the convention business in all fifteen conventions I chaired. When I assumed the chair for the first time in the 1982 National Convention, I had been trained in Robert's Rules and had an advantage over most of the delegates, but in the intervening years, the APWU convention delegates became more proficient in the rules of order, and my early advantage was neutralized. Among the most treasured memories of my lengthy career are those shared in convention discussions where after vigorous debate, the majority prevailed. I thank Andy Anderson, assistant director of Clerk Craft, and Phil Tabbita for keeping me abreast of the floor microphone rotation and Parliamentarian Loraine Buckley for her professionalism.

Final Convention

The 2010 National Convention was my final convention. I had the pleasure of inviting more than 125 delegates under the age of thirty-five to participate as guests at the national union's expense. The intent was to expose the next generation of postal employees to the democratic process of APWU conventions. They were permitted to be seated among the delegates without voice or vote, and several communicated with me their enjoyment in participating. I sincerely hope that many of these young postal employees elect to be leaders within the union and in their lives. They are the future of APWU.

During the convention, Liz Powell organized a moving tribute to my career. At one point, she had the delegates raise signs honoring me while thousands of balloons were released from the ceiling. Among the many other honors bestowed upon me was the motion to the executive board by Cliff Guffey to transfer title of the union automobile which I had been driving to my name. Then there were the awards organized by my friend, Joyce Robinson, national liaison to the APWU POWER Committee, and the POWER coordinators: Carolyn J Watson, Central Region; Rachel Walthall, Eastern Region; Ivona Palmer, Eastern Region; Gayle J Vincent, Southern Region; and M. Joanne Holiday, Western Region.

I will also remember that during the closing moments of the very last convention I had elected to vacate the chair and circulate among the delegates, unmindful that the convention was coming to a close. As we adjourned for the final hitting of the gavel at my last convention as APWU president, I was en route to the podium and was denied the opportunity to say good-bye.

The career that had dominated my life for more than a half century was coming to an end. I had so many fond memories and so many good friends, but I was moving on to a different phase in my life and welcomed the future challenges ahead.

The Last Contract

Prior to the ending of my career, we began the final negotiations in which I would participate. The union had an aggressive agenda, but at the last bargaining session that I attended as president, little had been finalized. The 2010 contract negotiations continued after my retirement under new leadership. While in attendance, Postmaster General Potter presented to me the Postal Medal of Freedom for my lengthy service from a substitute distribution clerk to the presidency. It had been a long and rewarding career during which time I was privileged to make many friends and the most cherished are those members of the American Postal Workers Union AFL–CIO.

The Record

As I entered what would be the end of my career as a union official, many of the obstacles that we inherited remained— excessive rate discounts, congressional interference, plant and office consolidations, and a host of labor management issues— but we made significant progress including

> Pay upgrades; air-conditioning for postal vehicles; bereavement leave; ban on the requirement to use personal vehicle in official duties; dependent care; reimbursement for travel; inter-level bidding; local memo protections; uniform local memo for small offices; elimination of PTFs; upgrade of PTFs in small offices; JCIM; administrative dispute procedure; interest on back pay; transfers; leave sharing; paid leave and LWOP; annual leave exchange; modified workweek; maximization; modified grievance procedure; allowing radio headsets; allowing tennis shoes; restrictions on casuals; travel pay; expedited payment for grievances; 90-10 compliance; court leave for PTFs; elimination of TEs; holiday leave; full-time increase of salary from $17,000 to $52,000.

These and many other changes were initiated over my career to improve conditions for postal employees, and though we made significant progress, many issues remain for future attention.

Vice President AFL

Among the many issues that had to be resolved before leaving office was my continuation as a vice president of the AFL. My continuing to serve in the position was not affected by my decision to retire as APWU president. My original decision was to retire from the AFL vice presidency concurrent with my retirement as president, but I was reluctant because of the dearth of African Americans serving on the council. Prior to a social meeting with AFL President Rich Trumka, I informed Cliff that upon leaving office I would resign my position on the AFL Executive Council and Executive Committee and recommended Cliff as my replacement. Several days later, I changed my mind because of the few numbers of African American Vice Presidents on the Council. I had serious reservations about reducing the anemic number of black representatives who were the face of the most loyal members of the Federation. In addition to my decision regarding the AFL position, the APWU constitution creates anomalies in the dates assigned for the results of the election, the counting of ballots, the installation of officers, and the conclusion of the term of office in the prior election. As a result of the constitutional conflict, the incoming officers are declared winners and, depending upon the availability of a ballroom for installation, have likely been given the oath of office prior to the constitutional expiration of the previous term. In the 2010 election when five of the resident officer positions changed hands, the newly elected officers were assuming offices filled with incumbents who had not yet completed their terms and were continuing to perform the constitutional duties of the positions. Being a stickler for living up to my oath of office, I continued to serve as president until the last moment of my term.

As a result, Cliff had been elected and sworn in while I continued as president.

The AFL–CIO elected positions are unrelated to the offices held in the international unions. They require a separate election, and it is not unusual for former international officers to continue in their elective position on the AFL–CIO Council after they leave office in their international union.

William LaSalle, a national business agent in the Maintenance Craft, communicated with me through my Burrus Journal Web site and inquired of my justification for continuing my service on the AFL–CIO Council. I explained in a public post that it was because of the disparity of the number of African-American leaders on the Council but that if requested by President Guffey to vacate the position, I would give the request serious consideration. On the following day, I received a garbled e-mail that I later learned was intended to be retrieved. The discernible part of the e-mail requested that "you step down from your position on the Council." On the following day, I received a letter, signed by Cliff confirming the contents of the e-mail. I was initially offended by the brevity of the request, but I realized that since I no longer represented the APWU members it would be appropriate to relinquish the position notwithstanding my reservations. On the same day I received the letter, I forwarded my official resignation to President Trumka with a copy to President Guffey. My services as a representative of postal employees had come to a conclusion.

From There to Here

I left office on November 11, 2010. Despite the unachieved objectives, my country and the US Postal Service are far different from when I began my career. Over that period, laws enforcing discrimination have been erased, and although we still have challenges, we are in a better place. Even though the postal service has experienced financial difficulties amid the continuing predictions that the Internet would relegate mail delivery to the romantic past—we have prevailed. Postal workers have succeeded in climbing the ladder to the middle class, and color is no longer the defining factor to success. We have moved from "there to here," and much of that success occurred on my watch. As a union official, I am most proud that I made a contribution to the continuation of uncapped COLA, and I played a role in the progression in the top wage from $17,276, at the time I assumed office in 1981 to $52,059 as I departed. Every APWU-represented employee was affected positively. Children have been educated, homes purchased, and medical conditions attended to. While we did not achieve all of our objectives, the record speaks for itself.

The retirement event honoring my service was special. Many union members and guests were in attendance, including my brother-in-law, Rev. Derrick Harkins; Congressman Bill Clay and his wife, Carol; Congressman Lou Stokes and his wife, Jay; my friend Doug Holbrook and his wife, Jackie; my children; grandchildren; and wife, Ethelda. Reverend Harkins presented the invocation, Congressman Clay gave a moving speech, and Doug Holbrook was the emcee. Among the many highlights of the evening was a rendition of "You Are My Hero," by Kolquist Edwards. The evening will be etched in my memory forever.

I was honored over my long career to be in the presence of presidents and prime ministers as the representative of American postal workers, but the meetings with President Barack Obama were particularly rewarding and hold a special place in my memories because of the struggles that I personally experienced. I was honored to receive from the president a personally signed letter of congratulations on my career and a set of White House cuff links that I treasure. I also had the opportunity to be interviewed on C-SPAN on several occasions and was listed among the two hundred most influential African Americans in *Ebony* magazine on many occasions. These honors were received on behalf of the millions of postal employees whom I was privileged to represent.

Upon assuming national office in November 1981 and writing my first column in the national magazine, I made the following promise to the APWU membership: "This election was an expression by the membership that they desire change. And change they shall get. There will be no dramatic turnarounds, but we hope that with a methodical approach we can improve working conditions for the membership."

I trust that I lived up to that promise I made thirty years ago.

So, after a career that spanned 633 months, 2,740 weeks, or 19,250 days, I am proud to leave the APWU in far better shape than when I arrived, and whatever role that I played in its progression, the members were deserving of more because the postal employees whom I was privileged to serve were the best. Thank you for contributing to my life, and to borrow Moe's phrase, "the struggle continues."

I can taste the wind and feel the fog!

Acknowledgments

There are so many people who allowed me to have such a long and successful career. I have mentioned many people in this book who have been instrumental in my successes, but there are many others who have contributed as well. Many of our advancements couldn't have been made without skilled counsel. Moe and I were privileged over the course of our presidencies to have a legal staff second to none. Upon assuming office in 1981, we retained the services of O'Donnell, Swartz, and Anderson, and over the ensuing thirty years, APWU was provided excellent legal representation in multiple arenas. They were the best and were good personal friends. I pay tribute to Darryl Anderson, Art Luby, Anton Hajjar, Susan Catler, Lee Jackson, and Mindy Holmes.

Professional staff makes the "train run on time," and I was fortunate to have the best. I set the course, and they did the work. Any success that I achieved must be credited to their dedication and skills.

Robin Bailey, Chief of Staff who served my office continuously from 1987
Sally Davidow, Director of Communications
Elizabeth Connolly, Comptroller
Twee Nguyen, Assistant Comptroller
Cory Thompson, Safety Representative
Andrea Chapman, Director Per Capita

Phil Tabbita, Special Assistant
Roger Cronk, Director of Information
Ron Collins, Logistics
Sue Peetoom, Human Resources
Roosevelt Stewart
Phil Tabbita
Hannah Lively
Lane Bodner

To all of the OPEIU- and Guild-represented employees, with special appreciation to Dave Curtis, Lisa Brunson, Holly Perrotti, and Conrad Carr. Dave attended to all of my computer needs at home and at the office, and Lisa was the bright spot at the office with the same pleasant demeanor day in and day out. Conrad would become my brother-in-law and, while serving as my driver, became my friend.

Thank you all.

Appendix

Bill Burrus, Chief Spokesperson
APWU
Opening Statement

APWU/USPS
Contract Negotiations
Opening Session

August 22, 2000

Good Afternoon:

I am joined today by the elected leaders of the American Postal Workers Union and the constitutionally constructed Rank-and-File Bargaining Advisory Committee prepared to engage in the democratic process of collective bargaining.

We represent the interest of 360,000 APWU members and 400,000 postal employees who, with their immediate families, equal more than one million American citizens.

We also represent the interest of the 260 million American citizens and businesses that depend upon a trustworthy and reliable postal service for the transportation, processing, and delivery of mail in the most advanced nation in our world.

As we begin the journey of the twenty-first century into a promising future for all mankind, these negotiations are an opportunity to rethink and retool archaic labor policies developed in a different age and ill-fitted for the rapidly changing world of tomorrow. Productivity and efficiency can no longer be sustained in an environment where "the boss knows best," and yesterday's solutions will not serve tomorrow's challenges. We must begin to empower the worker. This is the challenge of these negotiations. How do we provide workers with decision-making authority in the conduct of their work life?

Productive workers must be adequately compensated for their contribution in making ours the most productive and less costly postal system in the world. We will therefore be seeking significant wage increases that reflect this productivity and the employee commitment to serving the American public.

After hard bargaining and many disagreements, we expect to achieve a negotiated agreement that sends a message to our members—your employees—that they are valued assets and worthy of contractual improvements.

We enter a period of uncertainty as technology offers new and exciting means of communications. This is a product of peace and the ability of humankind to expand its universe. Let us not use tomorrow's uncertainties as an excuse for withholding the present entitlement of workers who built the foundation upon which the future will unfold.

A strong and committed postal service can face the future with confidence. A demoralized workforce will make this transition a perilous adventure.

We ask that you join with us in a commitment to build upon the negotiated agreement of 1998, the first in an eleven-year period.

Contracts governing the wages, hours, and working condition of employees should be negotiated by the parties rather than decided by an uninvolved third party.

Finally let me add a word of caution: While the American Postal Workers Union is prepared to engage in good faith negotiations, we will not be dictated to by inflexible decisions made outside the bargaining table. If necessary, we shall meet arbitrary limitations with the collective strength of our membership.

We ask that you join with us in this effort to reward workers for their contributions and demonstrate to the public and the major mailers of our country that we can jointly decide our future relationship.

We shall be available each day throughout the legally required ninety-day period of negotiations and will not accept the squandering of opportunities, designed to create panicked eleventh-hour discussions. Let us begin and apply our determinations to a promising bargain opportunity.

African American Labor Leaders' Economic Summit Summary and Report

Sponsored By
Harvard Trade Union

PROGRAM
The Department of Afro-American Studies
The A. Philip Randolph Institute
The Coalition of Black Trade Unionists with Support from the
Ford Foundation and Jerry Wurf Memorial Fund

Harvard University, October 8–10, 1998

The African American Labor Leaders' Economic Summit is an initiative designed to expand dialogue among labor leaders, academics, and policy experts. The 1990s may well represent a turning point in the history of the US labor force; today it has shriveled to 14 percent. This secular decline is creating pressures for new organizing strategies, calling on the energy and insight of people previously relegated to the margins of trade union leadership. In a revival of organized labor, African Americans will have a special role to play, as this community stands today as the most unionized and sympathetic to trade unions of any major group in the United States. According to a national survey of 1989 conducted by Associated Press-Media General, 56 percent of non-union African American workers answered yes to the question, "Would you join a union at your place of work?" compared to 46 percent of Hispanics and a mere 35 percent of non-Hispanic whites.

Bill Burrus delivered a paper, which addressed "the reality that the current occupants of urban areas do not have the resources (educational or financial) to transform the present decay into livable cities." Meanwhile, "those occupants who develop the means to escape their surroundings through education or employment move beyond the boundaries of the area at the first opportunity and deny the community the benefits of their upward mobility." These zones thus "progressively become home for those on fixed income, low employment, or unemployment." Burrus discussed a vision of the future in which a "dispersement of the population" might be encouraged, leading to "a proper mix of those who use available resources with a negative proportional contribution and those who generate resources beyond their personal needs." In his view, for urban zones to thrive "the ratio of the haves to the have-nots must be balanced."

Black nationalist intellectuals such as Harold Cruse opposed the integrationist impulse of the African American middle class, as he argued that their departure from the inner city upset the balance between the haves and have-nots. Burrus instead believes that urban planning committed to a cross-class pattern of dispersal might prevent the ghettoization of the truly disadvantaged.

Index

About the Author

William Burrus was born in Wheeling, West Virginia, to parents William H. and Gertrude Burrus. His parents separated, and his early childhood included foster care and relocation with his older sister, Billie Jane, to several cities in Ohio and West Virginia, where he completed schooling that was required by state law to be racially separated. His father remarried when he was drafted into the military during World War II, and his new wife, Blanche Pugh, became the primary care giver. At that point, the family unit was expanded to include her daughter, Effie Marva.

After returning to Wheeling after periods of residence in Columbus and Toledo, Burrus completed schooling in Lincoln High school, graduating with honors from a school system that was racially segregated. Therefore he was prohibited from attending any of the Wheeling colleges. Burrus volunteered to serve in the United States Army, where he attained the rank of sergeant over his three-year career. Upon his honorable discharge ,Burrus enrolled in West Virginia State College but soon relocated to Steubenville, Ohio, where he was housed by a close friend, Dorothy Smith. With few career opportunities available in the Steubenville community, Burrus qualified on the postal examination in Cleveland, Ohio, while residing with his sister Billie Jane Burrus.

He began his postal career as a clerk in February 1958, and in the years that followed, he was exposed to many coworkers who were experienced and highly educated. Postal employment was challenging as all clerks were required as a condition of employment to qualify twice per year on the scheme requirements assigned. Since he was not a native of Cleveland, it was especially difficult for Burrus to commit to memory over five thousand streets and addresses composing the Cleveland delivery zone.

Burrus married Claudette Vincent, a native of Steubenville, and they became the parents of two daughters, Valerie Jean and Doni Mari. In 1964, the marriage to Claudette dissolved in divorce. He then married Janice Reid, a postal employee, and they became parents to two daughters, Kimberly Elayne and Kristy Lanette. During this time, the wages of postal employees were not sufficient to support a growing family, so in addition to employment at the post office, Burrus worked a number of part-time jobs, most notably as a painter of homes and businesses.

He became interested in union affairs through his friendship with Anne Thomas, a coworker. After gaining membership in the National Postal Union (NPU), Burrus began his ascension through the leadership ranks under the tutelage of John R. Smith, an activist from Dayton, Ohio, who became a close friend and mentor. In 1974, he achieved the presidency of the Cleveland Ohio Local, where he served for seven years. The 1978 contract negotiations resulted in an agreement that limited the wage adjustment for cost of living increases, and this issue became the focus of progressives in the newly formed union. Burrus played a leading role in the membership rejection of the tentative agreement. Subsequent arbitration preserved the uncapped COLA, and Burrus emerged as a leader in postal unions.

In 1980, he joined with Moe Biller, the president of the New York Local, and John Richards, the president of the Pittsburgh Local, to form the Leadership Team and challenge the three top positions in the union; they succeeded in the election. In 1981, Burrus was elected as the executive vice president of the American Postal Workers Union, the second ranking officer in the 280,000 member union.

In 1985, Burrus married his current wife and soul mate, Ethelda Harkins, and they have formed an unbreakable bond. They are most proud of their ability to communicate and the two homes that they designed and built that reflect their mutual love.

Burrus served with Moe Biller, the elected president, for twenty-one years, and they succeeded in changing the union for the better in multiple ways. In 2000, Biller announced his retirement, and Burrus became a candidate for the presidency. He won the election handily and became the first and only African America elected by the membership to the presidency of a major union. He served as president for ten years before announcing his retirement after a fifty-three-year career as a postal employee and elected union official fighting to improve conditions for postal employees.

Upon his retirement, Burrus could look back over many achievements that changed postal employment from transient to a destination. Because of his efforts, homes have been purchased, children educated, illnesses attended to, and the quality of life fueled by dramatic employment improvements. Burrus acknowledges the foundation laid by his predecessors, Stu Filbey, Jim Rademaker, Moe Biller, and Vince Sombrotto, which he used to build a bright future for postal employees. He credits the many friends and coworkers who contributed to his efforts.

Burrus was listed in *Who's Who in Black America* and has appeared in numerous publications including *Business Week*, *Jet*, *Black Enterprise*, and *Ebony* magazine, where he was listed each year among the 150 most influential African Americans. He was appointed to the Ohio Advisory Board of the US Civil Rights Commission and was elected to the National Board of the A. Philip Randolph Institute. He served on the Federal Advisory Council on Occupational Safety and Health and on the Board of Directors of the National Black College Alumni Hall of Fame. While representing American postal workers, he was elected as a representative of the Communications International organization.

Photos

William Burrus, 1954

Jane Burrus, high school graduation

William Burrus, high school
senior, 1954

William Burrus Sr.

William Burrus Jr. with his
mother, Gertrude

William Burrus Sr. with his daughter,
Jane, and William Burrus Jr.

Gertrude Burrus, mother of William Burrus Jr.

Effie Burrus

Otis Burrus and William Burrus Sr.

Jane Burrus and J. R. Smith

First Row: Robert Huff, Wilbur Newsom, Joe Hart, Donald Burke, and William Burrus

Second Row: Coach Wiley Walker, Alley Minor, Earl Minor, Lawrence Hunter, James Galloway, and Manager Harold Minor.

William Burrus Jr. at age nine

Lincoln Panthers Win Regional Grid Honors

Football honors

William and Ethelda Burrus with Joseph Kennedy

American Postal Workers Union officers with President Clinton

Congressman Bill Clay, Ethelda and William Burrus,
and APWU President Moe Biller

Moe Biller, Doug Holbrook, and Bill Burrus,
1984 Biennial National Convention

William Burrus, Moe Biller, and Doug Holbrook

Bill Burrus and Congressman Bill Clay

Moe Biller, Bill Burrus, and John Richards

Moe Biller

Bill Burrus, Wallace Baldwin, Moe Biller, Coretta Scott King, and others

Bill Burrus, Moe Biller, and others

Roland Carter, Congressman Stokes, Congresswoman Mary Rose Okar, Bill Burrus, and others

Bill Burrus and J. R. Smith enjoy a light moment.

Bill Burrus shakes hands with President Obama at the
2008 AFL-CIO National Convention in Pittsburgh, Pennsylvania.

THE AMERICAN

Volume 39 • Number 1 • Jan./Feb. 2009

Postal Worker

YES WE CAN

APWU THE AMERICAN POSTAL WORKERS UNION

APWU 2008 Biennial National Convention—President Burrus
beams with pride.

Kim and Kristy Burrus   Kim Burrus

Kristy, James, Jammal, and Krisea Burrus

Valerie and Chastity Burrus

Doni Burrus

Misty Burrus

Mark Gardner of Mail Handlers, Bill Cantrell of NRLCA,
Bill Young of NALC, and Bill Burrus of APWU

Bill Burrus testifies before Congress.

Bill and Ethelda Burrus at home